f 1/10/86

GW00685015

The Strategy of
Sea Power

With a new introduction by Dr Geoffrey Till

For centuries sea power has been the first and last means both of defending our country and of striking at our enemies. What part, if any, can it play in an age of nuclear weapons and guided missiles? It is the argument of this clear and succinct historical survey that the principles and practices of war change much less than is often supposed. Each new invention and technological change provides a specious excuse to dismiss the study and analysis of past experience as an occupation fit only for the antiquarian and the academic. What lessons, it may be asked, could the wars of the eighteenth century, fought under sail, hold for the strategists of 1914 when our battle fleet was composed of heavily-armoured steamships and our merchantmen were threatened by submarines? It took, as the author shows, more than two years of heavy punishment to teach us that they were many and relevant. We see the same reluctant admission that convoy offered the best hope of defence and counter-attack. We recognise at the Battle of Jutland the same unhappy effects of a too-rigid method of fleet control that time and again in the eighteenth century had robbed us of victories that were there for the taking. And we see how neglect of the ancient art of combined operations lost us opportunities to strike telling blows at places of our own choice.

In war, as in life, the same situations recur. We seek to land an army or to carry out a commando raid, to supply a base or to protect our seaborne trade just as our ancestors did before us. Circumstances change, weapons change, tactics change, but the strategic principles remain. Like his great forerunners, Mahan and Richmond, Captain Roskill studies his subjects in the perspective of history, a perspective which is lengthened by his unrivalled command of the history of the war at sea between 1938 and 1945. His observations on our present defence policy are informed by the insights thus obtained, as well as by those to be expected from one who has made the sea his profession. This is a book that no one interested in naval history or in the present controversy over defence can afford to neglect.

The Strategy of
Sea Power

Captain S. W. Roskill, DSC, FRHistS, RN

JOHN GOODCHILD PUBLISHERS
AYLESBURY

John Goodchild Publishers
10 Mandeville Road
Aylesbury
Buckinghamshire HP21 8AA

John Goodchild Publishers is an imprint of Bookward Limited.

This edition published by permission of William Collins Sons & Co Ltd
First published in this edition 1986
© Copyright Mrs T. S. H. Till 1986, 1962
Introduction and Epilogue © Bookward Ltd 1986

Cover design by Graham Andrews
Printed by Nene Litho and bound by Woolnough Bookbinding Limited, both of
Irthlingborough Northants.

British Library Cataloguing in Publication Data
Roskill, S. W.
    The strategy of sea power.
    1. Naval strategy
    I. Title
    359. 4'3 V163

ISBN 0-86391-060-2

CONTENTS

FOREWORD

Admiral Sir John Fieldhouse, GCB, GBE, ADC

It is with a proper degree of humility that I produce the foreword to this edition of Captain Stephen Roskill's important work, *The Strategy of Sea Power*.

Stephen Roskill was the Royal Navy's foremost historian, and provided the officers and men of the Service he loved with their Naval background and traditions, inspiring the same sense of commitment and standards which are expected of Royal Naval people. Nevertheless, he was strong in his criticism when he believed the circumstances warranted it; such as the Royal Navy's tardy perception of the value of air power at sea or its failure to appreciate fully the submarine threat in the interwar period. In today's circumstances an examination of Britain's maritime strategy, encouraging informed debate on the Royal Navy's roles and execution of these roles, is as timely and as valuable as ever.

We are living through a period of great technological change and uncertainty. Powerful new sensors and weapons abound in areas of high political instability and it is important that the seagoing professionals and all those concerned in maritime affairs, which in a nation such as ours should mean most of us, understand the value of sea power. Naval history continues to be an important source of guidance even in an age of computer simulation. A navy which forgets its history is like a person without experience.

The exercise of comparing modern and historical experience is eminently worthwhile, but as well as demonstrating this, Stephen Roskill's message underlines the importance of the Royal Navy to the security and prosperity of our nation. I believe that in recent years strategic and political thought has been preoccupied with the scenario of direct NATO/Warsaw pact confrontation on the Central Front, to the detriment of the maritime consideration. The concept of a short conventional war leading inexorably to the final nuclear exchange is less credible than most other possibilities, and a visible capability to sustain the Atlantic link and in particular protect Reinforcement and Resupply shipping is vital – not only for the cohesion of the Alliance, but to give credibility to the forces on the ground. Equally important is the ability to respond to threats on NATO's flanks, to protect the West's economic resources and trade routes, and to cater for our defence commitments world-wide. Only maritime forces have the necessary flexibility and mobility, and can be given the breadth of capability to fulfil this wide range of tasks. Nearer to home, national waters are a highly important source of raw materials and energy and the 200 mile Exclusive Economic Zone requires policing and protecting. In all these many roles the value to the country of a strong and balanced Royal Navy has been demonstrated time and time again and the future is increasingly hazardous and unpredictable.

To quote Field Marshal Montgomery: "The lesson is this – in all history, the nation which has had control of the sea has in the end prevailed."

With that quotation in mind I regard this new edition as recognition of the continuing relevance of the work of Stephen Roskill as well as a tribute to the man himself.

INTRODUCTION

Dr Geoffrey Till

Stephen Roskill was born in 1903 and entered the Royal Naval College at Osborne thirteen years later. Early in his career he became a gunnery specialist, and at the beginning of the Second World War served in the Gunnery Division of the Naval Staff where his task was to help repair the deficiencies caused by the policy errors and financial stringency of the interwar period. In this capacity he crossed swords with Churchill's scientific adviser Professor Lindemann (later Lord Cherwell) and with Admiral Sir Frederic Dreyer, the officer charged with, amongst other things, the supervision of Merchant Navy Gunnery. Perhaps in partial consequence of this Roskill soon found himself, like other undeferential subordinates before him, posted to a cruiser on a distant station. In this case, it was H.M.S. *Leander* then serving in the Pacific. However Japan's subsequent entry into the war changed this backwater into one of the main areas of conflict and Roskill was soon engaged in the operations of war. He was wounded and decorated with the DSC for his part in H.M.S. *Leander*'s conduct during the battle of Kolombangara in the Solomons on the night of 12th/13th July 1943.

In 1944, however, Captain Roskill was posted to the British Admiralty Delegation in Washington, a position of responsibility and importance. His associations with the United States survived the ending of the war and he was the Senior British Observer at the atomic test on Bikini Atoll in 1946.

His next official naval posting as Deputy Director of Naval Intelligence 1947–8 was also his last. The reason for this was that occupational hazard of his generation of gunnery officers – deafness, an increasing disability which effectively precluded him from further positions of sea-going command. Recognising this, he asked for and was granted a premature retirement from the Navy on medical grounds in March 1949.

The end of one career was, however, the signal for the beginning of another yet more successful one. Roskill's academic gifts had been apparent from his entry into Osborne but the Navy of this era was hardly the place for them to be developed professionally. Accordingly, it was largely on the strength of the excellence of his report on the Bikini Atoll test of 1946 that he was charged with the writing of the official history of the naval operations of the Second World War. On the face of it, this was an extraordinary gamble but it paid off triumphantly. Originally conceived as a narrow operational history of the Atlantic War, Roskill's work blossomed into the mighty 'The War at Sea' series. The appearance of the first volume of this in 1954 made his name as an historian and proved highly popular with the book-reading public. Two more volumes appeared, the last in two parts, with Volume III, Part II being finally published in 1961.

In that year also Stephen Roskill accepted a Senior Research Fellowship at Churchill College, Cambridge, embarking on a career as a general naval historian. By 1964 he had produced a total of ten books, including the first edition in 1962 of *The Strategy of Sea Power*. He embarked on an intensely industrious research programme which eventually yielded a volume of *Documents Relating to the Naval Air Service* for the Naval Records Society; a major study on British *Naval Policy Between the Wars* in two volumes, and his three volume biography *Hankey, Man of Secrets*. On the strength of this, his contribution to University life and on his work of building up a prestigious archive centre at Churchill College, Cambridge, Roskill was elected Fellow, and then in 1970 a Pensioner Fellow of the College. He continued his work up to the end, producing *Churchill and the Admirals* in 1977 and *Admiral*

Lord Beatty, the Last Naval Hero in 1980. He died in Cambridge on 4th November 1982.

Stephen Roskill's success as an historian owed much to the tremendous efforts he made to get at all the facts relevant to the explanation of a particular situation. His determination to discover and print all the facets of the issue he was analysing, with a meticulous attention to the finest detail, demonstrated the true historian's concern to represent the unique and complex nature of his subject matter as fully and as fairly as he possibly could. Not for Roskill the glib and simplistic conclusions of the slipshod! In his case the findings of deep historical research were supplemented with the invaluable insights of one often actually involved in the events he studied and personally acquainted with many of their leading figures. The combination of these two advantages led to his work having an authority that verged on the magisterial. He was, moreover, able to present his narrative and his conclusions in a dignified yet readable fashion which appealed to the general book-buying public.

Roskill was also accustomed to controversy. As a naval officer he was willing to take on Professor Lindemann over such things as the notorious 'Naval Wire Barrage' and to suffer the consequences if necessary. As official historian, and one moreover who had the example of his illustrious but unfortunate predecessor of the First World War, Sir Julian Corbett, before him, he was prepared to withstand the mightiest in the land if he thought their explanations for what had happened differed substantially from what he believed to be the truth. The strength of his feelings on this issue can best be gauged by looking at his remarks about the lamentable consequences of censorship on pages 241–2 of his chapter on Perspectives and Prospects. Paradoxically enough, it was Mr. Churchill himself who in Roskill's case proved difficult over the publication of uncomfortable conclusions about such matters as the Dudley North affair or the despatch of the *Prince of Wales* and *Repulse* to the Far East in 1941.

Roskill was also determined, as a true historian, to protect his sources. He was at his most acid when confronted by those who sought to deny him access to records he knew existed or by the consequences of those modern Visigoths of the Admiralty who had wantonly destroyed so much of the record on which he and other historians must depend. He should, incidentally, take considerable credit for the fact that the record retention and weeding process is so much more sophisticated now than it was then.

As an historian he was, finally, not afraid of indulging in controversy with other historians. The most obvious example of this was that with the late Professor Arthur Marder, and, sadly, this dispute (largely over Churchill's role in the Admiralty 1939–40) was not always conducted with the detached objectivity that admirers of both these titans of modern naval history could have wished. But, happily, the two compromised before the end; this dispute, moreover, attracted a good deal of general interest in the subject they were arguing about and helped others to establish what the facts of the matter were.

Roskill's determination to get at the truth cost what it may and his capacity to weave a perceptive commentary on the overall significance of particular points, based on the highest standards of scholarship, into a clear and readable historical narrative are well displayed in *The Strategy of Sea Power*.

This book was an expanded version of the Lees-Knowles lectures which Roskill gave at Cambridge in the Spring of 1961. A modest man, he was pleased at their good reception:

> "The first lecture at Cambridge went, I think, quite well. They gave me one of the small lecture rooms in Mill Lane, and rather to my surprise it was full – almost entirely of undergraduates. Bearing in mind that it was a lovely evening and the river was packed with young people in punts pretending to study for their tripos, I thought it showed unexpected interest in my subject that so many should be

prepared to come indoors. I go for the second one on Monday with more confidence."

In turning his lectures into a book Roskill consulted other naval and academic authorities before passing the resultant manuscripts over to Collins the publishers. *The Strategy of Sea Power* appeared in February 1962; it was well received by reviewers and the general public alike. Inevitably there were some criticisms. In the *Telegraph* C. Northcote Parkinson pointed out that Roskill relied almost exclusively on the experience of the Royal Navy, to the exclusion of other navies; other academics argued that Roskill had artificially polarised the 'continental' and 'maritime' schools of strategy – the relationship between the two being in fact more complex than mere competition. Some senior naval officers still in uniform were concerned that Roskill's enthusiastic espousal of the submarine as the capital ship of the future would make it more difficult for them to get the new carriers they thought they needed. But generally *The Strategy of Sea Power* was recognised as a 'masterly feat of compression' as rich in its analysis of the past as it was stimulating in its guidance of the future. The book sold steadily, was reprinted, appeared in the United States and was translated into German. It has continued to maintain a steady readership ever since.

The Strategy of Sea Power can be looked at in two ways. Firstly, as a traditional naval history of Britain, it describes the evolution of British sea power from its earliest days and shows its importance in British history. As such it might be thought vulnerable to various sorts of criticism. In the first place, Roskill's use of the first person plural throughout his book would seem old-fashioned when set against the stern objectivity of modern historians. More substantially, a generalised tour d'horizon of the whole of Britain's maritime history is bound to be challengeable in the light of later, more detailed work on finer points. One of the biggest gaps in Roskill's treatment of the Second World War derives from the fact that he was not allowed to allude to the operational effects of ULTRA intelligence. Thus recent books on the Battle of the Atlantic such as Patrick Beesley's *Very Special Intelligence* or Jurgen Röhwer's *The Convoy Battles of March 1943* inevitably add a new and missing dimension to Roskill's coverage. Yet despite this, the broad thrust of his treatment of the conduct of this and other conflicts remains as valid now as it was when it first appeared. Indeed later scholarship has often demonstrated the succinct perceptiveness of Roskill's earlier commentary. His analysis of the despatch of the *Prince of Wales* and *Repulse* to the Far East in 1941 (pp. 174–5), for instance, is a miracle of accurate compression.

The thrust of *The Strategy of Sea Power* has also been challenged, less for its treatment of specific events than for the general assumptions on which it is founded. For instance Paul Kennedy's seminal and much admired book *The Rise and Fall of British Naval Mastery*, which appeared in 1976, took the usual navalist hypothesis, which plainly underlies Roskill's work, and turned it back to front: British sea power, by his account, was made possible by and determined by British economic power rather than the other way about. The importance of maritime power relative to other forms of power is thus challenged.

Moreover even the effectiveness of a strategy based on maritime power is open to debate. Roskill was aware of a sea power's limitations in dealing with a land power: he accepted that British sea power could not on its own have defeated Napoleon (p. 77); that the control of the land may often facilitate the control of the sea (pp. 162–3, p. 221); that conditions in the Far East were much more suited for the application of maritime power in the shape of blockade or amphibious operations than they were in Europe, and that the Russian army is due much of the credit for the final defeat of Germany (p. 240). There are those, however, who would argue that even accepting these qualifications, Roskill makes the maritime case too strongly. Perhaps sea power did determine the outcome of the war in the Mediterranean, but how strategically central was that campaign anyway? Many would dispute his closing conclusion on the Second World War: ". . . the strategy which brought about first the downfall of Italy, then the surrender of Germany, and finally that of Japan, was always predominantly maritime." (p. 234). A different perspective on these issues can be had, for example, from reading *The Sea Power of the State* by Admiral Sergei Gorshkov (until December 1985 Commander-in-Chief of the Soviet Navy). According to Gorshkov:

> "The war in the European theatre assumed an explicitly continental character and the operations of the fleets in the Atlantic theatre including the Mediterranean, Baltic and Black Seas were increasingly aimed at meeting the requirements of the land forces emphasizing the land nature of the greatest battle in history."

All this shows that Roskill's survey of British naval history dealt forcefully with some of the liveliest and most important of issues in contemporary debate about the history and development of war. No one hoping for a rounded understanding of the First or Second World Wars can possibly afford to neglect Stephen Roskill's work, even if they do not agree with his conclusions in their totality.

But *The Strategy of Sea Power* should also be read at a second level, too. The title of the book, the way in which Roskill makes constant use of historical analogy and comparative cross-referencing between historical parallels, his explicit discussion of the effect of new technology on ancient practices (as on p. 196–7 over the role of air power in the defence of shipping) and his concluding message that Britain's maritime experience has many implications for its present and future all show that Roskill's historical survey was a way of developing a general theory of the principles and practices of maritime strategy, nonetheless real for all that this was an unstated, implicit aim.

Roskill's philosophy of sea power was based on profound scholarship and personal experience. Every judgement and calculation in *The Strategy of Sea Power*, and for that matter nearly everything he wrote, is informed by his ideas about maritime strategy. Understanding these ideas is therefore important to a full appreciation of his treatment of the nature of war at sea in the past and maybe in the present and future too.

Although in *The Strategy of Sea Power* Roskill's theoretical analysis of such components of maritime strategy as sea control (p. 184), the nature of blockade (p. 48) and so on are scattered throughout his narrative, he in fact came closest to defining his philosophy explicitly in the first chapter of the first volume of *The War at Sea*, and it may be convenient briefly to recapitulate that philosophy here.

In the first paragraph of that work Roskill demonstrated a proper awareness of the value of maritime power particularly to the British:

> During the three centuries or so of our history as a world power it has several times happened that a far stronger continental coalition has pitted its might against Britain and her allies, has won a series of resounding victories on land only to find itself brought up against a method of waging war with which its leaders could not grapple and of which they had no clear understanding. Yet, ultimately, our maritime strategy, founded on centuries of experience of the sea, brought our enemies to utter defeat.
>
> When Britain and France took up the new German challenge in 1939 they took it up on the Continent. But when the enemy's land victories of 1939 and 1940 had deprived us of all our continental allies, a change of emphasis in our strategy became inevitable – if for no other reason, because only two methods of continuing the war against Germany remained open to us. One was the offensive use of our

initially small bomber force against German military and industrial targets; the other was to exploit to the utmost our traditional capacity to employ a maritime strategy as the means of bringing overwhelming forces to bear against the enemy in theatres of our own choice.

In common with other strategists of sea power Roskill considered it important to define what he thought were the basic constituents of sea power. In his view they are three:

The first comprises all the varied instruments of war which work on or beneath the surface of the sea or in the air above it. It can be called the Strength Element, for it is on their strength and numbers that maritime control greatly depends. Second comes the possession and safety of the bases from which all the instruments of maritime power must work. If bases are lacking, or are inadequately defended, the ships and aircraft cannot fulfil their functions. This can be called the Security Element. The third element of maritime power comprises the Merchant Navy, which must be adequate to feed our home population, to bring in the raw materials needed by our industries, to carry our exports overseas and to transport our armies and their multifarious supplies to the theatres where they are required to fight. Nor is the Merchant Navy by itself enough. It must be supported by an adequate shipbuilding and ship repairing industry to enable losses to be replaced and damaged ships to be returned rapidly to service. This can, perhaps, best be called the Transport Element. If it is inevitable that, in maritime war, the actions fought by the warships and aircraft gain most attention, it must never be forgotten that the purpose of those actions is, nearly always, the protection of the merchantmen; and without the steady devotion of the men who man those ships the whole structure of maritime power must crumble.

Such, then, appear to be the elements comprising maritime power in a modern context; and each of them must be present in adequate form if the nation's maritime strategy is to be fulfilled.

He was alert to the possibility that the precise form of these elements might vary over time. In the Second World War, for instance, aircraft of both the land and sea-based variety had come to exert a very great influence indeed over events at sea. Technology meant that the capacity to control the surface of the sea depended in large measure on control of the water beneath and the air above. The arrival of the aircraft and its impact on maritime operations made it necessary to redefine the elements of maritime power which used until then to bear considerable similarity to the ancient order of things when it was accepted that the fleet which controlled the sea routes and fought off all challengers must comprise three classes of warship. They were called the ships of the line or battleships, the cruisers and the flotilla vessels:

> The cruisers actually exercised control of our sea communications – supported by the battle fleets to prevent interference with our cruisers by more powerful enemy units – and the flotilla vessels acted as scouts for the battle fleet and carried out multifarious functions as escorts and in local defence.

But in the Second World War aircraft showed themselves capable of performing part or indeed sometimes the whole of the duties hitherto borne exclusively by the three types of surface warships. They attacked the enemy's principal naval units (the function of battleships), carried out increasingly effective reconnaissance and shadowing work (the function of cruisers), and supplemented the flotilla vessels in their multifarious duties in convoy escort, anti-submarine and fleet defence work. Very evidently the *material* may change, but the principles remain.

Turning to the conduct of war, Roskill believed that the experience of the Second World War showed that the prosecution of a maritime strategy tends to follow a common pattern:

> The experiences of the last war appear to reinforce those of earlier struggles which had shown that the prosecution of a maritime strategy passes through several phases. In the first it is probable that our strategy will be defensive, particularly if a new continental coalition has to be constructed. During this phase our maritime power is used to defend these islands from invasion, to cut the enemy off from the rest of the world and weaken his economy by enforcing a blockade, to hold and reinforce certain key points and areas overseas and to bring to this country the supplies which are essential to its survival. But while it may be necessary to accept that our strategy must, during this phase, remain defensive it is of cardinal importance that no opportunity should be lost to assume the tactical and local offensive against such enemy forces as may present themselves. If such opportunities are lost the period of the strategic defensive may bring about a decline of morale and of the will to fight. Assuming however that war remains such as it has been hitherto, and that our commanders seize every opportunity for local and tactical offensives, the period of the strategic defensive possesses certain inherent compensations. Chief among these is that, while our war economy develops, while our resources are mustered and our military strength expands, the enemy is forced, if he wishes to attack us, to do so across seas which he does not control. Such ventures, if made, expose his forces to drastic counter-measures and may result in expensive failures. The unwillingness of the Germans to accept such risks during the recent war is underlined by the immunity from attack of such key points as Iceland and the Azores. During the second phase our maritime forces continue to

carry out the functions which occupied their whole capacity during the first, but in addition the nation's offensive power is being developed. Forces of all armies are being built up, assembled and trained; and plans for their offensive employment are being prepared. This phase, which ends with the first major offensive operation, may well be entitled 'The Period of Balance' since the success or failure of the first offensive has yet to be decided. In the third phase the full advantages of the patient pursuit of a maritime strategy are reaped and our forces are transported overseas to assume the offensive.

The immediate aim of maritime strategy is, Roskill thought, to establish command of the sea, or sea control, but this need not necessarily be an absolute control.

The aim of maritime strategy is therefore not so much to establish complete control of all sea communications, which would be an ideal hardly attainable until final victory was almost won, as to develop the ability to establish zones of maritime control wherever and whenever they may be necessary for the prosecution of the war in accordance with the directions of the Government. And a zone of maritime control means no more than an ability to pass ships safely across an area of water which may be quite small in extent or may cover many thousands of square miles of ocean. Thus the enemy, mainly by the use of aircraft, established for some time a zone of maritime control in the central Mediterranean which, while it lasted, virtually denied to us the use of the communications through that sea. And the crisis of the whole struggle in the west developed, after the Battle of Britain had been won, from our need to establish a zone of maritime control over the entire length of the Atlantic shipping lanes and the enemy's sustained attempts to defeat that control. It must, however, be emphasised that complete control of even a restricted zone is rarely established, and that it is far more common for control to be in dispute than undisputed. Moreover, if control over a particular zone is lost by one belligerent it is by no means certain that it will pass to the other. In this stage it is more likely that control will remain in dispute and such, for example, was the condition in the English Channel in the summer of 1940. Furthermore, throughout the period when control of sea communications is in dispute, and even after the establishment of a reasonably firm zone of maritime control, sporadic attacks will remain a possibility. Such attacks on our sea communications persisted almost to the end of the recent war.

Wherever, therefore, a zone of maritime control is established, our own commercial and military seaborne traffic will be able to pass in reasonable safety. But there is a further effect of the establishment of such a zone. It will automatically bring about the denial to the enemy of the use of the same sea communications. In other words, the creation of such a zone produces a positive result to ourselves and a negative result to the enemy; and the latter can be as important as the former. Thus by creating a zone of maritime control in the focal area for shipping off the River Plate we protected our own South American trade and prevented the enemy from using the same routes; and when the zone of maritime control essential for the North African landings of 1942-43 had been completely established, we denied the enemy the use of sea communications adequately to succour and support his own armies in that continent.

This capacity to control the sea plainly demands flexibility in the application of maritime power and in the concentration of its instruments. This concentration is more than the simple massing of numbers of warships. It calls for an intelligent distribution of force so that on the one hand it can cope with possibly widespread and simultaneous calls on its services but can, on the other, still be wielded as a cohesive unit. The proper balance between the concentration and division of force is difficult to achieve. Roskill was, like Sir Julian Corbett (a strategist historian of the First World War whom he admired), suspicious of the tradition of massing forces as a prerequisite to seeking decision with the enemy by battle at sea.

This has long been a fundamental precept in our maritime services, and it is a tradition of immense power and value. None the less it is a precept which can be carried too far, and our history contains examples where it has only led to indecisive battles. It must, in truth, be constantly tempered by the judgment and experience of those responsible for the conduct of operations, since it is well established that, if enthusiasm for battle outruns judgment, the blow will fall upon air; whereas by waiting with forces correctly disposed we shall compel the enemy ultimately to offer an opportunity for action. It happened many times in the war that the commanders of our maritime forces assumed the tactical offensive, often against superior strength, with great gallantry and most favourable results; and it now seems that our adversaries sometimes sacrificed a potential advantage through reluctance (often imposed on them by higher direction) to do likewise. None the less the well-known capacity of a defensive strategy in certain conditions to inflict grievous injury on the enemy and to stultify his purpose still holds good. Perhaps the outstanding example from the last war relates to the defeat of the enemy's attack on our merchant shipping. Though it was not at once accepted there now seems no doubt at all that it was the defensive strategy of sailing ships in convoy and of providing the convoys with powerful surface and air escorts which did most to accomplish that decisive victory. Yet it was the desire at once to assume the offensive against the U-boats which led to the persistent employment, during the first year and more of the war, of flotilla vessels to hunt enemy submarines in the vast ocean spaces instead of using them to escort our convoys. Not only did the early hunting groups achieve negligible success, but the dispersal of our slender resources in that manner led to our convoys being inadequately escorted, and so suffering heavy losses, and to many good opportunities to destroy the submarines which attacked them being missed. Equally the view that bomber aircraft could contribute most to the defeat of the U-boat by taking the offensive against the enemy's bases and his building and repair yards rather than by escorting and protecting the convoys far out at sea, is not substantiated by post-war analysis of their achievements. It is today impossible to avoid the conclusion that the most effective way of defeating the U-boat was by waiting for it in the vicinity of the prey which it was seeking.

The chief difficulty in implementing this policy of waiting is the reluctance of public opinion to believe that it can be a deliberate strategical move and not an example of timidity or pusillanimity on the part of our commanders. Yet the truth is that nearly all of the really effective blows struck at our enemies' maritime power have come about through a deliberate tempering of the desire to seek and destroy the enemy by judgment and experience, which had taught that the object would be more assuredly achieved by offering the enemy a bait and then waiting for him to present himself. The sinking of the *Bismarck* and of the *Scharnhorst* provide examples of this, though in the case of the latter ship it was necessary to wait many months before she came to her destruction. All the major warships of the Japanese Navy which could be made fit for sea also came, ultimately, of their own accord to meet their end.

Roskill and Corbett both attributed the fatal tendency to concentrate too much on the exciting business of preparing for a decisive battle to a failure properly to appreciate that command of the sea and the control of sea communications was not an end in itself but simply a means to an end. The point of maritime power was to be able to use the sea for one's own use and to prevent the enemy from using it for his. Roskill believed that the Royal Navy sometimes suffered from devoting too many of its assets to winning command and not enough to the tasks of exploiting it.

He recognized that the sea is vital as a means of transportation of men and material essential for the conduct of war. It followed that one corollary of having the necessary command to use the sea in this way could be to stop the enemy from doing the same.

> The denial to the enemy of the use of sea communications is accomplished by the application of all the various instruments comprising maritime power, but the sum total of their effects can be described as being the establishment of a blockade. This is one of the chief means whereby a nation which is stronger at sea may be able to impose its will on one which, though stronger on land, is not self-supporting in food and raw materials. In spite of German arguments to the contrary, which read strangely from a nation well versed in the exaction of all sorts of rights, penalties and requisitions from nations subjugated by continental campaigns, it is a relatively humane form of war. In common, however, with other aspects of the exercise of maritime power it is slow and cumulative in its effects; on the other hand, it starts to function from the day on which hostilities open.

Control of the sea is also a prerequisite to operations against the shore. By denying it to the enemy, the navy can prevent him from launching a successful invasion.

> Maritime strategy in face of a threat to invade our shores also requires some special consideration. There is a tendency, in

such circumstances, for the public to demand the massing of our forces around our coasts. Such a policy, if adopted, would be a false concentration; the attitude adopted would be wholly defensive, and the initiative would rest with the enemy who might thereby be given the very opportunity he seeks. The traditional British policy, and it has been successfully applied many times in our history, is quite different. In the first place the enemy transports which are assembling to carry, or are actually carrying his army, displace his warships as the primary object of our maritime forces. A firm grip over the assembly of the transports is established by blockade. Today this includes bombing, bombardment and minelaying as well as constant watch and patrol off his assembly ports. The blockade is enforced by flotilla vessels and aircraft, but they must be supported by greater strength and covered by the battle force in the background. The threat of invasion is clearly visible to the layman; the counter-measures are probably concealed from him. But they are none the less effective for their invisibility from the land, and there should be no uneasiness in British homes as long as the old methods are applied and the strength and vigour of our maritime forces remain unimpaired.

Assuming, however, that the old policy is adopted, the enemy must try either to force his invasion army through in one large mass, or slip through whilst evading our blockading forces. The second choice can hardly be applicable to a modern expedition attempting to cross narrow seas. The first choice is extremely favourable to the defence; it produces exactly the conditions for which we have always hoped and has, again and again in our history, led to decisive sea battles. It appears that Hitler intended to adopt this course in 1940, thereby following in the path of many earlier continental strategists, and that the British policy which frustrated and defeated the intentions of his forerunners also destroyed his plans. Indeed, study of contemporary German documents leaves little doubt that the quarrelsome vacillations of the German leaders were chiefly caused by the uneasiness which always seems to be produced among our enemies when it becomes apparent that an invasion is to be launched across seas which they do not adequately control. The lessons of 1940 appear to reinforce our knowledge that, although continental enemies have repeatedly tried to find a way to invade these islands without first defeating our maritime forces, no such short cut exists.

By the same token, with the necessary control of the sea the navy can make possible those operations against the enemy's shore which are at once the final aim and crowning glory of a successfully conducted maritime war.

Finally – and this point is placed last in this discussion because it is not reached until the application of our maritime strategy has begun to bear fruit and the early strategic defensive can be exchanged for the offensive – we must consider the employment of maritime power to transport our armies overseas, to place them on shore in the chosen theatres, to support and supply them as may be necessary and to shift their bases forward as their land campaigns advance. It is plain that the establishment of an adequate and effective zone of maritime control in the approaches to, and the coastal waters off the disembarkation area is an absolute prerequisite for success in this type of operation. The functions of our maritime forces in an amphibious expedition of this nature differ considerably from those of the forces employed on mercantile convoy work. In the latter case their duties end with the safe arrival of the convoy in port; but in the former case they must continue to support and assist the army after it has landed, and continue to maintain the maritime control on which success on land hinges. Their function, in fact, ceases to be purely maritime; they become a part of one vast and integrated organisation comprising all arms of all services, and all working towards the common end of defeating the enemy's land forces.

The great merits of amphibious expeditions of this nature are their mobility and secrecy. By making good use of strategic and tactical feints and defeating the enemy's reconnaissance it is possible to achieve surprise in both spheres, as, contrary to all expectations, occurred in the case of all three major enterprises (North Africa, Sicily and Normandy) launched by us and our Allies against our European enemies during the late war.

Provided that the planning and organisation of the whole vast and complex undertaking are meticulously based on inter-service understanding and co-operation, fortunate is the nation to whom the ability to undertake such expeditions falls. Though the exercise of maritime power in defence of trade is essential to the nation's war economy, and it alone can produce the conditions from which the final decisive offensive will be launched, it is by exercising this same heritage in the despatch of great military expeditions overseas that a maritime strategy can be crowned by final victory.

Knowing Stephen Roskill's philosophy of seapower helps us of course to understand his general analysis of the past and his more detailed commentaries on particular events. But it also helps us to establish his views for the present and future, a theme he approached in the final chapter of his book. Since over 20 years has elapsed since the first appearance of *The Strategy of Sea Power*, a brief concluding review of maritime developments since 1962 has been added at the end of this edition.

Finally, I would like to record my thanks to Mr. Nicholas Roskill for inviting me to supervise the preparation of this second edition of *The Strategy of Sea Power* and to the publisher, Mr. John

Goodchild for his support – and patience – throughout the project. My thanks are due to Peter Brown of the British Academy for the use of an advance copy of John Ehrman's memoir of Stephen Roskill in the *Proceedings of the British Academy*. Marion Stuart and the staff of the Churchill College Archive Centre were very helpful and so also were Kathy Mason, Jean Taylor and the typing pool of the Royal Naval College, Greenwich. I am grateful to the Chief of the Defence Staff, Admiral Sir John Fieldhouse, and his staff, for the timely reminder that Stephen Roskill's work is as valuable now as ever it was. My wife Cherry provided her usual support and forbearance throughout. But I am, of course, most indebted to Stephen Roskill himself to whose memory this edition is most gratefully and respectfully dedicated.

Royal Naval College   GEOFFREY TILL
Greenwich
December 1985

CAPTAIN S. W. ROSKILL

D.S.C., F.R.HIST.S., R.N.(RETD.)
FELLOW OF CHURCHILL COLLEGE, CAMBRIDGE

The Strategy of
Sea Power

ITS DEVELOPMENT AND
APPLICATION

Based on the Lees-Knowles Lectures
delivered in the University
of Cambridge, 1961

Facts are the mere dross of history. It is from the abstract truth which interpenetrates them, and lies latent among them like gold in the ore, that the mass derives its value.

LORD MACAULAY, *Essay on History*

As for the historian himself . . . he must approach his material as any other creative artist does— with the sense that it contains some essential and permanent truths which it may be his skill or good fortune to release.

C. V. WEDGWOOD, *Truth and Opinion in History*

At this point I find myself compelled to express an opinion which I know most people will object to; nevertheless as I believe it to be true, I will not suppress it.

HERODOTUS, *The Histories*, VII

FOREWORD

This short account of the development and application of maritime strategy is based on the Lees-Knowles lectures given in Cambridge University in 1961. The debt I owe to three historians who studied Britain's earlier maritime wars, and analysed the working of sea power, will be plain to all who are familiar with the work of Rear-Admiral A. T. Mahan, u.s.n., Sir Julian Corbett and Admiral Sir Herbert Richmond; and the fact that in all three cases I have found occasion sometimes to disagree with them, and in a few instances to correct them on matters of fact, vitiates my respect for their work but little; since the study of history must, after all, be an ever-continuing process. Nor does the acknowledgment of what I owe to those three writers by any means mark the limit of my indebtedness to others. Among contemporary or near-contemporary historians the authoritative works of S. R. Gardiner, Dr. A. L. Rowse, Sir John Neale, Mr. David Ogg and Dr. J. A. Williamson on their special periods have all proved quite invaluable.

Although it may seem bold to the point of rashness to consider how far the theses and theories of Mahan, Corbett and Richmond remain valid in an age when man's insatiable urge to discovery is plainly leading him towards such revolutionary accomplishments as the conquest of space, such an attempt has here been made. The justification for this temerity lies in the belief that, while historical experience must require constant revision and reconsideration, and must in any case always be viewed with cautious scepticism, its neglect has in several recent instances proved premature, if not

wholly mistaken. Thus there may be found in these pages a warning against rejection of principles and practices which, although
their continued validity certainly cannot be guaranteed, have yet
to be proved obsolete.

In assessing the strategy employed in the First World War the
historian is handicapped by the fact that, although forty-five years
have now elapsed since the battle of Jutland was fought, a considerable number of important documents are, by direction of
trustees or literary executors, still 'reserved' from scrutiny. Such
are some of the papers of Admiral of the Fleet Earl Jellicoe, and also
the only surviving unexpurgated copy of Captain J. E. T. Harper's
Jutland Record. On the other hand I have been greatly aided by
the kindness of individuals who have lent or given me letters and
papers dealing with the same period, for use without any re-
striction other than that imposed by the law of copyright. In
particular I would thank Sir Shane Leslie, Bart., for the gift of a
very interesting collection of letters written by Admiral of the Fleet
Earl Beatty between 1917 and 1921 to Lady Godfrey-Faussett, for
allowing me to see the typescript of his forthcoming book based on
Commander Oswald Frewen's diaries, and for sparing me time to
discuss the events and personalities of the 1914-18 war. Mr. Wilfred
Clarke has also been generous in giving me the whole of the papers
which he collected on the battle of Jutland as a result of his service
in the Admiralty. Analysis of the strategy employed in the Second
World War has proved considerably easier than the first, and I have
been particularly fortunate in having the use of all the private papers
of Admirals of the Fleet Sir Charles Forbes and Lord Cunningham.
Other senior officers, too many to name individually, have also
made generous gifts or loans of their letters and papers, and to them
collectively I would extend my cordial thanks.

I am deeply indebted to Dr. J. A. Williamson, M.A., D.LIT., to
Professor Michael Lewis, C.B.E., M.A., and to Professor Christopher
Lloyd, M.A., for reading and criticising the whole or parts of this
work; while Professor A. J. Marder of the University of Honolulu,

has kindly allowed me to read his forthcoming book *From the Dreadnought to Scapa Flow* in typescript and to quote certain passages from it. Mr. Richard Ollard of Collins and Co. has gone far beyond what a writer can reasonably expect by way of advice from his publisher, and Commander Geoffrey Hare, D.S.C., R.N., has again helped with the tedious work of checking dates and quotations, and has prepared for me yet another excellent index. My devoted secretary, Miss Edith Eales, has dealt most efficiently with the innumerable redrafts and amendments I have made, while my wife has coped very patiently and successfully with the difficult task of combining literature with matrimony, and has given much time to checking my typescript. Finally I must thank Lord Adrian, O.M., F.R.S., Master of Trinity College, Cambridge, for inviting me to give the lectures which set my feet in the path which has led to the production of this book.

S. W. ROSKILL

Blounce,
South Warnborough,
Basingstoke, Hants.
June 1961

CONTENTS

I

===

From early times to
the end of the
Seven Years'
War

The function of maritime power is to win and keep control of the seas for one's own use, and to deny such control to one's adversaries. Though the aim of mercantile states and nations has always been the acquisition of wealth, there is a distinction between the aggressive and predatory methods of some, and the desire of others to enjoy the benefits of a peaceful exchange of goods carried by sea; and we may here note that, in the course of evolution, it has been quite common for a nation to change from the first category to the second. Such a metamorphosis is indeed apparent in the development of our own country.

The exchange of goods by sea has been called 'Mercantilism', which Murray's dictionary defines as 'devotion to trade and commerce'; but because to-day 'Mercantilism' has come to be generally used in a narrow sense in the field of economics, it should be made clear that here it is used to cover all maritime enterprise. Although devotion to trade and commerce may not be the most elevated of human activities, it does seem to fulfil one of man's strongest instincts. Moreover without it the spread of civilisation all over the world could hardly have come to pass. From the dawn of history one finds evidence of mercantilism in the activities of states; and the preference for the movement of goods by sea rather than by land is easily explained by the fact that about three-quarters of the earth's surface is covered by salt water, and that it has generally been found both cheaper and safer to transport goods on that element.

Joseph Conrad rightly called the Mediterranean 'the cradle of oversea traffic and of the art of naval combats'; and he has given us a vivid picture of the profound influence of 'that tideless basin freed from hidden shoals and treacherous currents . . . which has led mankind gently from headland to headland, from bay to bay, from island to island, out into the promise of world-wide oceans'.[1] The Phoenicians of ancient times, the Athenians during their greatest period, the Carthaginians for much of their history, the Venetians and Genoese at the height of their wealth and influence, the Spaniards and Portuguese of the medieval era, were all trading nations or states; and their wide influence lends force to Dr. Johnson's remark that 'Almost everything that sets us above the savages has come to us from the shores of the Mediterranean'. Finally the influence of those maritime states reached these small islands—'the sea-defended green spot Clas Merdin' of the Celts[2] and caused their people to look outwards from their shores over the wide sea horizon.

But devotion to trade being an acquisitive practice, and the accumulation and enjoyment of wealth by man having always aroused the envy of his neighbours, it has invariably been necessary for a trading community to defend the ships and craft which carry its goods to and fro across the sea; for if the sea is not *ruled* as well as *used* losses are bound to be suffered, and may reach such dimensions as will imperil the community's existence. This principle has been understood and applied in varying degree by the rulers of such states. Thucydides for instance quotes Pericles as saying 'the rule of the sea is indeed a great matter'; and one finds echoes of that view in the words and writings of English philosophers, such as Francis Bacon, and of statesmen such as Burleigh and the elder Pitt, from the beginning of our own mercantile period down to recent times. In sum it seems true to say that the exchange of goods by sea must lead to the development of the instruments of sea power; and once a nation has provided itself with such instruments the

[1] *The Mirror of the Sea* (Dent, Collected Works Ed., 1946, pp. 148 and 152).
[2] Cambro-Briton, Vol. I, p. 8 (London, 1820).

manner in which they may be employed to the best advantage, which we define as strategy, is bound to become important.

But long before England became 'devoted to trade and commerce' its primitive people became aware of another aspect in which the rule of the sea had immense influence on their lives. Foreign raiders were constantly attacking our coasts for plunder, and in some cases stayed on as settlers, establishing their own form of government. Thus Julius Caesar's invasions in 55 and 54 B.C. are, thanks to his own chronicles, well known; but the arrival of Claudius's expeditionary force in A.D. 43 actually had much longer lasting influence, since it was after that date that Roman rule and law were extended over the greater part of these islands. In the ten centuries which separate Claudius from the arrival of William of Normandy in A.D. 1066 there were, however, a number of other invasions: for the Angles, the Jutes and the Danes all then came by sea; and it is not until the 9th century A.D. that we find the dawn of the realisation that only by meeting and engaging such invaders while they were yet at sea could their purposes be frustrated. Though Alfred the Great may reasonably be regarded as the originator of British sea power, many more centuries were to elapse before the principle he learnt from his long struggle with the Danes—that 'there is no advantage in living on an island unless you control the waters that wash its shores'—came to be recognised as essential to national policy. We thus arrive at the second function of sea power —to give security against invasion; and in passing we may note that William of Normandy's cross-Channel operation in 1066 might well have ended in disaster had Harold Godwinson not dispersed his fleet a short while previously, and had the invaders not been very fortunate in the weather they encountered. As Julius Caesar discovered on his first reconnaissance in 55 B.C., and many other continental would-be conquerors have since learnt, the fickleness of the weather in the English Channel and the strength of the tidal currents which sweep through it are among the most effective guardians of England's security.

As every mercantile nation has expanded its activities it has experienced the need to provide protection for its trading ships in waters far distant from as well as adjacent to the homeland. To meet this need bases must be established along the trade routes, where ships can water, victual and refit. Again the bases themselves cannot fulfil their purpose unless they are made secure, and that has always necessitated both the stationing of a garrison in them and the presence of armed ships to control the local waters. Without a garrison a base may at any time fall to a surprise attack from the land or sea, and without an adequate naval force to work from it the base cannot possibly fulfil its functions—as the fate of Singapore in 1942 forcibly reminded us. Though we will return to the subject of overseas bases when we review the spread of English trade all over the world, we should here note that, even though the number of the essential bases and their proximity to each other will be reduced as the speed and endurance of the trading ships increase, they always have been and still are an essential element in the application of a maritime strategy.

We have now reached a stage in our thesis where we can define the fundamental requirements for the enjoyment of fruitful commerce in peace, and for the prosecution of a maritime strategy in war. First comes the need to render the homeland secure against invasion, and the overseas bases secure against sudden attack or blockade. Second we may place the possession of a sufficient fleet of trading vessels to carry the nation's goods hither and thither across the seas and oceans, in war as well as in peace; and a natural corollary of that requirement is the creation and support of an adequate ship-building and ship-repairing industry. Third come the instruments necessary to protect the trading ships during their voyages against legalised or unlegalised marauders. Last, but by no means the least important, comes the need for a maritime nation to foster the profession of the sea: for without seamen experienced in all the vagaries of the element on which they live no fighting fleet can work successfully in war. In England the fisheries and the short-sea traders have always provided many of our finest seamen: and in recent times their ranks have been strengthened by the yachtsmen and amateur sailors who have, in ever-increasing numbers, sought their recreation on the waters. But the chief source of our maritime strength has for at least three centuries been the men who have made the profession of the sea their life's work in the Royal and Merchant Navies.

Nations devoted to trade have generally employed statutory means to secure to themselves what they regard as their rightful share (and that is always the largest possible share) of world commerce. Such was the long series of English Navigation Acts, the first of which dates from the reign of Richard II; and their purpose always has been to restrict, or if possible prohibit the carriage of goods to and from our ports by foreign vessels. The less fortunate nations have commonly employed diplomacy in the first instance to endeavour to improve their position, and have reinforced their diplomatic moves by seeking alliances. If diplomacy fails, or the strength of the alliance is deemed adequate, a state which we would call ' cold war ' has often followed; and the cold war has not seldom led to an outbreak of open hostilities. Thus England and Spain were in a state of ' cold war ' from about 1569 to 1585, when—for all Elizabeth's endeavours to preserve peace with her Spanish brother-in-law—the trade rivalry became so acute that Philip II decided to rid himself of his troublesome adversaries by force.[1] Before leaving the subject of statutory measures designed to secure as large as possible a share of the world's commerce, it is worth remarking that, although the English Navigation Acts were relaxed early in the 19th century, and were virtually repealed at the dawn of the Free Trade era in the middle of that century, at the present time the subsidising by governments of uneconomical shipping, and such devices as ' Cargo Preference Acts ' and ' Flags of Convenience ' serve, and are intended to serve exactly the same purpose.

[1] Sir John Neale in his essay *The Via Media in Politics* (*Essays in Elizabethan History*, Cape, 1958) lends his authority to the description of the conflict without arms in Elizabeth I's reign as ' cold war '.

19

Though our subject here is maritime strategy, and the instruments of sea power therefore take first place, it must be made clear that, although many wars have been decided mainly by sea power, rarely, if ever, have they been decided by sea power alone. In the first place an island nation like Britain can seldom avoid some commitment on the adjacent continent. We have fought to keep a strategically placed port, such as Antwerp, from passing into unfriendly hands. We have extended to Europe wars that had their origin in other continents, as in our long struggles against the Dutch and the French. For all these purposes we have had to form alliances; and once they have been concluded the call to send military support to the ally in the event of war is bound to arise. Thus there has always been a clash between those who have considered that land operations against the common enemy will be more fruitful than sea operations designed to weaken his economy and so his military condition—in other words between what are commonly called the ' Continental' and the ' Maritime' schools of strategy; and it has been a first, and most difficult task for our statesmen to decide which to adopt. In the majority of our wars an effort has been made to find a satisfactory compromise, but the Continental school has, as we shall see, more often gained its way than the Maritime. Even where our strategy has been predominantly maritime it has not been the use of naval forces alone, but the skilful deployment of naval and military forces working to achieve a clearly understood common purpose, that has brought success. Convincing examples of that fact can be found in the annals of the Seven Years' War (1756-63) and of the second war against Germany; and we may here note that, since the conquest of the air has had so profound an effect on all strategic and tactical considerations, it has become essential to integrate the new instruments of war into the broad strategic pattern. In sum it seems true to say that although sea power has often proved itself the most important single factor in war, and a predominantly maritime strategy has sometimes brought striking rewards, a decision cannot be won without the support and collaboration of the military and, latterly, the air services.

We left the development of English maritime enterprise at the time of its false dawn under Alfred the Great; and the 10th to the mid-15th centuries of our history can be briefly dismissed, since during the rule of the Norman and Angevin kings the country was too fully occupied by the struggle for power at home and in France to look outwards beyond the sea horizon. However we should take note of two important developments of the 13th century. The first is the rise and influence of the Cinque Ports (originally, Hastings, Romney, Hythe, Dover and Sandwich) as a factor in the control of the short-sea trade routes to and from Europe; and the second is the export of English wool, initially in the raw state and later in manufactured form, across the narrow seas. The privileges granted to the Cinque Ports in respect of that trade and of the fisheries, and the responsibilities for defence placed upon them in return, made their private navies the backbone of medieval English sea power. And the Portsmen of the medieval era can justifiably be regarded as the progenitors of the tough, hard-bitten inshore fishermen to whom this country has long owed a very great but rarely acknowledged debt—not least for their work in the mine-sweeping service during the wars of this century. Ruthless and unscrupulous the Portsmen certainly were; but they understood as no one else the vagaries of wind and weather, and of the tides and currents in that shingle-strewn stretch of coast between Dungeness and the North Foreland, which has had so profound an influence on English history. With the decline of the Cinque Ports in the 15th century, caused largely by the silting up of their harbours, the responsibilities of the Portsmen were inherited by the seamen of Bristol, Plymouth and Falmouth in the west, and by those working from the harbours around the Thames estuary in the east; but of recent times one of the Cinque Ports, Dover, has recovered a good deal of its earlier importance, thanks to the construction of an artificial harbour. In defence of our coastal waters the key points have altered many times, the principles never. The fishermen of Lowestoft, Hull, Grimsby and Aberdeen occupy to-day as important a place in the general scheme as did their forbears who sailed out of Rye, Winchelsea and Hastings. ' Give up the fishery ' Admiral Sir Charles Saunders, of Quebec fame, told the House of Commons in 1774 ' and you lose your breed of seamen '.

The Norman and Angevin Kings of England themselves often owned some ships capable of fighting at sea; but for their warlike purposes they depended more on those which the Cinque Ports, and certain similar but less powerful organisations, had to lend to the King on demand. That there was really no such thing as a permanent ' Navy Royal ' is proved by Henry V's ships being sold on his death to pay his debts—rather sad obsequies for the victor of Agincourt. From the 12th to the 15th century there was a great deal of cross-Channel raiding in both directions, especially during the Hundred Years' War (1339-1453); but the sea fights of that period, such as the Battle of Sluys in 1340, were really extensions of the land campaigns, which happened to take place afloat. Thus, apart from the continuous struggle in the narrow seas, the period cannot be said to mark any significant development in maritime strategy; and the only sign of an awakening to the possibilities inherent in control of the seas is that Edward III's victory at Sluys enabled him to send an expeditionary force to France.

In about 1436, however, there appeared a remarkable document entitled ' The Libelle of Englyshe Policie '. It was in verse, and was possibly written by Adam de Moleyns, Bishop of the maritime See of Chichester; and in it are clear signs that the author understood both the benefits to be gained by commerce, and the basic principles underlying a maritime strategy. Thus the writer of the ' Libelle ' urged on his countrymen the need to ' Cherish merchandise, kepe the Admiraltie ', and in the realm of strategy to ' kepe then the sea that is the wall of England, and then is England kept by Goddes hand '; which, remembering 1940, has a remarkably modern ring about it.

In 1485 there took place an event which was to have far-reaching influence on the development of English seaborne trade; for Henry Tudor, Earl of Richmond, landed at Milford Haven with the object of 'liberating' (as this century would put it) the country from the yoke of Richard III, and on 22nd August he won the crown of England on Bosworth Field. Like its many predecessors this successful invasion, which founded the Tudor dynasty, would have been impossible had the defending forces maintained control of the narrow seas.

But to any student of maritime strategy Henry VII's reign demands attention for far weightier reasons than his having conducted a successful invasion; for he was the first king to apply the principles enunciated fifty years earlier in the 'Libelle'. Not only was Henry a shrewd business-man who certainly 'cherished merchandise', but he provided, though in a small way, the first instruments designed to make such a policy prosper. Though he actually built few King's ships, and never possessed more than about half a score of them, he used them cleverly and effectively. He dared neither to challenge Spain in the New World, nor quarrel with the powerful Hanseatic League in the Old; but his reign saw the passing of two Navigation Acts (1486 and 1489), he won valuable trading concessions in Flanders, he gained the first entry into the Mediterranean trade, and by authorising the Venetian John Cabot's crossing of the Atlantic in 1497 he inaugurated the golden age of English exploration. By the time that he died in 1509 the mercantile tonnage owned by his countrymen had increased considerably;[1] and he bequeathed to his son a small but compact Navy with, for the first time, an administrative machine behind it, and the beginnings of a proper home base for it at Portsmouth.

It was, however, his son Henry VIII—an altogether more colourful personality—who was the first to give real impetus to the

[1] Dr. Williamson has drawn my attention to the fact that customs receipts increased by about 30% during Henry VII's reign, and that it is probable that the English share of trade increased in relation to that carried in foreign ships. But the increase can hardly have been as great as sixfold, as suggested by Professor Lewis in *The History of the British Navy*, p. 29 (Allen & Unwin, 1959).

development of a fighting fleet. Moreover the purpose for which he built it was the eminently sound one of frustrating the efforts of France and Spain to carry their quarrel with him into his own kingdom. To the half-dozen ships that he inherited he added more than ninety, of which he built about half;[1] and among them were proper fighting ships, as distinct from the armed trading vessels which were all that his predecessors had possessed. This was a revolutionary development, since, outside the Mediterranean, no ships had previously been built with the sole purpose of fighting other ships. Henry VIII can therefore be regarded as the founder of the Battle Fleet which, as the primary instrument of our sea power, was to last for four and a half centuries. And, by creating the Navy Board, he also founded the administrative machine of Admiralty which still endures. Nor was Henry's influence on tactics less important than his building programme; since the heavy guns which he insisted on sending to sea had to be mounted low down on the broadsides of his larger ships, instead of high up in the forecastle and aftercastle. That technical revolution rang the death-knell of the oar-propelled galley which, especially in the Mediterranean, had for centuries been the chief instrument of sea power. One may compare the displacement of the galley by the heavy gun with the supersession of the latter by the airborne instruments of our own time. Technical changes have always had a profound influence on strategy and tactics which, as Sir Julian Corbett remarked,[2] are dictated by the dominant weapon in use at any period.

Nor was the obsolescence imposed on the galley the only influence of the new weapons introduced in Henry VIII's reign, since the mounting of guns on the broadside made it essential to fight so that they could bear on the enemy; and that could only be done by engaging in line ahead, or nearly so. It is likely that the firing of the first English broadsides, which was as revolutionary an

[1] See M. Oppenheim, *The Administration of the Royal Navy* 1509-1660 (Lane, 1896), Vol. I, pp. 48-9.
[2] Preface to *Fighting Instructions* (Navy Records Society, 1905).

occasion as the successful launching of the first guided missile, took place against the French fleet off Shoreham on 15th August, 1545; and thereafter the broadside remained the principal instrument of maritime power right down to recent times.

At his death in 1547 Henry VIII thus left a large and powerful fleet. But its strategic possibilities were as yet but dimly understood —for he had built it chiefly, if not solely, for defence against invasion; and that, as we have seen, is but one of the fundamental functions of maritime power. Though the encouragement of maritime enterprise was not a dominant purpose with Henry VIII, and he did not use his fleet to secure and expand the country's commerce, it seems certain that he did at least encourage trade with Spain and the Netherlands during the conflict between the Emperor Charles V, with whom he was generally in alliance, and France. What is certain is that, by the creation of efficient instruments of sea power he had in fact made possible the policy which his father had studiously avoided—namely a challenge to the influence of Spain, and to that country's monopoly of trade with the New World.

The age of the first Elizabeth is, in its own rights, an unfailing and fascinating source of study for historians. Whether their interest lies in politics or in war, in social development or in exploration, in literature or poetry, there is in the period ample material for a lifetime of study. What is common ground to all students of the period is that between the middle of the sixteenth century and the early years of the seventeenth England undoubtedly bred a remarkable galaxy of talented men. Moreover it was the prelude to the period when the use of the English language in prose and verse reached, in G. M. Trevelyan's apt words, ' its brief perfection '. Perhaps the closest parallel is Athens between the defeat of the third Persian invasion in 480 B.C. and the disasters of the Peloponnesian war some 80 years later; for in Elizabethan England and in republican Athens a sudden burgeoning of the arts was combined with a great extension of wealth and influence. The spirit of the age was adventurous, and once men are drawn to adventure their creative faculty seems to soar to unprecedented heights. It was, of course, on the sea that the Elizabethans sought and found adventure, and a fair proportion of the men of genius applied their skills to the challenges of discovery and trade. It would go to far to say that Gloriana herself had any deep grasp of the sea affair, or a clear understanding of maritime strategy. Her chief interests were always the security of her throne, and the state of her treasury; and although she more often hindered her seamen with conditions and restrictions than she helped them, she certainly had no objection to filling her coffers with the fruits of their efforts.

Edward VI and Mary Tudor had, during their brief reigns, neglected the Navy Royal, and its ships were in none too good condition when Elizabeth came to the throne in 1558; but Sebastian Cabot had returned to England ten years earlier, and a revival of Henry VII's mercantile policy was much in the air. Very soon the explorers were setting out again into the unknown. First Willoughby and Chancellor to the North-East in 1553, then the great John Hawkins to the West Indies: 1572 saw Drake's adventures on the Isthmus of Panama where, according to Keats, 'Stout Cortez' and his men 'looked at each other with wild surmise silent upon a peak in Darien'.[1] Drake's men were silent too, though not with wonder at the sight of the Pacific, but because they were intent upon ambushing the mule train carrying the treasure of Peru across the isthmus. In the same year Frobisher sailed to seek the North-West Passage, and between 1577 and 1580 Drake in the *Golden Hind* circumnavigated the globe, to return home with his holds full of Spanish treasure. Gilbert's voyage to Newfoundland, Raleigh's Virginian enterprise, and John Davis's three expeditions in the footsteps of Frobisher soon followed. The primary object of all these voyages across unknown seas in tiny vessels was, of course, financial gain. Technically, and in many cases more than technically, they infringed the papal award of 1493 dividing the globe between

[1] As a matter of historical fact it was Balboa who, in 1513, first saw the Pacific.

the Spaniards and the Portuguese. Disaster on sea or on land over-took not a few ships' companies. But the ports of Plymouth and London hummed with tales of adventure overseas, and of fantastic wealth to be won: and the rewards of success were so great that volunteers for new enterprises were, despite all the hazards, never lacking. As a step towards the expansion of trade the Elizabethan voyages of exploration were immensely important, for they made the people of these islands far more conscious of the world beyond the wide sea horizon than they had ever been before; and the next step was bound to be a more lively understanding of maritime strategy.

Mention of the great discoveries of the Elizabethan era leads naturally to consideration of the influence of geography on strategy. The opening up of the new lands led inevitably to searches for the easiest routes by which they could be reached, and to the selection and development of the harbours which would serve best as depots for the collection and loading of goods, and as stations for the troops required to provide security in the area. Gradually the harbours such as Santo Domingo, Porto Bello and Cartagena became the key strategic bases in the New World, and throughout the period of Anglo-Spanish commercial rivalry the contest for possession of them was continuous.

In 1585, for all Elizabeth's efforts to preserve peace with Spain, the 'cold war' over religion, trade and treasure moved into a phase not far removed from open conflict, and it was now that what we would call 'amphibious operations' were first extensively exploited by the English. We soon discovered not only the im-mense benefits to be derived from that method of exploiting sea power, but that the risks entailed in such undertakings were always serious.

Though Drake's attacks on Santo Domingo, the administrative capital of all the Spanish islands, and on Cartagena, one of their treasure collecting centres in 1585, were completely successful, and his expedition to Cadiz two years later provided us with an epigram which has passed into the language, he failed badly at Lisbon in 1589—as he had failed earlier at Nombre de Dios. Personally I am convinced that when Drake spoke about ' singeing the King of Spain's beard' he meant it in a deprecatory rather than a boastful sense:[1] for he was too shrewd to believe that his blow at Cadiz could frustrate the entire Armada project. The suggestion is confirmed by his subsequent seizure of Cape Chagres in the approaches to Gibraltar, for use as a base from which to operate against Spain's vitally important Mediterranean trade. Professor Mattingly has pointed out in his brilliant study of the Armada campaign that this latter action had far more serious consequences on Philip's invasion plans than the Cadiz raid.[2] And it was from Cape Chagres that Drake enunciated to his oft-times difficult mistress another principle of maritime strategy: that ' the advantage of time and place in all martial actions is half a victory, which being lost is irrecoverable '. Forgetfulness of that principle has contributed to the failure of many combined operations from that time to this. Indeed Elizabethan experiences taught us lessons about amphibious warfare which we have too often had to relearn. First that anything less than the most careful and secret planning will jeopardise the entire undertaking: secondly that any diversity of purposes, such as there was in the Lisbon expedition already mentioned, is fatal: and lastly that quarrels between the naval and military commanders—aptly stigmatised by Sir Julian Corbett as ' the corrupting blight '—will ruin any such enterprise. As Sir Herbert Richmond put it ' Combined operations are always difficult. They demand vast care in preparation, a just estimate of strength, and a clear understanding on the parts of both those who initiate them and those who command them, of the primary object of the enterprise '.[3] Yet if the seemingly

---

[1] The authority for attributing this saying to Drake himself, which has sometimes been disputed, rests on Francis Bacon's Essay *Considerations touching a war with Spain* (1624), in which he wrote ' I remember Drake, in the vaunting stile of a soldier, would call this enterprise [i.e. the raid on Cadiz, 1587] the singeing of the King of Spain's beard '. (Francis Bacon, *Works*, Vol. III, p. 517, London, 1824.)

[2] *The Defeat of the Spanish Armada* (Jonathan Cape, 1959).

[3] *Amphibious Warfare in British History* (Historical Association Pamphlet No. 119, 1941).

obvious pitfalls can be avoided, the rewards which can be gained by exploiting maritime power to strike *at points of one's own choice* can, as the experiences of the Elizabethan seamen first proved, be out of all proportion to the effort made. Though we will return to the subject later, when we review amphibious warfare in a modern context, here is a case of a historic principle whose validity, at least over a matter of 400 years, remains quite unchanged. Leaving out for the moment large-scale seaborne invasions of enemy territory, such as the Peninsular War of 1808-1814 or the landings in North Africa of 1942 which, although based on sea power, belong to the field of major strategy, the purposes of amphibious operations are many. Richmond analysed them under half a dozen headings,[1] such as the capture of a source of wealth: the destruction of an enemy force in its base: the seizure of a new base, or the ejection of the enemy from one of his. Though it leaps down several centuries at one bound we may here note that all such purposes of amphibious expeditions have gained renewed validity from very recent experiences.

To continue with the development of maritime strategy in the Elizabethan era, there was one man who was far ahead of his time in his grasp of the vital requirements. In 1589 Sir John Hawkins made clear to his royal mistress that if the flow of treasure from the New World to Spain was stopped, Philip II could not rebuild his fleet and would have to give up the struggle; and he put forward detailed plans to accomplish that purpose. Twelve of the Queen's ships and a flotilla of six pinnaces were to be allotted to blockading the Azores, the key to control of the routes across the central Atlantic, while the rest of the Queen's ships (12 or 13) were to be kept in home waters to secure control of the Channel. The ships of the blockading force were to be divided into two equal squadrons, one of which was to be constantly on station while the other was refitting and replenishing; and Hawkins, as Administrator of the Navy, was fully competent to judge the endurance and sea-keeping

[1] Ibid.

capacity of its ships. Indeed in 1586 he had proved his ability to victual a squadron for four months, with a margin of safety; and he was confident that his strategy, if it did not result in capturing one or more of the treasure fleets, would prevent them sailing.[1] Sir Julian Corbett has stigmatised Hawkins's plan as mere commerce destruction, and has declared that it failed.[2] But such a view is open to a strong challenge, since the plan was very much more than commerce destruction; and as it was never tried it cannot be said to have failed. Instead only isolated cruises were made to the vital area, and during the intervals between them the treasure fleets, strongly convoyed by fighting ships, got through—even in 1589, when our Lisbon expedition was on the coast; and in 1597 another made harbour in the Azores almost within sight of the English cruising squadron. Recent studies having fully confirmed Spain's utter dependence on the arrival of the treasure fleets,[3] it is difficult not to conclude that the strategy urged by Hawkins was correct.

This leads to consideration of how far the Queen herself understood the basic requirements of a maritime strategy. Raleigh complained bitterly that ' Her Majesty did all things by halves, and by petty invasions taught the Spaniard how to defend himself . . .'[4] But the historian should surely show caution before accepting the strictures of a commander (and especially of a highly emotional character such as Raleigh) against those responsible for the strategy they are required to apply. Unfortunately Sir Herbert Richmond accepted and enlarged upon Raleigh's criticisms of the Queen,[5] and not a few other naval historians have followed him blindly. Yet, far from there being sound evidence to support such a view, there is a great deal that can be cited to the opposite effect—as Dr.

[1] See Hawkins's *Discourse for obtaining a good peace, December* 1587 quoted in J. A. Williamson, *Sir John Hawkins* (Oxford U.P., 1927), pp. 451-4. The same work contains a convincing analysis of the merits of the strategic proposals propounded by Hawkins.

[2] In *Drake and the Tudor Navy*, Vol. I, pp. 315-16 (Longmans, Green, 1898).

[3] See for example A. L. Rowse, *The Expansion of Elizabethan England* Chapters VII and VIII (Macmillan, 1955).

[4] E. Edwards, *Life of Sir Walter Raleigh*, Vol. I, p. 245 (Macmillan, 1868).

[5] In *Statesmen and Sea Power* (O.U.P., 1946).

A. L. Rowse has convincingly demonstrated.[1] Thus for the 1589 expedition to Spain, which might well have struck a decisive blow at Philip's navy, the Queen's orders to Drake and Sir John Norris were quite unequivocal. They were ' to take and distress the King of Spain's navy and ships where they lay '[2]—namely in San Sebastian and Santander. Yet they acted quite differently—and accomplished almost nothing at Corunna, Lisbon or Vigo: while the treasure fleet came home safely that summer. It was now the Queen's turn to complain, and she angrily retorted that ' they went to places more for profit than for service ', and did not employ Drake again until six years later. There is in truth more justice in her comment than in the strictures of Raleigh—which, indeed only reflect the tendency of commanders to criticise the makers of strategy—a phenomenon which has not been uncommon in our own times.

On the question of English involvement in the Netherlands campaign the issue is perhaps rather less clear cut. Certainly Hawkins warned against expeditions to Europe, which he regarded as expensive and profitless. On the other hand the threat latent in a Spanish hegemony in the Low Countries was very real, and the pressure for intervention on the continent was, as in many later conflicts, strong. The Queen has often been accused of ' niggardliness ' towards her soldiers in the Netherlands. But here too a convincing case has been made in her defence,[3] and it is probable that the complaints of Sir Roger Williams, her valiant and sorely-tried veteran of those campaigns, that she frittered away her resources ' in consuming little fires ' have as little justice in them as Raleigh's strictures on her strategy at sea.

To sum up Elizabeth's understanding of maritime strategy and principles, she certainly showed foresight in fostering the expansion of the sea-faring section of her people. In the case of the 1589

[1] In *The Expansion of Elizabethan England*, Chapter VIII (Macmillan, 1955).
[2] See R. B. Wernham, articles in *The English Historical Review*, January and April, 1951.
[3] By Sir John Neale in *Elizabeth and the Netherlands* (English Historical Review, July 1930).

expedition she saw that the true objective was the surviving ships of the Spanish fleet. And the issue by her of the first contraband list in the same year, together with her stout defence of the right of a belligerent to stop the carriage of goods to the enemy in neutral bottoms, foreshadowed the policy of the younger Pitt.[1] Indeed in the understanding of the importance of economic blockade she was well in advance of her contemporaries. Thus even if one may regret the failure to adopt Hawkins's strategy, a great deal can be cited in the Queen's favour. And the failure to achieve a decision certainly cannot be laid entirely at her door. Spain itself, though embarrassed by our raids in the New World, and shocked by the disaster to the Armada, was not brought anywhere near to admitting defeat—and indeed her Navy made a remarkable recovery in the 1590s. The war thus dragged on until Elizabeth's death in 1603; and shortly after his accession James I concluded a somewhat hasty peace, and then proceeded to lay up virtually the whole of the Navy.

The period that followed was a very unhappy one for England, since with her coastal waters wide open to marauders, pirates from North Africa enjoyed just as happy a time as Dönitz's U-boats enjoyed in our western approaches in 1940-41. We do not know how many English ships the 17th century Barbary corsairs seized, carrying off their crews to slavery: but reliable estimates give the figure of nearly 500 ships captured between 1609 and 1616. Trade of course was disrupted, and the country soon faced bankruptcy. Such was the price paid for forgetting the principle that Alfred the Great had enunciated regarding the vital importance of controlling our coastal waters.

Charles I inherited many difficult problems from his father, and very soon created new ones on his own account; but he did understand that the old Navy, composed of a mixture of Royal and privately owned ships, was incapable of meeting the situation. He saw that only a state service could do so, and tried to provide the

[1] See p. 56.

necessary instruments; but by levying 'ship money' to pay for them he made his troubles with Parliament worse. From his point of view the tragedy was that, on the outbreak of the civil war, almost the whole of the naval service joined the Parliamentary faction. And, although its influence on the outcome has attracted little attention from historians of the period, there is no doubt at all that possession of the fleet in fact decided the issue—because it made intervention by Louis XIII and Richelieu impossible, and saved the port of London from a blockade which would have ruined the City's trade and so the Parliamentary cause. The Commonwealth leaders certainly appreciated the importance of the part that sea power had played in making their success possible; and probably for that reason they kept their promises to its officers and men. Moreover the selection by Cromwell of Robert Blake, Deane and Popham as his first 'Generals-at-Sea', was a stroke of genius; and Blake and George Monk (later Duke of Albemarle), another soldier, were to have a most profound influence on every aspect of naval warfare—administrative and technical, strategic and tactical.

The quarrel with Holland, which led to the outbreak of war in 1652 was, like the earlier quarrel with Spain, essentially a struggle for trade. Monk stated the bare truth when he said that 'the Dutch had too much of it and the English were resolved to take it from them'. The directors of maritime enterprise have become more polite since the 17th century! In the Dutch wars the geographical advantage lay with England; since all her adversary's trading ships had to pass through the Channel or round the north of Scotland, and our ships, based on the flank of those routes could attack at will—very much in the manner that the German forces in north Norway were able to choose their moments to strike against our Arctic convoys in the last war. Moreover, whereas the English enjoyed unified naval command under Cromwell's 'Generals-at-Sea', the Dutch were handicapped by their forces being provided by the five semi-independent United Provinces. One of Cromwell's

chief anxieties was to secure the Baltic trade, on which his expanded fleet greatly depended for mast timber and other naval
stores; and it was the need to keep the Sound open that caused him,
after the war was over, to take strong steps against Denmark, to
conclude a treaty with Sweden, and to seek alternative sources of
supply in North America. Throughout the era of the sailing ship
the need to maintain and defend the Baltic trade exerted a profound
influence on our strategy and maritime dispositions: and Milton's
choice of metaphor, in his description of Satan's accoutrements in
Paradise Lost—

> *His spear, to equal which the tallest pine,*
> *Hewn on Norwegian hills to be the mast*
> *Of some great ammiral, were but a wand*[1]

suggests that in the 17th century knowledge of the importance of
Scandinavian timber, and of its quality, was not confined to the sea-
faring section of the populace. We may here remark how, in recent
times, our dependence on oil supplies from overseas has produced
precisely similar problems.

Cromwell's strategic direction of the war did not at once reveal
that firm grasp of essentials which was to distinguish the later phases.
After the successful fight off the Kentish Knock in September, 1652,
he committed the serious error of detaching a considerable part of
the fleet to the Mediterranean on trade protection duties, so allowing
the Dutch to regain command of our home waters. Thereafter,
however, Cromwell and his advisers did concentrate on the primary
purpose of destroying the enemy's main fleet; and after a succession
of very stubborn battles their strategy brought success—though
only by a narrow margin. Then Cromwell extended his aims by
attacking Spain, and his strategy was based, correctly, on blockading
that country's coast, in order to catch the treasure convoys and
destroy the enemy's main fleet, what time he sent an amphibious

---

[1] Book I, lines 292-5. (The author is indebted to Mr. Richard Ollard for drawing his
attention to this very apt quotation.)

expedition to the West Indies. Though it failed to capture Santo Domingo in 1654, it did succeed, almost accidentally, in winning Jamaica—so providing us with our first overseas base; while Blake's blockade of Cadiz was so effective that in 1656 he captured an entire treasure fleet worth a million pounds. In the following year, hearing that the Mexico fleet had arrived at Tenerife in the Canaries, he attacked and destroyed all the shipping in the harbour; and the effects of those successes at sea were at once felt by the Spanish armies in Portugal and Flanders. In general the strategy conceived by Cromwell, and applied principally by Blake, was far more effective than that of Elizabeth I.

Nor did the Restoration at first bring any change in the policy of maintaining our sea power; and when in 1662, Catherine of Braganza brought Tangier to England as part of her dowry, Charles II gained the Mediterranean base which his predecessors had sorely lacked. In the Second Dutch War, which Charles provoked in 1664, the background was again trade rivalry; and again the British strategy was to defeat the enemy's main fleet in battle. But corruption and venality in high places had meanwhile been eating away the service's efficiency, and in 1665 the outbreak of plague added to the administrative confusion. After Albemarle's victory of St. James's Day (25th July, 1666) the government committed the colossal blunder of laying up the main fleet in the Medway. De Ruyter was quick to see the chance and on 14th June, 1667, penetrated right up the river, and inflicted one of the most humiliating defeats ever suffered by British arms. How, one may ask, could it have been forgotten that control of the narrow seas demands everlasting vigilance, and that two can play at the raiding game at which Drake and Blake had shown themselves so adept? Luckily Dutch suspicions of Louis XIV's intentions—soon to be shown to be well-founded—enabled us to sign a treaty of peace at Breda, which was far more favourable than we deserved; and although it was scarcely noticed at the time, by giving up New Amsterdam (later New York) the Dutch virtually handed over to us control of the eastern seaboard of what are now the United States.

The Third Dutch War (1672-1674) came about through a discreditable deal by which Charles II virtually hired the Royal Navy to Louis XIV to prosecute his quarrel with the Dutch; whereas England's true interest should have been to help the Dutch to defeat Louis's plan to gain control of the Scheldt estuary, with its great port of Antwerp right opposite the Thames. Antwerp in Spanish hands had been dangerous enough, as the Armada campaign had shown; but an expansionist France established in the Low Countries was an infinitely more dangerous prospect—as we were to learn in course of the next century. Under de Ruyter the Dutch continued to fight stubbornly and well, the French squadrons with the English fleet played an inglorious part, and general disgust over so unnecessary a war soon forced Charles to withdraw from the conflict. In the succeeding years neutral England succeeded in swallowing a large share of belligerent Holland's trade.

The year 1688 saw the arrival of William of Orange in Torbay on the wings of the ' Protestant wind ', and the flight of James II. This was the last of the long series of successful invasions of these islands: for Prince Charles's landing at Inverness in 1745 was not an invasion in the commonly understood meaning of the word. Though William actually encountered no opposition he came prepared to fight; for he was indeed ' intervening by force in the domestic concerns of his father-in-law, prosecuting a design quite indistinguishable from an act of war '.[1] But James's fleet, though the greater part was initially loyal to him, was beset by the listlessness which can destroy the efficiency of a fighting service when it lacks enthusiasm for the cause to which it is required to bend its efforts; and it was this, as much as the changes in the weather and the chance circumstance of the easterly wind keeping Lord Dartmouth's ships in the Thames, that allowed William to win control of the Channel so easily. Certain it is that the invasion of 1688 provides

[1] E. B. Powley, *The English Navy in the Revolution of 1688*, p. 2 (Cambridge U.P., 1928).

' one of the most ambiguous episodes in the history of the Royal Navy '.[1]

These events, however, marked the end of the second phase of British maritime development. The country now had in the Royal Navy a permanent state service, manned by a growing band of officers who had made the service their career, and backed by a reasonably well-organised and efficient administrative machine. In the realm of tactics a Battle Fleet had been created to replace the heterogeneous collection of part-fighting and part-trading ships which were the legacy of the Tudors; and by the Fighting Instructions of 1653, and still more by those issued by James, Duke of York, twenty years later, the happy-go-lucky endeavours of the previous century had been replaced by disciplined movements based on the line ahead formation. In weapons there had been a great advance from the early light artillery to the heavy ship-killing weapons mounted on the broadside. Maritime enterprise was recognised to signpost the road to wealth and prosperity, and the need to protect the trading ships against licensed marauders or plain piracy was beginning to be understood. Also in the field of strategy the experience of the early years of the century, when the Barbary corsairs had swarmed around our coasts, had taught a lesson which the disgrace in the Medway of 1667 had re-affirmed—namely that control of the seas that wash its shores is essential to the prosperity and safety of a maritime nation. As to carrying the war into the enemy's camp, the capacity of amphibious power to strike shrewd blows at times and at places of our own choosing had several times been demonstrated; but the planning and organisation of such undertakings were as yet very imperfectly grasped. Nor had any statesman yet arisen who realised that amphibious power could also be exploited as the decisive instrument in major strategy. For that we were to have to wait another half century.

The accession of William III inevitably meant a re-orientation of

[1] D. Ogg, *England in the reigns of James II and William III* (Oxford U.P., 1955, p. 215). E. B. Powley, Op. Cit., brings out very clearly the effects of the weather on the activities of the English fleet.

British policy, for William was the sworn foe of Louis XIV of France. Thus began the long series of no less than seven Anglo-French wars, which, with short interludes of uneasy peace, lasted until 1815. The first two—those of the English and Spanish Succession were partly dynastic and partly arose out of apprehension over the growth of French power. Not until the middle three—the War of the Austrian Succession, the Seven Years' War, and the War of American Independence, did trade and colonies become the main issues. In the last two, the wars of the French Revolution and the Napoleonic War, mercantile aspirations took second place to the containment of revolutionary principles and of French aggrandisement respectively. But the period 1688-1815, taken as a whole saw first the hesitant beginning, then the gradual development, and finally the full flowering of a truly maritime British strategy; and it is therefore essential to glance briefly at the course of events which brought that about.

The wars of William and Mary's and Queen Anne's reigns, generally called the War of the English Succession (1689-1697) and the War of the Spanish Succession (1702-1713), introduced totally new strategic problems; for instead of fighting alone, or with one ally, England became a member of a continental coalition of states. Although we still enjoyed considerable geographic advantages, our new adversary was less dependent on overseas trade than Spain or Holland, and therefore less susceptible to the pressure of sea power. On the other hand England (or rather one should say Britain after the union with Scotland in 1707) was more vulnerable to invasion by forces assembled on the Channel or Biscay coasts of France; and her economy was now more dependent on overseas trade. Moreover naval developments, particularly in the field of hygiene and supply (or ' logistics ' as we would call it nowadays) had not yet reached a point where close and continuous blockade of enemy bases, which in the new circumstances was bound to be an important strategic requirement, was practicable. Though Dutch sea power was in decline, and was to deteriorate still further in the first two decades of the 18th century, in the 1690s the joint maritime resources of England and Holland were superior to those of France; and except in the Mediterranean (for Charles II had abandoned Tangier in 1683) we also held the advantage in the matter of bases. As long as Spain was our ally Cadiz was available for our fleets. But that fine harbour was too far to the west to serve satisfactorily for a fleet required to work inside the Mediterranean; and we were soon to learn, not for the last time, about the fickleness of alliances, and that dependence on a friendly country for bases can be no satisfactory substitute for firm possession.

The main strategic issue in King William's war was whether we could help the anti-French coalition best by sending military forces to the continent or by weakening France at sea: and so arose the conflict between the 'Continental' and 'Maritime' strategic schools, mentioned earlier, which has lasted down to our own times. In general William was continental in outlook; while the most effective spokesman for the maritime school was, rather surprisingly, Dean Swift—coloured though his views were by allegiance to the Tories, whose outlook was 'maritime' chiefly because the country gentlemen, not having forgotten the activities of Cromwell's major-generals, feared a strong central government with a standing army at its disposal. Neither school thought in terms of using the Army and Navy as a combined force, and the maritime school was at fault in advocating a direct attack on enemy trade and colonies in preference to making the destruction, or at least the neutralisation of his fleet the main objective. Furthermore our endeavours to stop neutral countries supplying the enemy in their own ships were as unsuccessful as they had been in the Dutch wars; and Holland herself, while still an ally, continued to trade actively with France. Not for another half century did we succeed in establishing the right to control the carriage of contraband to our enemies in neutral bottoms.

At the start of King William's war the English fleet was in its customary state of unreadiness; and that enabled the French to land in Ireland, and overrun it up to the walls of Londonderry. Then in 1690, after the defeat of Torrington's Channel Fleet off Beachy Head and his withdrawal to the Thames to keep his fleet ' in being ' (he was the inventor of that hard worked aphorism), Tourville gained complete control of the narrow seas, and England was wide open to invasion. Happily the French were quite unready to exploit the opportunity, our scattered squadrons were given time to concentrate, and in the summer of 1692 the twin battles of Barfleur and La Hogue eliminated the invasion threat. Meanwhile the relief of Londonderry by Rooke in 1689 had saved Ireland, and at the Battle of the Boyne in the following year William decisively defeated the French invaders. Thus, after two years of war, we were in a position to adopt an offensive strategy; while the French for their part, having failed in their invasion project, had turned to the *guerre de course* against our trade—very much as Hitler was to do with his U-boats after his failure to invade these islands in 1940.

In 1691 and '92 the main English effort was made on the continent: but the land campaigns went badly for us. Then, in the following year the Brest fleet, which had been left intact through our concentration on a continental strategy, went south and caught our very valuable Smyrna convoy off Cadiz. That disaster spurred the government into making an amphibious attack on Brest in 1694. But lack of security in England, or some have said treachery in high places, gave the French warning of our intentions, and the result was a costly fiasco. In the same year we sent a powerful fleet to the Mediterranean with the object of frustrating Louis XIV's intended offensive against Catalonia and Savoy; and William ordered it to winter at Cadiz for the first time. This marked the beginning of the long search for a base in the western Mediterranean from which our fleet could make its presence effectively felt.

The adoption of the *guerre de course* by Louis XIV provides the opportunity to review the prospects and limitations of such a strategy more closely; for it has frequently happened that a continental enemy who has been frustrated in his attempt to gain command at sea, or whose plan to invade these islands has been defeated, has turned to attacking our trade.

The traditional defence against commerce raiders has always been the strategy of convoy-and-escort: by which is meant the assembly of the homeward-bound merchantmen in an overseas base, whence they sail in company of protecting warships. Such a practice is in fact very ancient. Thus in the mid-16th century Spain introduced convoy to guard the ships bringing her treasure home from the New World: and from Commonwealth times to the beginning of the 19th century we ourselves used it extensively in every war in which we were involved. With the introduction of steam, however, convoy seems to have fallen into disrepute in British circles—its technical and administrative difficulties being exaggerated at the expense of its strategic merits. Yet the truth is that, up to the present time, it has invariably proved effective both in limiting the depredations of raiders of all types—whether they worked on, above or beneath the surface of the sea—and in enabling the convoy escorts to retaliate effectively against them. In terms of strategy the convoy function is of course defensive; but it has been many times shown also to have an important offensive influence in that it creates opportunities for an energetic local counter-attack. The reason is that commerce raiders, who may work in flotillas and squadrons as well as singly, are as sure to be attracted to the convoys as bees to honey; and that is bound to give the escorts, provided that they are energetically led, the opportunity to bring them to action. Again and again in history have attempts to molest our convoys led to important sea fights; and it has gradually become a tradition among Royal Navy convoy escorts that, in the protection of their charges, they should unhesitatingly engage the enemy regardless of the odds. We may also here note that so far the *guerre de course* against merchant shipping has never *by itself* brought victory. In the present century Germany has twice, in 1917 and again in 1943, come within what has seemed to be measurable distance of success in that form of warfare; yet each time it was defeated in time, if only just in time, by the escort-of-convoy strategy. On the other hand the American onslaught on Japanese shipping in 1944-45 probably came very near to being decisive: but in that case Japanese sea power had already been destroyed in the series of fleet actions which began with the Battle of Midway in June, 1942 and ended off Leyte Gulf in October, 1944.[1] It therefore appears that Mahan's dictum regarding the inability of the *guerre de course* to achieve a decision requires qualification. For its prospects must surely depend on the extent to which the nation against which it is waged is dependent on seaborne trade. To Philip II of Spain the treasure of the New World was, as already pointed out, vital:[2] and in the last war Japan was scarcely less dependent on imports from overseas—as was Britain in both conflicts of this century. To-day, with this country more dependent than ever before on foreign food and raw materials, and especially oil fuel, the possibility of the *guerre de course* achieving a clear-cut decision is surely greater.

By 1697, the French economy was suffering severely, and Louis XIV was ready for peace. But the Treaty of Ryswick, signed in that year, proved only a temporary truce, and in 1702 the war was renewed over the need to prevent Louis XIV's grandson mounting the throne of Spain, so establishing a French hegemony over western Europe, stretching from Gibraltar to Antwerp. England and Holland were again allies, again the initial strategic issue was whether we should strengthen the armies on the continent or weaken our adversary's economy and military effort by concentrating on the offensive at sea; and again the continental view prevailed. None the less the importance of commanding the western Mediterranean was recognised: and the hopes of capturing Toulon, which William had entertained eight years earlier, were revived under Queen Anne. Cadiz however was now an enemy port, and an expedition sent out in 1702 to seize it was so ill-prepared and so circumscribed by the restrictions placed on the commanders that it was an utter failure. Thus the fleet was severely handicapped in

[1] See pp. 188 and 218-19.   [2] See pp. 29-30.

furthering the design against Toulon until, in the following year the Methuen Treaty gained us the use of Lisbon. In 1704 the outlook improved. Marlborough, who was one of those rare leaders with a clear understanding of naval and military interdependence, was in firm control of our strategy; and he was a strong advocate of the plan against Toulon. In July of that year Rooke seized Gibraltar with his Marines, and the prompt attempt by the Toulon fleet to recapture it was frustrated by the battle of Malaga. This was one of those indecisive actions which left the side which had the worst of the fighting in possession of the strategic objective about which it was fought. Thereafter our squadron at Lisbon managed to cover and secure the new base against repeated attempts to recapture it: but the margin by which it was saved was at times very narrow. Though the base problem was now improved, it was by no means solved; for the acquisition of a harbour inside the Mediterranean was essential if we were to control the western basin of this sea effectively. Indeed the attempt to do so from Gibraltar and Lisbon was imposing dreadful hardships on our warship crews. None the less in 1705 Barcelona was captured, and in consequence all Catalonia soon came under the control of our allies. In spite of this success the cause which we supported fared ill elsewhere in Spain; but in 1706 Marlborough's victory at Ramillies opened up new prospects for a Mediterranean offensive by invading the south of France. Though the attempt failed—largely because our ally the Emperor Joseph did not understand the working of sea power, it led directly to the self-destruction of the Toulon fleet; and that brought immense relief. Then in 1708 by seizing Port Mahon in Minorca we at last gained a satisfactory advanced base, and at once our control of the western Mediterranean became far firmer. Had this been accomplished earlier it is likely that, as Marlborough clearly understood, the war would have been decided in that theatre. But the amphibious projects against Toulon and the south coast of France had foundered on the deficiencies in our maritime services, on the failure to agree with our allies and apply a consistent joint strategy, and on the long delay in acquiring the essential bases in the vital area. The influence of Lisbon, Gibraltar and Port Mahon on Queen Anne's war provides convincing evidence of the part that bases always play in strategy.

In the final phase of the war, from 1709-13, we instituted an economic blockade of France, making corn contraband for the first time; and we also carried out a series of diversionary raids in the Channel and Mediterranean. But we had a hard struggle to maintain our own trade against the French heavy raiding squadrons. Though it was chiefly Marlborough's great victories which forced France to accept terms of peace in which she made wide concessions— especially in the New World—he himself certainly recognised the influence which the operations in the western Mediterranean had on the course of the war, and that it was the pressure of our sea power which brought France to the verge of bankruptcy. England on the other hand ended the war more prosperous than she had been at the beginning—for all that her shipping losses had been very heavy; and the famous ' Convoys and Cruizers Act '[1] of 1708 had, by allocating a definite number of warships to trade defence in our home waters, established the principle of naval responsibility for the safety of our mercantile traffic. Furthermore by the Crown surrendering to the captors its right to a share in Prize Money the Act gave a great fillip to privateering.

The years of peace that followed the Treaty of Utrecht of 1713 were in fact very uneasy—a period somewhat similar to that through which we are now passing. In the first place anxiety for the safety of our trade in naval stores from the Baltic states was continuous; and it became a cardinal principle of British strategy that we would allow no one power—Russia, Sweden or Denmark—to gain such a predominance that she could close the Sound at will against our shipping. In 1700 we had sent a fleet to support the Swedes against the Danes, and in almost every year between 1715 and 1727 we again made our sea power felt in those waters. Then in 1718 there was trouble in the Mediterranean over Spanish designs to seize

---

[1] 6. Anne. C.13.

Sardinia and Sicily in violation of the Treaty of Utrecht; but the destruction of the Spanish fleet off Cape Passero (11th August, 1718), and the seaborne support given to the Austrian army in Sicily, totally frustrated such purposes. Seven years later Spain and Austria were concerting together to regain Gibraltar and Minorca, and in retaliation we sent a fleet to the West Indies to stop the sailing of Spanish treasure ships. In each of those cases—the Baltic, the Mediterranean and the West Indies—we used our sea power to uphold treaties, to stop aggression or to localise conflicts. But, for all the effectiveness of that policy, by the end of the 1730s, when tension between Britain and the Bourbon powers (France and Spain) was again rising, our Navy was in poor condition—undermanned, ill-equipped and riddled with corruption and political disaffection.

After a two-year preliminary skirmish with Spain over trade, generally called the War of Jenkins's Ear, the third of the Anglo-French conflicts opened in 1740, when we showed our determination to stop the dismemberment of the Holy Roman Empire. For a time France only gave covert assistance to Spain, but in 1744 she joined in openly with the object of seizing the Austrian Netherlands. At the beginning of this second phase, which lasted until 1748, the British Government had neither policy nor plans: nor had any preparations for the plainly approaching conflict been made. In marked antithesis to Cromwell's strategy, Cadiz was not blockaded, and no attempt was made to deal with the Spanish fleet. But this unhappy period did produce a brilliantly successful amphibious attack by Admiral Vernon against Porto Bello in the Isthmus of Panama, which showed how much could be accomplished with very small forces, given careful planning and good organisation. Two years later, using much larger forces, we tried to strike a similar blow against Cartagena; but the long delay in launching the operation, and faulty tactics, brought failure.[1]

[1] A clear, but unheeded warning of the disastrous consequences which would follow any long delay over launching expeditions in the West Indies had been given by Admiral Vernon a few weeks before his successful assault on Porto Bello. See his letter of 31st October, 1739

When in 1744 the conflict in Europe widened, the primary purpose to which our sea power was put was to help Austria by commanding the western Mediterranean, so stopping the transport of Spanish troops to Italy. But the French threat to the Netherlands produced the old clash between the ' Continental ' and ' Maritime ' schools; and, as so often, it was the Continental school that prevailed. The defeat we suffered at Fontenoy in 1745 merely underlined how much more effectively we could have injured the Bourbon powers had we disposed of adequate maritime forces, and used them with enterprise.

The first fleet action of the war took place off Toulon in February, 1744, and its indecisiveness makes it necessary to introduce a brief digression into the field of tactics. Earlier in that century Rooke's Fighting Instructions of 1703 had been made ' Permanent ', thus elevating them to the status of a sacred and immutable doctrine, from which a flag officer could only depart at his peril.[1] It was true that one Article (No. 25) of the Instructions permitted the ordering of a General Chase: but only if the enemy was already on the run. Any idea of seizing a favourable tactical opportunity, of breaking the enemy's line, or of producing a mêlée in which superior fire power would be decisive, was wholly lacking. Professor Lewis, in his lucid analysis of the period 1692-1782,[2] has pointed out that fifteen ' line ' actions were then fought without a single enemy ship being sunk or captured; and that the six clear-cut British victories were all of them ' chase ' battles. We may also here note that during periods of tactical sterility, such as prevailed in the mid-18th century and in the 1914-1918 war against Germany, it will be the strategic disposition of maritime forces that decides the issue; since even though the actual battles are indecisive, the pressure exerted on the enemy by blockade and by control of sea routes can be immensely influential. That is, of course, not an argu-

to the Duke of Newcastle, printed in Richmond, *The Navy in the War of* 1739-48, Vol. I, p. 44 (Cambridge U. P., 1920).

[1] See Corbett, *Fighting Instructions,* 1530-1816. (Navy Records Society, 1905.)

[2] *The History of the British Navy* (Allen and Unwin, 1959).

ment in favour of unenterprising tactics: rather is it an explanation of why wars throughout which tactical sterility has prevailed have none the less sometimes ended in success to the British cause.

While we were failing to contain, let alone defeat the Toulon fleet in 1744, the Brest fleet was able to leave harbour more or less at will; and that produced two highly unfavourable strategic consequences—a threat of invasion, which was frustrated by a timely gale rather than by any skill on our part:[1] and the reinforcement of the French possessions in North America, which boded ill for the British colonists. In 1745, however, Admiral Vernon who was now in command of the Channel Fleet, stressed the need to establish a ' Western Squadron ', disposed off the entrance to the Channel. From that station it could take full advantage of the prevailing south-westerly winds, it could protect our trade, and also provide the chief defence against invasion.[2] This strategy was actually adopted by Anson two years later, with the most fortunate results. Also in 1745 a colonial expedition organised in Massachusetts captured Louisburg on Cape Breton Island, the key to the St. Lawrence river and so to French Canada; and that success cast a ray of light on a period of dreary indecision and strategic incompetence. We should however note that our sea power in home waters was sufficiently strong to prevent French reinforcements being sent to the aid of the Young Pretender, who had landed at Inverness with a few companions, and reached Derby in November, 1745; and that accomplishment possibly preserved the throne of England to the Hanoverians.

The adoption of the strategically disposed Western Squadron in 1747 enabled us at last to blockade Brest effectively, and the consequence was that the tide turned sharply in our favour. Hawke's and Anson's substantial victories, both of them chasing actions and both named after Cape Finisterre, followed in the same year: the

---

[1] At the time of this invasion threat the Channel Fleet was under Admiral Sir John Norris, who had just assumed command at the age of 84.

[2] Vernon to Duke of Bedford, 5th August, 1745, and to the Secretary of the Admiralty, 17th August, 1745. *Vernon Papers* Nos. 370 and 379 (Navy Records Society, 1958).

transport of French reinforcements to Canada was entirely stopped, and their trade was brought almost to a standstill. Thus did a single well-conceived strategic measure at sea offset all the French successes on the continent, and in 1748 we were able to conclude a reasonably satisfactory treaty of peace at Aix-la-Chapelle. But we handed back Louisburg to the French.

The foregoing brief account of the favourable developments of 1747 leads naturally to consideration of the place of blockade in maritime strategy. As Sir Julian Corbett has pointed out,[1] there are two kinds—the naval and the economic or commercial: and although the two have quite commonly overlapped, the blockades of the 18th and 19th centuries were generally of the naval class. Such blockades are always instituted with the object of destroying, or at least immobilising, the main enemy fleet; but they can be enforced in two ways. If we keep the fleet more or less permanently off the enemy base the blockade is said to be of the 'close' type: but if it watches enemy activities from a distance, cruising periodically off the base and exerting only a general control over the local waters, it is said to be of the 'open' type. The distinction between the two can best be decided according to whether supplies are sent to the blockading squadrons to be embarked while on their station, or whether the squadrons return to their home ports to replenish. In a close blockade success will depend almost entirely on overcoming the formidable difficulties of hygiene and supply. But it is in any case very difficult to maintain for long periods, certainly without the possession of a substantial superiority over the enemy: and of all naval operations it is the most exhausting. Its merit lies in the fact that it produces by far the better chance of effectively immobilising or destroying the enemy fleet. Thus Hawke's blockade of Brest in 1758-59 was of the close variety, as were those of St. Vincent, Cornwallis and Keith in the Napoleonic War, and also Collingwood's long blockade of Toulon after Trafalgar. Nelson often declared that his blockades of Toulon aimed to allow the

[1] *Some Principles of Maritime Strategy*, pp. 164-187 (Longmans, Green, 1918).

enemy to come out, in order that he might bring him to battle—
not to keep him in harbour: but they were none the less close
blockades. On the other hand in the War of American Independence we employed open blockade of Brest, and it was generally
not successful in preventing French warships and reinforcements
crossing the Atlantic. Of recent times developments in weapons—
and especially the torpedo, the mine and the aircraft—have made
close blockade impracticable. Thus in both wars of this century our
blockades were of the open variety and had economic as well as
naval purposes. Moreover in the second of those conflicts shore-
based and carrier-borne aircraft proved extremely effective instruments of blockade both in containing or neutralising the enemy's
principal naval forces, and in stopping the flow of his coastal trade.

The influence of geography and, to a lesser extent of meteorology
on strategy was mentioned earlier in connection with the struggle
for the trade of the New World in Elizabethan times. Here we may
note the favourable effects of the geographic situation of the British
Isles in relation to France and Spain; since it had a most important
influence on strategy throughout the era of the sailing ship. Not only
are these islands separated from the continent by the narrow stretch
of tide-swept water which has so often proved our chief defence
against invasion, but whereas the south coast of England is lavishly
provided with fine harbours, the Channel coast of France possesses
few capable of taking deep-draught ships. In the field of meteorology the fact that the prevailing winds around Britain are south-
westerly also brought us strategic benefits in the era of the sailing
ship; for our squadrons were able to seek shelter in British harbours
secure in the knowledge that the wind that had blown them off
station would keep their adversaries in port. Though the introduction of steam has eliminated the benefits gained from the
westerly winds, Britain has continued to derive substantial strategic
advantages from her geographical position, as will be seen when we
come to discuss the German wars of the present century.

The War of the Austrian Succession, in spite of its disastrous beginning, confirmed certain earlier strategic principles, and saw the development of others. Thus while control of the narrow seas was again shown to be the essential ingredient in defence against invasion, the establishment of the Western Squadron proved to be a very effective offensive-defensive strategy against the main French fleet in Brest. Amphibious operations had received a fillip from Vernon's attack on Porto Bello, and the later failures had underlined all the old lessons regarding the need for careful planning and preparation. In sum, after a very shaky start, we had moved a step nearer to becoming the principal mercantile nation, armed with the instruments requisite for a maritime strategy, and equipped with a clearer understanding of the manner in which they should be used. The advance was the more fortunate because the peace of Aix-la-Chapelle of 1748 proved only a truce in the long Anglo-French struggle. But by allowing the strength and condition of the fleet to decline to a point at which France could pursue her aims in India and North America unhindered, we nearly sacrificed all that had been gained from the previous war. Indeed the period 1748-56 closely resembles the 1930s, when Germany and Italy were openly arming, and were taking little trouble to disguise their aggressive intentions. The note of warning sounded by Pitt in the former case was heeded as little as that sounded by Churchill in the latter.

Fighting was actually renewed in America in 1755, before war was declared; and an attempt to intercept French reinforcements on the far side of the Atlantic provided our first failure. Next, when a threat to Minorca was plainly developing from Toulon, the government, perhaps remembering the unhappy results of dividing the fleet in 1653 and again in 1690,[1] hesitated to reinforce the Mediterranean. But the French invasion preparations of 1756 actually seem to have been a strategic bluff; and, if that is so, they succeeded as completely as the deceptive measures we took to convince Hitler that we intended to invade Norway in 1944. A weak

[1] That is after the English victory of the Kentish Knock (28th September, 1652) and at the time of the defeat of Torrington by Tourville off Beachy Head (30th June, 1690). See pp. 34 and 40.

fleet was finally sent to the Mediterranean, and the indecisive battle it fought led directly to the loss of Minorca. When war was actually declared in May, 1756, strategic considerations were at once complicated by the need to defend Hanover for George II. Pitt, who was out of office, spoke against the continental commitment; but the opposite view prevailed, and an alliance was concluded with Prussia.

Although in America the French strategy of hemming in the English colonists between the mountains and the sea made steady progress, in India Clive had defeated his rival Dupleix, and our sea power had proved sufficient—though only just sufficient—to prevent the French reversing that decision. The first year of actual war continued very unhappily for Britain, with the loss of Calcutta and further reverses in America. Then the mainly Hanoverian army under the Duke of Cumberland was caught with its back to the sea near the mouth of the Elbe, with no supporting fleet to relieve or remove it, and the politely described 'Convention of Klosterzeven' was in fact a surrender. However, in the same year that we lost Minorca, Pitt became Secretary of State under the nominal leadership of the Duke of Devonshire; and, much like Churchill in 1940, he quickly inspired his countrymen, and transformed the conduct of the war. Supremely confident in himself, he declared that 'I am sure that I can save this country, and that no one else can ';[1] and it is hard to believe that the great leader of 1756-1761 was the man who only a few years earlier had suffered from manic-depressive insanity. His strategy was based on five principles. First, opposition to France on the continent was to be organised and supported by British subsidies paid to Prussia; and we may note how after 1941 we supported and subsidised Russia against Germany by delivering to her vast quantities of war material. Secondly diversionary raids were made against the French coast to force the enemy to keep large numbers of men locked up in sterile garrison duties; and the same type of amphibious pin-pricking was carried out from Britain all

---

[1] Macaulay, *Essays*, Vol. II, p. 189 (Longmans Ed., 1843).

along the coast of Hitler's ' Festung Europa ' from 1940-44 with, we now know, a high degree of success. Thirdly Pitt and his naval advisers carried Anson's strategy one step further by blockading the enemy's main base; and in both wars of this century the same policy was applied, though modern developments forced us in general to employ open instead of close blockade. Fourthly Pitt used our sea power to strike far overseas at enemy colonies and bases at times and places of our own choosing; and that strategy, as in the last war, reaped immense rewards at astonishingly small cost. Lastly, by his ' Rule of War, 1756 ' he established, and thereafter firmly upheld, our right to stop neutral ships trading with the enemy —a purpose in which we had been singularly unsuccessful in our earlier wars with France and Holland. In sum it may be said that Pitt regarded North America as the vital theatre, on which our main effort should be concentrated: and that in addition he employed our sea power to gain a firm grip over the main French fleets, to force a dispersal of strength on the enemy, and to weaken him by economic blockade.

Between 1755 and '57 our blockades of the French Biscay and Mediterranean bases had not been effective enough to prevent substantial reinforcements reaching Canada, but by 1758 they had been immensely tightened. In that year Pitt's eyes were focused on Louisburg, the key to the St. Lawrence River; and not a single French ship from Europe succeeded in reaching the scene of the decisive operation. In July the combined expedition against Louisburg, with Amherst and Wolfe in command of the land forces and Boscawen leading a powerful detachment from the Home Fleet, was completely successful. Meanwhile what we would call Commando raids were being carried out against the French Channel and Biscay coasts, but they were not an unqualified success either tactically or strategically. For the Rochefort expedition of 1757 foundered on the rocks of the commanding General's timidity, and in the following year we unwisely tried to repeat a highly successful attack on St. Malo. Moreover we now know that the troops flung ashore did not in general stay long enough to force the enemy to divert substantial forces in order to contain them.

And so we come to 1759—'the year of victories'. The recapture of Louisburg had opened the way for the expedition to Quebec; and it is worth quoting in full Pitt's secret instruction to General Wolfe regarding the new undertaking. 'Whereas the success of this expedition' he wrote 'will very much depend upon an entire good understanding between our land and sea officers, we do hereby strictly enjoin and require you, on your part to maintain and cultivate such a good understanding and agreement . . . as the Commander-in-Chief of our squadron (i.e. Saunders) is instructed, on his part, to entertain the same good understanding and agreement'.[1] Evidently Pitt was fully alive to the danger of the 'corrupting blight' of inter-service strife, and determined to insure against it. Then in August, Boscawen destroyed de la Clue's Toulon squadron, which was trying to join the Brest fleet as a preliminary to invading this country, in Lagos Bay; and Hanover was saved on the field of Minden. Next on a wild and stormy November afternoon Hawke, flying the signal for General Chase, led his fleet in among the jagged rocks of Quiberon Bay, and completely shattered the Brest squadron. Lagos and Quiberon Bay not only frustrated Choiseul's ambitious plan to send an invasion army from Flanders to the Essex coast, supported by powerful diversionary attacks against Scotland and Ireland, but secured to England a command at sea more complete than she had ever heretofore enjoyed; and rich were the rewards she thereby gained—especially after Spain had injudiciously joined hands with France.

For 1761 Pitt's strategy aimed to eliminate France from India and the West Indies; but in June, Belleisle in the Bay of Biscay was captured by a combined operation in order to provide us with a base in between Brest and Cadiz at a time when Spain's attitude was becoming increasingly unfriendly. Unfortunately the refusal of Pitt's colleagues to agree to a pre-emptive attack on the Spanish

[1] Secret Instructions dated 5th February, 1759. (Public Record Office Ref. C.O. 5/214).

53

treasure fleets brought about his resignation, and it was left to others to reap what he had sown. Early in 1762 war was declared on Spain, the Mediterranean fleet was at once reinforced, and Cadiz was blockaded so effectively that aid to France was rendered nugatory. In India Pondicherry, the last French base, was captured in 1761: in the West Indies, Martinique, Guadeloupe and all the lesser French sugar islands in the Antilles had fallen to English amphibious power; Havana, the main depot of Spanish wealth in the west was captured with a vast treasure, though at a needlessly heavy cost in lives, in 1762; and in the far Pacific Manila in the rich Philippine group succumbed to the same strategy. As a contemporary observer truly remarked ' the fleet and army acting in concert seem to be the natural bulwark of this Kingdom '.[1]

In 1763, the British Government, misled by what Macaulay has called the ' specious objects which Lord Bute professed to procure ', and probably influenced by George III's dislike of Pitt and his apprehensions regarding the possible return of the great statesman to power, signed an astonishingly hasty peace at Paris; and much that we had won was handed back to its former possessors. None the less the Seven Years' War marks the real beginning of our imperial story, and the first triumph of a predominantly maritime strategy. As Mahan put it ' The one nation that gained in this war was that which used the sea in peace to earn its wealth, and ruled it in war by the extent of its navy . . . and by its numerous bases of operations scattered over the globe '.[2] Although between 1756 and 1760 French privateers captured over 2,500 English merchant ships, the *guerre de course* was again shown to be incapable of defeating a nation which firmly based its strategy on the maritime principles which had been slowly evolved during the previous two centuries. In fact the very size of our losses was in a sense a tribute to our expanding trade, for we had over 8,000 merchant ships at sea during the war, and each year saw an increase in English commerce and a

---

[1] Thomas More Molyneux, *Conjunct Expeditions* (1759).
[2] *The Influence of Sea Power on History* (1889), pp. 328-9.

decline in the enemy's. Mahan does however comment that 'the inattention of merchant ships to the orders of convoying vessels' was a cause of many unnecessary losses;[1] and that has a very modern ring. For in both wars of this century one of the greatest troubles that beset our escort commanders, and one of the most common causes of avoidable losses, was the tendency of merchantmen to romp ahead of or straggle astern of their convoys.

Finally one may remark how striking is the analogy not only between Pitt's conduct of the Seven Years' War and the strategy for which Churchill argued so persistently and persuasively during the recent struggle with Germany, but between the characters and influence of these two great statesmen. For Macaulay's summing up of Pitt's achievements: 'and history, while for the warning of vehement, high and daring natures, she notes his many errors, will yet deliberately pronounce, that, among the eminent men whose bones lie near his, scarcely one has left a more stainless and none a more splendid name',[2] might well have been inspired by the 20th-century Prime Minister. And all who came into close personal contact with Churchill during the last war must surely have felt the influence that Isaac Barré attributed to Pitt—namely that ' no man ever went in to [his] closet, who did not feel himself, if possible, braver at his return than when he went in'.[3]

The end of the Seven Years' War is a convenient stage at which to break the story of the development and application of our maritime strategy—not because it ends on a note of high success, with the reaping of a wonderful harvest, but because it leaves to be told how in the next phase much that had gone before was forgotten, and we were thus forced to pass through another of those periods of sore trial and testing adversity which are so repetitive a feature in our country's history.

[1] Ibid. p. 319.
[2] Essay on the Earl of Chatham. (*Literary and Historical Essays*, Vol. III, p. 626, Longman's Ed., 1854.)
[3] Speech in House of Commons, 13th May, 1778. Taylor and Pringle, *The Chatham Correspondence*, Vol. IV, p. 525.

II

From adversity through triumph to 'Pax Britannica'

We saw in the last chapter how in the Seven Years' War, Britain first employed a fully developed maritime strategy. But for all the benefits which the genius of the elder Pitt then brought to us, the period that followed was one of the most discreditable through which this country has ever passed. While the Duc de Choiseul and his successors were doing their utmost to reconstruct and foster French sea power, corrupt and forgetful British governments did the exact opposite. It was of course inevitable that peace should bring retrenchment to the Navy, but what was inexcusable was to allow the ships which were retained to decline into a state of neglect and inefficiency. It was not as though the period was one of assured peace: for in 1770 there was a sudden alarm over the seizure of the Falkland Islands by Spain, and a squadron had to be hastily mobilised. Pitt, now Earl of Chatham, used the occasion to call for a two-ocean Navy, capable of dealing with a new Bourbon coalition in the Atlantic and Mediterranean. But his foresight went unheeded, and two years later Lord North, the Prime Minister, actually told the First Lord that 'I do not recollect to have seen a more pacific appearance of affairs than there is at this moment'[1]—a striking example of the not uncommon tendency of politicians to take a short view, as against the longer view forced on those responsible for and experienced in maritime affairs. The blindness shown by our statesmen towards the likelihood of France renewing the challenge may indeed be compared with our attitude towards renascent Germany in between the two wars of this century.

[1] To Lord Sandwich, 10th September, 1772. Sandwich Papers Vol. I, p. 20 (Navy Records Society, 1932).

When the American colonies broke into open revolt in 1775 the policy of France was at first to give them clandestine aid, and to do all she could to prevent a reconciliation with the mother country. American privateers, towards whom France acted in a most un-neutral manner, soon began to attack our trade, and our fleet was far too weak to afford it adequate protection, as well as escort our troops overseas, and blockade the American seaports. Moreover the revolt brought an added danger to the Royal Navy by threatening to stop the shipment of naval stores from the colonies, which were the only alternative to the Scandinavian countries as a source of supply; and the loss of such stores was bound to make it even harder to commission new ships. The first phase ended with Burgoyne's surrender at Saratoga in October, 1777, and in the following March, France, confident that the moment for revenge had come, joined in openly. Because we could spare no ships for the Mediterranean, the Toulon squadron was able to cross the Atlantic unhindered, and the impact of French sea power on the continental war very soon began to be felt. In July, 1778, the Brest fleet put to sea, and the indecisive action fought by an ill-equipped and ill-trained Home Fleet off Ushant went a long way towards deciding the fate of America. For the French were able to remedy the colonists' lack of sea power, so saving them from a blockade which we would otherwise have been bound to enforce with increasing severity.

The declaration of war by France brought about a change in British strategy, which now aimed to strike at French colonies and trade whilst conducting a defensive land campaign in America; and it was for this reason that the West Indies became an active theatre. But no lasting benefits can possibly derive from a strategy which leaves the enemy's main fleet intact, and concentrates on secondary objectives whose fate will in any case follow the success or failure of the principal operations. To cite an instance, after Spain had joined France in 1779, a Franco-Spanish fleet came into the Channel and we were too weak to engage it. This was the best opportunity to invade these islands that had come the French way since 1690; but they totally failed to seize their chance.[1] It was indeed 'not British preparations but the inefficiency of our enemies' that saved us.[2] For France and Spain, by concentrating on winning West Indian islands and regaining Gibraltar respectively, went a long way towards compensating us for our failure to defeat or contain the Toulon and Brest fleets. At the end of 1780 we declared war on the United Provinces, who had refused to honour the terms of the alliance of 1678 and were insisting, as neutral nations always do, on trading with our enemies. But our action in stopping Dutch trade led to the 'uncommitted nations'—Sweden, Denmark, Prussia, Austria and, later, Portugal—forming themselves into an Armed Neutrality, whose aim it was to curtail, and if possible destroy the maritime rights to which the elder Pitt had attached such great importance. The claim that the nationality of a ship covers its cargo, which has been called the doctrine of 'free ships, free goods', or in our own time 'the freedom of the seas', is one that has recurred in one form or another in every war since the 17th century; but in the 1780s the government stood firm on the general principle involved, and the Armed Neutrality actually accomplished little.

Our naval weakness, however, continued to cause us serious difficulties farther overseas, especially in the matter of securing our vital bases. Though Gibraltar survived a three-year siege, the despatch of a fleet to relieve it in 1781 allowed a French squadron to leave Brest for the Indian Ocean: and on its way south its commander, Suffren, whom Sir John Laughton has rightly called 'one of the most dangerous enemies the English fleets ever met'[3] defeated an expedition we had sent to seize the Cape of Good Hope—then a Dutch possession. On arriving at his destination

[1] A. T. Patterson's new and authoritative study, *The Other Armada* (Manchester U.P., 1960), brings out very clearly the extent to which the Franco-Spanish failure was due to a breakdown in supply, and to the severe incidence of scurvy in their fleet, rather than to British counter-measures.

[2] Laird Clowes and others, *The Royal Navy, a History*, Vol. III, p. 445.

[3] *Studies in Naval History* (Longmans, Green, 1887).

Suffren quickly recaptured Trincomalee—the base on which control of the Indian Ocean chiefly depended; and it was only the arrival cf a timely reinforcement for the British Admiral Hughes, and the interception of two supply convoys destined for Suffren, which saved us from losing India. Thus do the actions of quite small maritime forces in a remote theatre decide vast issues. Indeed it is never the mere strength of fleets that is decisive, but the ability to achieve command of the sea in face of whatever opposition the enemy may be able to offer—as is shown by the fact that from 1779-82 Hughes had only six battleships, yet was able to achieve complete command of the Indian Ocean and to capture Trinco-malee. But Suffren's arrival, and his skilful strategy and tactics, quickly, though only temporarily, reversed the British advantage. The second base that we lost was Minorca in March, 1782, after another indecisive battle; and that disaster restored command of the western Mediterranean to the French.

While one part of the Brest fleet was on passage to the Indian Ocean under Suffren another and larger part sailed for the West Indies, whence its able commander de Grasse, took it up to the Chesapeake. There on 5th September, 1781, he was met by Admiral Graves, admittedly with slightly inferior strength; and the inde-cisive action which he fought, in spite of having begun the day with a distinct tactical advantage, led directly to Cornwallis's surrender at Yorktown. If it was Keppel's action off Ushant that brought salvation to the American colonists, Graves's failure in the Chesa-peake sealed the issue. It is interesting to find how deeply conscious Washington was that the success of the revolt depended chiefly on sea power: as late as April, 1781, when de Grasse was actually on his way across the Atlantic, he was extremely anxious. ' If France delays timely aid ' he then wrote ' it will avail us nothing if she attempts it hereafter. We are at the end of our tether, and now or never deliverance must come '.[1]

---

[1] *Writings of George Washington from the Original Manuscript Sources*, Vol. 21, p. 439 (Ed. John Fitzpatrick, Washington Bicentennial Commission).

Luckily the slow recovery of our sea power, and our adversaries' failure to take advantage of their opportunities at home, saved us from irremediable disaster. In April, 1782, Rodney defeated de Grasse in the West Indies in a battle which came too late to exert any strategic influence, but which is tactically important; he seized a favourable chance to break the enemy's line, and in the ensuing mêlée captured five ships, including de Grasse's splendid *Ville de Paris*. It is possible that, had Rodney been in command at Ushant or off the Chesapeake, the course of history would have been quite different. But the battle of the Saintes did at least help to destroy what Sir Julian Corbett has aptly called the ' sterile fetish ' of the line of battle.[1]

After Yorktown everyone in England (except the King) realised that the American colonies were irretrievably lost, and that the vital theatre had shifted to India—not only for its own commerce but because possession of the bases on the coasts of the sub-continent and in Ceylon would give control of the far eastern trade, which was then increasing rapidly and rivalling in importance that of the West Indies. By the winter of 1782, France was so exhausted that the Comte de Vergennes, the Foreign Secretary, knew that she could hardly sustain another year of war. He and Lord Shelburne (later Marquis of Lansdowne) engaged in protracted negotiations for peace, each hoping for decisive news from India. But when the news came it was clear that, for all Suffren's brilliance, it was the British Admiral Hughes who had won the campaign.[2] Indeed it is no exaggeration to say that Hughes laid the foundation of the British Empire as we have known it. In 1783 the treaty of peace was signed at Versailles. Though Britain had suffered a profound loss of prestige in the West, it was to a considerable extent offset by her success—narrow though the margin was—in the East; and the years of adversity had proved a good training ground for the school of sea officers who were to serve her so well in the next struggle.

[1] *Fighting Instructions* (Navy Records Society, 1905).
[2] See V. T. Harlow, *The Founding of the Second British Empire*, Vol. I, pp. 363-83 (Longmans, Green, 1952).

Furthermore we derived unlooked for benefits from the three voyages made by Captain James Cook on behalf of the Admiralty between 1768 and 1779, which laid the foundations of new dominions, and opened up new opportunities for trade, in undeserved compensation for what we had lost in America.

Because the ineffectiveness of the British tactics in the battles of Ushant and the Chesapeake had such far-reaching influence in the outcome of the War of American Independence, we may here make a brief digression to review the various factors which ultimately brought about a complete, though unfortunately not a long-lasting revolution in the handling of our fleets in battle. In the first place an efficient signal system is an absolute pre-requisite to the rapid and unambiguous communication of the Admiral's intentions, and the system in force during the greater part of the 18th century had not met that requirement—as the misunderstandings which arose in actions such as Mathews fought off Toulon in February, 1744, amply demonstrated. In the 1770s, however, Admiral Kempenfelt put forward proposals for a numeral signal code, and the signal book which Howe introduced in 1782, which was based on Kempenfelt's ideas, marked a great step forward in the ease and assurance, and above all the clarity with which a flag officer could transmit his orders. For the second development we were chiefly indebted to a small but distinguished band of French students of naval warfare, and to the school of study which grew out of their writings in the latter half of the 18th century. The originator of that school was Père Paul Hoste whose *L'art des armées navales, ou traité des évolutions navales* had appeared at the instigation of the Comte de Tourville, as early as 1697. Parts of that work were published in English in 1762, though for a complete translation we had to wait as late as 1834. None the less Rodney and Howe both unquestionably studied Hoste, and on several occasions applied the principles suggested in his treatise. Next in the field was Sebastien-François, Vicomte Bigot de Morogues, whose *Tactique Navale, ou traité des évolutions et des Signaux* was published privately in 1763, but attracted little attention until it was reprinted in Amsterdam sixteen years later. In 1782 a Scottish laird called Clerk of Eldin, who had probably never been nearer to the sea than Leith docks, published his *Essay on Naval Tactics*: and five years later there appeared the Vicomte de Grenier's *L'Art de la Guerre sur Mer*. The most interesting point about this sudden burgeoning of intellectual study of naval warfare is that the treatises of Morogues, Clerk of Eldin and de Grenier all showed a clear antipathy to the set-piece action in line of battle; and although it is impossible to prove it historically there is little doubt that between them they influenced tactical thought in the Royal Navy very markedly. For example there is in Nelson's famous Trafalgar Memorandum more than a hint of the suggestions put forward by Clerk of Eldin. Be that as it may, there is no doubt that by 1790 the Royal Navy was in far better shape to face the trials ahead of it than it had been at the beginning of the previous war. An experienced, and in some instances brilliant band of sea officers, hardened in the furnace of recent adversity was available: the long tactical thraldom of the mandatory Fighting Instructions was shaken, if not actually shattered: a simple but efficient communications system was in use: and Sir Charles Middleton (later Lord Barham), one of the most capable administrators and strategists the Admiralty has known, held the key office of Controller of the Navy. Furthermore William Pitt the younger had formed his first administration in 1783, and it was his policy to restore the Navy to the condition and efficiency which had enabled his father to achieve such striking successes in the Seven Years' War.

The decade that passed between the Treaty of Versailles, by which the American colonies gained their independence, and the outbreak of the War of the French Revolution in 1793 was one of almost continuous tension, first between Britain and one or both of the Bourbon powers, and then with Russia. The French government's policy had the double aim of gaining control of the United Provinces, which was bound to revive our ancient determination that no major naval power should control Antwerp and the Scheldt, and of regaining India. While the fact that the Cape of Good Hope and Ceylon were held by the Dutch (we having lost Trincomalee in 1782), and that Mauritius was a French possession, produced the plain danger that if France conquered Holland she would gain complete control of the sea route to India. Furthermore our use of the alternative route to India by way of the Mediterranean and Egypt, which was important even before the opening of the Suez Canal, had been rendered insecure by the loss of Minorca. And that disaster had again made it very doubtful whether our fleet could assert itself effectively against the combined power of France and Spain in the western Mediterranean. When, however, a crisis arose in 1787, Pitt had the fleet ready, the immediate French threat was averted, and Dutch independence was preserved. Three years later the Spanish seizure of Nootka Sound (Vancouver) brought another crisis, and again peace was only preserved because Pitt showed his ability and readiness to use our sea power; but he was unsuccessful in frustrating Russian designs against Poland and Turkey in 1789—in the latter case because his colleagues refused to support the use of the fleet.

The French threat to Holland had, however, brought up the old question whether, in the event of war, we would need continental alliances to support our aims, or whether we should do better to concentrate on using our sea power to weaken the enemy. Because France was much less dependent on trade than Holland or Spain, and was indeed nearly self-supporting in food, and because it was certain that sea power could not alone save the United Provinces, Pitt deemed it essential to contract alliances, and between 1787 and '88 he therefore brought Hesse and Prussia, as well as the Dutch, into his coalition. This, of course, inevitably imposed on Britain continental commitments which might—and indeed did—weaken the application of a maritime strategy.

In spite of the recurrent crises of the 1780s, in 1792 the prospects of peace seemed good, and Pitt therefore agreed to reductions in the Army and Navy. These untimely measures produced difficulties which became all too plain when, in the following year, war broke out. The chief naval weaknesses arose from the shortage of seamen, caused by successive governments having failed to put the vital matter of manning on a sound basis, and from the insufficiency of the smaller warships (frigates) needed to carry out the multifarious duties which always fall on the class of ships which can generically be classed as cruisers or flotilla vessels. We were, however, confident that the French Navy's efficiency had been seriously undermined by the revolution, and the consequential loss of many of its best officers; and with Holland and Spain initially on our side it was certain that we would hold the numerical advantage in battleships. But both our allies quickly proved broken reeds: for they acted very ambiguously for a time, then concluded peace treaties with France, and finally joined hands with her. Thus were we once again taught how dangerous it is to base defence plans on the help which may be gained from alliances.

In the field of strategy Pitt did not show the clear grasp of essentials, and the firmness in pursuing the most important purposes, that had distinguished his father's conduct of the Seven Years' War. As always a large number of different projects were put forward; and there was the usual conflict between the continental and the maritime schools of thought. While the former wished to make our primary effort in Flanders, and to put an end to the Jacobin movement by capturing Paris, Burke wished to send support to the Royalist rising in the Vendée, Dundas (the Secretary of War) favoured peripheral operations, especially in the West Indies, while the Duke of Richmond saw great benefits in attacks on French naval bases. In fact we tried to achieve a compromise between the various strategic ideas put forward, and that led to a costly and ineffective dissipation of resources in Flanders, in the West Indies, and especially at Toulon, where an anti-Jacobin revolt broke out in 1793. Furthermore when we were forced to abandon that base at the end of the year we failed to destroy most of the French battleships in the harbour; and they formed the nucleus of the fleet whose containment was to absorb a vast effort during the succeeding years.

The defection of Holland in 1794, and of Spain in the following year provided the French with a string of admirable bases stretching from the North Sea to the Mediterranean. But we acted quickly to occupy the Cape of Good Hope and Ceylon, so averting the threat to India which Pitt had foreseen ten years earlier, we secured Corsica as a substitute for Minorca, and we also prepared to defend Lisbon against a Spanish attack. One may find a parallel to these actions taken to limit the dangers produced by the collapse of the coalition in the occupation of Iceland after Hitler had overrun Denmark and Norway in 1940, and in the preparations we put in hand in the same year to occupy the Spanish and Portuguese Atlantic islands in the event of the Germans marching into Spain, and thus rendering Gibraltar useless to us.

Though the first three years of the War of the French Revolution were thus chiefly a period of contest for bases, they did produce two fleet actions, and a number of lesser clashes between British and French squadrons. In the first major battle, which was fought far out in the Atlantic between 28th May and 1st June, 1794, Howe with the Channel Fleet out-manoeuvred and out-fought the French Brest squadron. However the corn convoy from America which Villaret-Joyeuse had been sent out to cover, and whose safe arrival was, on account of a bad harvest, a critical matter for France, slipped through unscathed. The second action took place in the Bay of Biscay in June, 1795, and was little more decisive than the two partial actions fought by Admiral Hotham against the Toulon fleet in March and May of the same year. If, as Mahan has observed, those clashes exhibited the ' extreme circumspection characterising the early naval operations of the British ',[1] the results did convince the French government that they could not hope to win command at sea. They therefore decided to concentrate their efforts on the *guerre de*

[1] *The Influence of Sea Power on the French Revolution and Empire*, Vol. I, p. 178 (Sampson, Low, Marston, 1892).

course—exactly as Louis XIV had done when, nearly a century earlier, similar conditions had arisen during the War of the Spanish Succession. This caused us considerable losses, and forced on us a great dispersal of cruisers, of which we never had enough. But, as in earlier wars, it never appeared likely to produce a decision. Nor did our own colonial campaigns of 1793-96 bear greater strategic fruits than the French *guerre de course*: and the cost in lives of the West Indian operations was appallingly heavy.

The attempts, during the first phase of the war, to do too much with inadequate resources placed an excessively heavy strain on the Royal Navy. It had been required to support the Austrians in southern France and north Italy, to cover our vital Baltic trade against the Dutch fleet, to deal with numerous privateers on the oceans, and to try and protect the Mediterranean sea routes, which were now very exposed. Moreover the importance of that theatre was enhanced when, in 1796, Bonaparte invaded Piedmont, and the condition of our Austrian allies soon became critical. By the middle of that year we were faced with a major crisis; for the loss of north Italy and the declaration of war by Spain in July placed the fleet which had been working in the Gulf of Lyon in a perilous situation. The government therefore decided to evacuate the Mediterranean. Corsica, which we had gone to such lengths to secure two years earlier, was abandoned, and on 21st December, 1796, Sir John Jervis anchored his exhausted and battered ships in the Tagus. Thus did we return to the precarious state of affairs that had prevailed at the beginning of the War of the Spanish Succession, before the capture of Minorca in 1708. The chief cause of this retreat, by which the Mediterranean virtually became a French lake, was our failure to destroy the main Toulon fleet—first when it was actually in our hands at the time of the evacuation of our forces from the base, and then on at least two occasions (Hotham's actions of March and May, 1795), when it was encountered at sea. But as all our operations in this theatre had been grievously handicapped by the lack of a well-equipped base, the loss of Minorca in 1782 must surely be regarded as a major contributory cause.

Nor was the evacuation of the Mediterranean the only unfavourable development of the closing months of 1796: for in the north our army was withdrawn from Europe, leaving the great ports of the Scheldt and Rhine in French hands—the very circumstance which we had striven to avoid ever since the days of Spanish dominance of the Low Countries: the Austrian armies in Italy had been shattered, and Naples had been forced into neutrality: while the revolt in the Vendée, which we had vainly tried to support had been crushed. Detachments from the Toulon fleet were preying upon our convoys out in the Atlantic and in the Levant; and in the winter of 1796-97 a French attempt to invade Ireland was defeated by the weather rather than by any particular effort or activity on the part of the Channel Fleet under Lord Bridport, which was supposed to be blockading Brest.

It is impossible not to feel that during the first phase of the war, from 1793-1797, both the strategic direction and, in many instances, the naval leadership were faulty. For the blockade of Brest was not properly enforced, nor was that of Toulon between the recapture of the base by the French and the arrival of Jervis to take command of our fleet; nor was the powerful ' Western Squadron ' properly maintained in the manner suggested by Vernon half a century earlier.[1] As to the naval commanders, if Bridport was supine and inefficient, the elderly Hood was certainly a difficult man to work with. In the Corsican operations there were bitter quarrels between him and the soldiers, relieved only by the unflagging and disinterested efforts of Nelson; and it is probably also the case that more could have been done to support and encourage the Austrian army—ill-led though it certainly was. When Hood's mantle descended on Hotham the latter—stigmatised by Mahan as ' this leisurely Commander in Chief '[2]—showed himself mediocre in

---

[1] See p. 47.
[2] *The Influence of Sea Power on the French Revolution and Empire*, Vol. I, p. 202.

leadership and lacking in determination; while his second-in-command, Admiral Mann, was certainly no better. In war it is probably inevitable that it takes time to discover the officers who are best capable of exercising the responsibilities of high command, but between 1793 and 1797 we seem to have been very slow in weeding out those who could not do so.

The analogy between the events of the autumn of 1796 and those of the summer of 1940 are obvious; and in the latter crisis the Admiralty again considered evacuating the Mediterranean. But the staunchness of Churchill and of the naval commanders concerned —Admirals Cunningham and Somerville—quickly caused the proposal to be dropped. Nor was the tide long in turning in the earlier war. For on 14th February, 1797, off Cape St. Vincent, Admiral Jervis, aided by an unorthodox but brilliant tactical manoeuvre by Nelson, frustrated the junction of the Cadiz and Brest fleets, which the French had planned as the first step to invading these islands; and in the following October, Admiral Duncan utterly crushed the Dutch fleet off Camperdown. Those two victories frustrated Bonaparte's hope of building up an overwhelming maritime coalition against us, and restored to the Royal Navy the confidence in itself and its leaders which had been such a marked and beneficial feature of the latter part of the Seven Years' War. And they put a term—though only temporarily—to the long-enduring tactical sterility produced by the rigid line of battle.

By the spring of 1798, the situation was, thanks to the reassertion of our maritime superiority in the North Sea and Atlantic, a good deal more reassuring: since Austria was showing a conditional readiness to re-enter the fray—provided that we sent a fleet into the Mediterranean and paid her a large subsidy. But if the victories of St. Vincent and Camperdown had checked the French invasion strategy on the North Sea and Atlantic flanks of our sea frontier, they still had a good deal of room for manoeuvre in the ocean spaces in between them. Thus they persevered in their intention to send an expedition to Ireland, and in August and September, 1798, two strong raiding forces therefore sailed from the Biscay bases. The first evaded our patrols, and successfully landed its troops: but they were soon all rounded up. The second was intercepted at sea, and the French flagship and three other prizes were captured. These experiences underlined the old lesson that, while it is always possible for an enemy to fling a small force ashore, an effective degree of maritime control is the essential preliminary to a serious invasion. Moreover at the same period our light forces in the Channel carried out their traditional function of harassing the flotillas which the enemy was assembling to invade these islands. Sometimes the naval raids and minor combined operations succeeded: on other occasions we attempted too much and were repulsed. In sum, however, the strategy of striking at the invasion fleet in its harbours was successful: for it fully re-affirmed our control of the narrow seas.

While these events were in progress in the north the Admiralty was growing anxious about the purpose of the French expedition which they knew to be preparing in Toulon. Naples, Portugal or Ireland were considered the most likely destinations, and Egypt was not mentioned in the first instructions sent to Lord St. Vincent. In June, 1798, however, Dundas, for all that his judgment on strategic issues was by no means always sound, expressed ' the perhaps whimsical belief' that the enemy's objective might be Egypt and then India. Evidence soon began to accumulate that such was the case, and early in May, St. Vincent sent Nelson into the Mediterranean with a small squadron to watch Toulon and report the movements of the French fleet. On the same day that he was detached the British Government and Admiralty took a courageous decision. They told St. Vincent to divide his fleet and reinforce Nelson, and ordered reinforcements out from home to replace those sent into the Mediterranean—in spite of the invasion threat. There is a close analogy between the bold strategic moves of 1798 and those of 1940, when the Admiralty quickly sent a powerful squadron (mostly from the Home Fleet) to Gibraltar to replace lost French maritime power—in disregard of the German armies massing on the other side of the Straits of Dover.

In fact Bonaparte's eyes had turned to the east — towards Egypt and India—soon after Austria had made peace in April, 1797. The French expedition sailed from Toulon on 19th May, 1798— only five days before the reinforcements from St. Vincent's fleet reached Nelson; and during the long pursuit he again narrowly missed it to the south of Crete. Speculation on what the course of events might have been had he caught the cumbrous transports in the Gulf of Lyon or off Cape Matapan provides a fascinating example of what John Buchan has called ' the causal and the casual ' in history.[1] Certain it is that the whole course of the war, and of Anglo-French relations in the 19th century, would have been different. As it was, Nelson's crushing victory in Aboukir Bay on 1st August, 1798, destroyed Bonaparte's prospects in the Middle East, and also brought into being the Second Coalition against him. Though Austria continued to vacillate, Turkey, Russia and Naples all now joined in the war, a Russo-Turkish fleet came into the eastern Mediterranean, British ships blockaded Malta, and Port Mahon in Minorca was retaken by a combined operation. Thus, within a few weeks of Nelson's victory, did the Allies regain complete control of the whole Mediterranean. Finally the simultaneous ending of the costly West Indian operations brought hopes that we would in the near future possess what Richmond has aptly called a ' disposable military force '[2] capable of making its influence felt in a vital theatre.

For 1799 our strategy in the Mediterranean theatre was to make the protection of the ' Two Sicilies ' a first charge on our resources, to keep the French Army isolated in Egypt, to blockade Malta, and to co-operate with the Russians in the Aegean. But the government also reopened the question of attacking the enemy fleets in their home bases—a proposal which had been considered but rejected at the beginning of the war. The Dutch ships which had survived Camper-

[1] Rede Lecture, (Cambridge U.P., 1929).
[2] *Statesmen and Sea Power*, p. 124 (O.U.P., 1946).

down were made the first objective, and in August a Russo-British expedition landed on Texel with the object of destroying them, of driving the French out of Holland, and of acting as a diversion in favour of Austria, on whom France had declared war in March. Pitt, whose strategic views were always coloured by his excessive optimism, hoped to follow up this considerable undertaking with an attack on Brest. But, as in the war of 1939-45, shortage of shipping cramped all our strategic purposes. Thus although the expedition to Texel achieved the capture of the Dutch warships, it failed to regain Holland or to achieve its diversionary purpose. Subsequent attempts against Belleisle, Ferrol and Cadiz were, for a variety of reasons, even less productive. The troops sent to Belleisle were hastily withdrawn in June to support the Austrians in Italy; but they arrived too late to take part in the battle of Marengo, where their presence might well have turned defeat into victory. This was a clear case of failure to establish and adhere to firm strategic priorities. The entire campaign against enemy bases thus accomplished little, and again our 'disposable military force' had been dissipated. The causes lay in the lack of clear decision and constancy on the part of the home government, and in its dispersal of effort on too many undertakings; while in the military field the time taken to mount the various expeditions had been far too long. One may remember that as lately as 1956, exactly the same chain of cause and effect frustrated the rapid organisation and despatch of an expedition to Egypt. Early in December, 1800, Bonaparte crushed the Austrians at Hohenlinden, and in the following February they made peace. So ended the Second Coalition against the French: and we were again forced back on to the defensive, with nothing except our sea power standing between our enemies and world domination.

Towards the end of 1800, the northern European powers formed themselves, as they had done in 1781, into an 'Armed Neutrality', whose object it was to close the Baltic and establish the principle of 'free ships, free goods'. This was a plain threat not only to the

74

maintenance of our fleets, whose vital stores would be cut off, but to the exercise of our essential belligerent rights. However, the British Government stood as firm as the elder Pitt had done in 1756 on the same issue. It must indeed ever be a fundamental right of a maritime power to insist that neutral nations shall not supply its enemies—and reap vast profits in doing so. In 1801, a fleet was promptly sent to the Baltic and Nelson ' as though again drawn by some mysterious influence, to be at hand for services which he alone could render ',[1] was appointed second-in-command. It was largely by a combination of skill, tact, courage and bluff on his part that, at the end of a very hard day's fighting off Copenhagen, the Armed Neutrality was brought to nought. The measures taken in 1801 to secure the supply of our naval stores may be compared to the prompt reaction to the threat of German infiltration into Iraq and Iran in 1941, when it was our oil supplies—the 20th-century equivalent to timber and cordage—which were threatened.

In September, 1800, Malta, which had been blockaded for two years, surrendered. The Russians, however, laid claim to the island; and our refusal to hand it over to them involved us in a very protracted dispute. Next Bonaparte persuaded Spain to invade Portugal, with the object of depriving our fleet of the use of the Tagus. But such a loss was not nearly as serious in 1800 as it would have been four years earlier; since with Minorca and Malta in our possession the fleet was assured of well-placed bases inside the Mediterranean. We did, however, take the precaution of occupying Portuguese Madeira—for the same reason that, in 1940, we made preparations to occupy some or all of the Spanish and Portuguese Atlantic islands. In the autumn of 1800, the British Government, undeterred by the threat of invasion at home or by the loss of the Portuguese bases, determined to send an army to settle the issue in Egypt, where General Kléber's troops had been trapped ever since Bonaparte's attempt to break out by way of Palestine had been

---

[1] A. T. Mahan, *The Influence of Sea Power on the French Revolution and Empire* (1892), Vol. II, p. 37.

frustrated at Acre in May, 1799—largely thanks to the activity of the naval squadron under Sir Sidney Smith. As so often the assembly of the new expedition was delayed by shortage of shipping, and it was not until October, 1800, that it sailed from Gibraltar. The troops landed on 8th March, 1801, and on 19th Alexandria was captured. So ended an attempt to conduct a land campaign across seas which the invader could not adequately control. Churchill's simile, applied to another army stranded in Africa as hostage to British sea power nearly a century and a half later, is equally valid in the case of Kléber's: for it did indeed resemble ' cut flowers in a vase '. An interesting sidelight on the seaborne military movements of 1800 is Wellesley's far-sighted assembly of an expeditionary force at Trincomalee, whence it could be despatched either to Java or the Red Sea, as the home government might decide. It was finally ordered to the Egyptian theatre, where it was joined by other forces sent out by way of the Cape. Though it arrived too late to influence the land operations in lower Egypt, it provides an almost exact analogy to the despatch of reinforcements from India and the British Isles to East Africa and the Middle East early in the last war.

Although we had made an astonishing recovery since the crisis of 1796, and our sea power was gaining all the time in strength and effectiveness, in October, 1801, the Addington ministry concluded a hasty peace, whereby we surrendered all our overseas gains except Trinidad and Ceylon, and even agreed that Malta should be returned to the totally ineffective rule of the Knights of St. John. Worse still was the fact that, although it quickly became clear that Bonaparte's ambitions were far from assuaged, we at once began to reduce our Army and Navy.

During the truce which followed the Treaty of Amiens, and immediately after the renewal of the war in 1803, British sea power played a key role in deciding two issues which arose in the western hemisphere. Haiti had become a French possession in 1795, and when a negro revolt broke out six years later they sent strong forces to suppress it. We gave help to the rebels, and blockaded the island's coast. The French expedition ended in a costly failure, thus confirming the reputation of the West Indies as a graveyard for overseas enterprises—unless, as Admiral Vernon had urged more than fifty years earlier, they were carried out at the right season of the year and accomplished their purposes quickly.[1] The second issue concerned the state of Louisiana, which France had regained from Spain in 1800. When, however, the war was renewed our maritime control made it impossible for Bonaparte to make any strategic use of the colony, and he finally sold it to the United States for a few cents an acre. The acquisition by the young Republic of that vast and rich territory was thus an unacknowledged benefit derived from British sea power.

On the outbreak of the Napoleonic War our initial strategy was again defensive; but because the defeat of the renewed invasion threat, the close blockade of French ports, and the protection of our trade could not by themselves bring victory it became essential to build up another continental coalition. Russia, however, was still demanding Malta, and was also pressing us to modify our maritime code: and Pitt's refusal to yield on either issue brought about an impasse over her joining the alliance. Then in July, 1804, we took pre-emptive steps against Spain, who had refused to stop allowing the French Navy to use her ports, and our attack on one of her treasure fleets led to a declaration of war. We then extended our blockade to the whole enemy-held coast.

From 1803-1805, 130,000 of the most brilliant soldiery of all time were massed on the heights above Boulogne, while a smaller contingent was assembled in the Low Countries; and the whole effort of France was concentrated on providing the means and producing the conditions for their transport across twenty miles of salt water. But barring the way lay the Channel Fleet under Lord Keith, whose flotillas constantly harried and raided the invasion ports; away to the west Cornwallis was watching Brest, Collingwood and Pellew were blockading Rochefort and Ferrol, while off Toulon

[1] See p. 45 footnote (1)

Nelson was wearing himself out in battling with the storms of the Gulf of Lyon. Unless those squadrons could be driven off or defeated Napoleon had no hope of concentrating his fleet in the north to gain even temporary command of the Channel.

Napoleon's final plan for 1805 is well known. Villeneuve's Toulon fleet was to break out of the Mediterranean, pick up Gravina's Spanish squadron at Cadiz, and then cross the Atlantic to Martinique. Ganteaume's Brest fleet was to come south to Ferrol, drive off the blockading ships, join hands with the squadron from that port, and then follow Villeneuve to the West Indies. When the Combined Fleet had concentrated, it was to return to the east, defeat Cornwallis in the Channel approaches, and then make for Boulogne to cover the passage of the invasion flotillas. Had the plan worked out as intended we would have been faced by some 50 battleships in the chops of the Channel—about double the strength normally available to Cornwallis off Brest. But there were grave weaknesses in Napoleon's plan. Its success depended on his various forces slipping through our blockading squadrons at the right moment, on their avoiding engagement on the way to the West Indies or after arrival there, and on their then returning undisturbed 3,000 miles to the east. Indeed it took so little account of British reactions that it almost seems as though Napoleon expected our various fleets and squadrons to fall in tamely with his wishes: whereas in fact the Admiralty under Lord Barham had a very firm grasp of the best means of frustrating them. Corbett has justly stigmatised Napoleon's plan as ' the work of a self-confident amateur blind to the essential differences between land and sea warfare '.[1] The small Rochefort squadron did break out in January, 1805, and, after several false starts Villeneuve got away from Toulon, picked up five Spanish ships from Cadiz and reached the West Indies on 12th May. But that marked the limit of success to Napoleon's preliminary concentration: for Nelson, once he was certain of the Combined Fleet's destination, had set off in hot pursuit. Although he narrowly

[1] *The Campaign of Trafalgar* (Longmans, Green, 1910).

missed Villeneuve in the West Indies his arrival caused his adversary to return to Europe without extending his period of waiting for the Brest squadron—which was actually still blockaded in port; and on 13th June, four days behind Villeneuve, Nelson also set sail to the east. Though everything turned out happily in the end there will always remain some doubt whether Nelson's pursuit of his adversary was a sound move. For it certainly contravened the principle on which British strategy rested—namely that in the event of the French squadrons eluding our blockading forces the latter would fall back on Cornwallis off Brest, so establishing as powerful a concentration as possible in the western approaches to the Channel. In fact it could be argued that it was Nelson who presented the French with the best opportunity of bringing Napoleon's plan to fruition. On the other hand his action undoubtedly saved our West Indian possessions: and, perhaps more important, he understood his opponent's failings sufficiently clearly to realise that hot pursuit was the most probable way of destroying the last remnants of his self-confidence, and so leading him into error.

Just as in 1940 we can say with some precision that it was Hitler's order of 17th September, postponing his invasion plan 'indefinitely', that marked his admission of defeat, so it is clear that when Villeneuve turned south from Ferrol on 13th August, 1805, instead of north for Brest, Napoleon must have known that the whole edifice of his strategy had failed. On the 25th of that month he told Talleyrand ' My decision is taken ... three weeks hence I shall be in Germany with 200,000 men '. The vast camps at Boulogne were struck, and so began the march to the Danube which ended at Ulm on 20th October.

It was actually Napoleon's order to the Combined Fleet to move into the Mediterranean and recover Sicily that brought about the battle of Trafalgar. Yet the fight was in truth the climax of two years of defensive strategy, based upon our grip on the main enemy fleets in their bases. And one may admire the calm confidence with which the Admiralty, while holding steadfastly to the essential measure of control in the western approaches, switched its forces to effect concentrations at danger points—notably by ordering Cornwallis to reinforce the squadron off Ferrol as soon as they learnt that Villeneuve was on his way back towards Finisterre. Indeed one cannot but feel sympathy for Villeneuve who, for all his deficiencies as a commander, was not only saddled with the execution of an impossible project, but had to endeavour to carry it out in face of opponents whose maritime skill and experience surpassed that of his own men by as wide a margin as the strategic insight of Lord Barham and his colleagues at the Admiralty was superior to that of his master.

Here we are concerned with strategy rather than with battle tactics, and so much has been written about Trafalgar that it would in any case be redundant to attempt to describe the battle. One point must, however, be made clear, namely that, even though there is still some uncertainty regarding Nelson's true tactical intentions, there is no room for doubt about the general purpose of his Trafalgar Memorandum. He meant to break up the opposing fleet and bring about a mêlée in which the superior gunnery of his ships would be decisive. There was to be no rigid line of battle—' the order of sailing will be the order of battle '—and a very wide discretion was given to subordinates. ' Something ' he wrote ' must be left to chance ': and, finally, ' no captain can do very wrong if he places his ship alongside that of an enemy '. The whole Memorandum is in fact the complete antithesis to the rigid Fighting Instructions of the 18th century discussed earlier; and, as Corbett remarked, it contains ' a clear note of denunciation against the old order of battle in single line '.[1] Yet hardly had the body of the nation's hero been lowered into its grave than the lessons he had taught were forgotten. As early as 1816 a newly issued signal book reveals with devastating clarity ' the full impression of the extent to which tactical thought had degenerated and Nelson's seed had been choked '; for ' the movements and formations for which signals are provided are

[1]*Fighting Instructions* (Navy Records Society, 1905), p. 283.

stubbornly on the old lines of 1799 '.[1] And that retrograde state of affairs was to remain unchallenged throughout the succeeding century, and even gained strength after the arrival of the steamship had eliminated most of the old limitations of manoeuvring under sail. Fighting Instructions, if they never became mandatory again, certainly remained rigid and formalist; and not until air power had spelled the doom of the entire conception of the battle fleet in the last war did senior officers of British squadrons again cast off the shackles which Hawke and Rodney had first loosened, and Nelson had shattered into fragments, but which were then sedulously refastened by his successors. It is one of the greatest puzzles of history how a service which has never ceased to worship the *memory* of Nelson has remained so blind to the chief reason for his successes, and after his death followed with almost monotonous regularity the opposite course to that which he himself adopted. But it is worth remembering that until 1876, when the Admiralty decided to turn Greenwich Hospital into a naval university, and the future Sir John Laughton *sought permission* to introduce history into the curriculum, that subject had been completely neglected in the service.[2] Mahan, whose *Influence of Sea Power on History* startled the world in 1890, has admitted his discipleship of Laughton, who in 1893 founded the Navy Records Society; and it was in one of that society's volumes, published exactly 100 years after Trafalgar, that Sir Julian Corbett made the critical analysis of Nelson's various Memoranda which might have, but did not lead to a reassessment of the tactics enshrined in current and future Fighting Instructions. We will discuss later the impact of that omission on the wars of this century, but it is apposite to remark here that the ultimate harvest of bitter herbs was reaped in the North Sea as the last day of May, 1916 drew to a close.

Trafalgar did not of course decide the outcome of the Napol-

[1] Ibid., p. 339.

[2] The naval college was transferred from Portsmouth to Greenwich on the Royal Hospital being closed in 1869, but it was not until 1873 that the Royal Naval College, Greenwich, was established by Order in Council. There was at the time no chair of history in the college—only a Professorship of Fortifications!

eonic War; but it did produce the conditions which made certain the ultimate downfall of France. In Mahan's famous words ' to the strife of arms with the great Sea Power succeeded the strife of endurance . . . for ten years to come . . . amid all the tramping to and fro over Europe of the French armies . . . there went on unceasingly that noiseless pressure upon the vitals of France, that compulsion whose silence . . . becomes to the observer the most striking and awful mark of the working of Sea Power '.[1] But while the long blockades of Brest and Toulon, which were the chief manifestation of that ' noiseless pressure ', continued unremittingly, our sea power enabled us to make a clean sweep of French, and later of Dutch overseas possessions. It was in this period that we retook the Cape of Good Hope, all the French West Indian Islands, Mauritius and the Seychelles group in the Indian Ocean, and finally the Dutch East Indies. Though the network of bases then established all round the world helped us to protect our merchantmen against French privateers, our losses none the less continued at a high level. And in November, 1806, Napoleon introduced measures which were potentially more dangerous to the British economy than the *guerre de course*; for by the ' Continental System ' he endeavoured to cut us off from all trade with the European mainland. We retaliated by an Order in Council prohibiting trade with all French ports, by enforcing a licensing system on the movement of goods by neutrals, and by giving overt support to the smuggling of our own produce into the continent—so frustrating the French object of destroying our export trade.

In June, 1807, Napoleon crushed the Russians at Friedland, and by the Tilsit agreement that followed, Sweden, Denmark, Austria and Portugal were forced to close their ports to British ships. Canning acted promptly in reply, ordering naval expeditions to be sent to the Baltic and Constantinople—the former with the purpose of securing our Baltic trade and depriving the French of the Danish fleet, and the latter with the object of forcing Turkey to make peace

[1] *The Influence of Sea Power on the French Revolution and Empire*, Vol. II, p. 184.

with Russia. The expedition to the Baltic, which was prepared in the deepest secrecy, was completely successful, and Admiral Gambier returned with the entire Danish Navy; but the attempt to coerce Turkey was a dismal failure. Although after considerable delays Admiral Duckworth succeeded in forcing the Dardanelles and arrived off Constantinople, his threats to bombard the town had no effect, and he finally beat an ignominious retreat—suffering considerable losses at the hands of the Turkish forts on the way down the Straits. The chief causes of this fiasco were that a preliminary reconnaissance had given warning of our intentions, and so allowed time for the Turks to man and strengthen the defences commanding the narrows. Worse still, no troops were sent with the expedition to seize the forts, and so ensure that the fleet could pass to and from its destination in safety. But Duckworth's weakness and hesitancy were also contributory factors. As we were to learn at vastly greater cost in 1915, nothing short of a well-planned and well-executed combined operation could win command of the approaches to Constantinople from the south: yet the errors of 1807 were then very precisely repeated.

We were more successful in dealing with Napoleon's renewed threat to Portugal, for in October, 1807, we removed that country's fleet to Brazil; and, as we had done six years earlier, we also took the precaution of occupying Madeira. Napoleon next carried his economic warfare one step further by the Milan Decree, and we retaliated by further Orders in Council strengthening our control over neutral trade.

By the beginning of 1808, Britain was thus engaged in a single-handed contest with all the rest of Europe, except Sicily and Sardinia: and they, if safe under the protection of the British fleet, could contribute nothing to our cause. In general, however, the neutral nations seem to have realised that we were fighting for their freedom as well as our own: and of the two evils between which they had to choose they preferred British interference with their trade to domination, and possibly occupation by the French. So it was to prove again in our struggle with Germany in the 1940s. Moreover, although the French economic blockade caused us great hardship and anxiety, our counter-measures were in the sum more effective; and it was therefore France that suffered the more. As Mahan put it ' By her persistent enmity to the spirit of aggression . . . by her own sustained and unshaken strength, she [Britain] drove the enemy into the battlefield of the Continental System, where his final ruin was certain '.[1]

The spring of 1808 produced a call for help from Sweden, and again we sent a powerful fleet to the Baltic. It stayed there for the next five years, securing our trade and blockading Russian bases; but Sweden herself proved highly unco-operative. In 1809, she joined the Continental coalition and closed her ports to us, and in the following year declared war. None the less our control of the Baltic had far-reaching strategic consequences—especially in the encouragement it gave to Russia to throw off the Napoleonic yoke. At the other end of the continent the revolt of Spain in 1808 produced opportunities for an equally convincing demonstration of the effectiveness of a maritime strategy; for an expeditionary force was carried to the Peninsula, and that resulted in the French forces leaving Portugal after Wellesley's victory at Vimeiro. Sir John Moore's advance into Spain followed, and it was our sea power that enabled his army to be rescued from Soult's clutches after the retreat to Corunna in January, 1809. Then came Wellesley's second campaign, and, after his retreat to Torres Vedras in 1810, the fleet kept his forces nourished and supplied until the time arrived when he could again take the offensive. Finally, after Spain had been liberated, came the advance into southern France in 1813, during which the fleet supported the army's seaborne flank and carried its supplies right up to the front. The enormous contribution made by our sea power, first to averting the worst consequences of the early disasters, then to building up our strength in the Peninsula, and finally to the winning of victory cannot be better expressed than by

[1] *The Influence of Sea Power on the French Revolution and Empire*, Vol. II, p. 401.

Wellington's own words. 'If anyone wishes to know the history of this war' he said to the Admiral commanding our supporting fleet 'I will tell them it is our maritime superiority gives me the power of maintaining my army, while the enemy are unable to do so'.[1]

Unhappily in 1809, at the time when the campaign in the Peninsula was first showing signs of developing into the 'Spanish ulcer', which was to suck away so much of Napoleon's military strength, we dissipated considerable resources on another expedition to Holland. The strategic purposes were reasonable enough—to spur the feeble King of Prussia into action, to produce a diversion in favour of the Austrians, and to prevent Napoleon building up a fleet at Antwerp. But in execution the expedition produced none of the rapidity of action and resolution in leadership which every previous amphibious enterprise had shown to be essential to success. Though 'Walcheren 1809' has become a by-word for incompetence in the conduct of a combined operation, and the 40,000 men involved would probably have been better employed in the Peninsula, it did cause Napoleon serious anxiety, and had it succeeded the rewards would have been great. Between 1808 and 1810 we also sent a new series of expeditions to the West Indies, this time with the defensive purpose of protecting our trade against French privateers. In addition to achieving this we retook all the French islands which had been returned under the Treaty of Amiens.

The tremendous strain which the operations in the Baltic, in Holland, the Peninsula and the West Indies threw on the Royal Navy at a time when the close blockades of Brest and Toulon had to be maintained and convoys provided for all our shipping, will be plain. Fortunately in 1812, Russia declared war on France, and we were therefore able to recall the fleet from the Baltic. But, almost simultaneously with that favourable development, we had to face a new enemy on the other side of the Atlantic, and it is therefore

[1] Quoted by Rear-Admiral T. Byam Martin in his despatch to Lord Keith of 21st September, 1813. (Navy Records Society, Vol. XII, p. 409.)

necessary to discuss briefly how it came to pass that the United States declared war on the country which for the preceding nine years, had, often alone, borne the main burden of opposing the designs and aggressions of the continental dictator. As is always the case with neutral nations in time of war the Americans had benefited enormously from the increased trade which had come to them, and the restrictions which our Orders in Council imposed on their profits were therefore deeply resented. Secondly we were desperately short of seamen—for no British government had yet placed the manning of the fleet on a sound and permanent basis; and we were aware that numbers of British deserters were serving in American ships, often under false naturalisation papers, at far higher rates of pay than they could gain in the Royal Navy. We therefore made it a practice to stop and search American ships for deserters, and to remove those whom we found. No doubt our action was high-handed, and it is also probable that some genuine American citizens were impressed; but a dispute over such issues should surely have been settled by negotiation. On our side there was a good deal of feeling against the American Embargo Act of 1807, which forbade trade with belligerent countries, and against its successor the Non-Intercourse Act of 1809. Just as in 1939 we sorely needed munitions from America, but were unable to obtain them until the Neutrality Act of 1935 had been repealed, so did we need stores from the United States to supply our Army in the Peninsula during the Napoleonic War. In June, 1812, we did actually modify our Orders in Council to mollify American opinion: but President Madison had declared war a week earlier. Then for nearly six months we actually refrained from warlike acts against the United States. When, however, American designs on Canada became clear, and their privateers and raiders began to play havoc among our shipping, we were forced to take the quarrel seriously. The issue was fought in three theatres: first on the oceans, where we suffered heavy shipping losses: secondly on the Great Lakes, where the fighting between improvised fleets went in the Americans' favour: and, thirdly, off the eastern seaboard of the United States, which we did not begin to blockade effectively until 1813. Though the successes in single combats achieved by the heavily-armed American frigates such as the *Constitution* and *President* (which corresponded to the German pocket-battleships of the last war), were a shock to the Royal Navy's pride, neither those setbacks, nor the *guerre de course* waged by the hordes of lesser privateers, nor the fighting on the Great Lakes was likely to produce a decision. On the other hand once we began to apply our sea power in conventional manner American trade was crippled, and the young Republic's future prospects became exceedingly grim—especially after the fall of Napoleon in 1814 had enabled us to send strong naval and military reinforcements across the Atlantic, and to launch amphibious expeditions at various points from the coast of Maine to the mouth of the Mississippi. With British squadrons commanding Long Island Sound and the Chesapeake, and the American treasury empty, President Madison was forced to admit defeat, and in December, 1814, an end was put to this unnecessary war by the Treaty of Ghent. Neither side achieved the full purposes for which it had been fighting. Canada remained British, but we gave way on the matter of impressment; while the attempt by the Americans to gain more trade and profit out of the war resulted only in their suffering heavy losses. It should however be remarked that at the Peace Conference of 1814, Castlereagh, like both the Pitts before him, stood out firmly against continental proposals that we should modify our Maritime Code.

And so the day came when the greatest continental conqueror since Alexander of Macedon, and perhaps the greatest military strategist of all time, set foot in defeat on the deck of one of those 'far-distant storm-beaten ships' of Britain to be carried to his final place of exile. No matter how great were the contributions of the Russian winter, of the efforts of our various continental Allies, and of Wellington's brilliantly conducted Peninsula campaign, the chief cause of Napoleon's downfall was our maritime strategy; and the instruments by which that strategy was applied were the ships of the Royal Navy. Nearly 400 years had passed since the author of the ' Libelle of Englyshe Policie ' had suggested that fruitful commerce and a maritime strategy were necessarily linked together, and that certain broad principles underlay the successful application of such purposes.[1] Those centuries had been marked by a great deal of empiricism, since the causes of failures were hardly ever investigated; and that inevitably resulted in similar failures recurring again and again from what we now see to have been similar causes. One might, however, have expected that the experiences of the Seven Years' War and the Napoleonic War would together have endowed the British people with a mature and widespread understanding of the means whereby they had achieved such great successes. Yet such was not the case. Indeed the best part of another century was to elapse before historical analysis elucidated the means and methods whereby the few million people of a tiny island off north-west Europe had not only created a flourishing world-wide trading system, but had repeatedly defended it successfully against continental enemies whose resources were in many respects vastly superior.

This harassed age is inclined to look back on the 19th century with nostalgia, regarding it as a period when any threat to peace was promptly and effectively dealt with by the omnipresent Royal Navy; but such a conception is a travesty of history. During the 30 years after Waterloo we twice came to the verge of war with France. There were revolts against the established régimes in Greece, in Italy and all over South America: there were colonial or trade wars in Burma, in New Zealand, and in China: and there were frequent outbreaks of piracy (always a source of concern to a mercantile nation) in the Indian Ocean, the Mediterranean, and the Far East. Then, in the middle of the century, we became involved in the Crimean War, and the period of Germanic expansion started

[1] See p. 22

soon afterwards with Bismarck's acts of aggression against Denmark and Austria. In the same decade the young republic across the Atlantic was torn in two by the long civil war—still referred to by many Americans as ' *the* war '—in which Britain herself nearly became involved. Parenthetically we may note that it was the naval blockade which the Federal government was finally able to establish that decided the outcome of that conflict. In truth the 19th century was very far from being a period of undisturbed ' Pax Britannica '.

As to the Royal Navy itself, the Industrial Revolution had actually completed its first phase before the end of the Napoleonic War, and in the next two decades technological developments began to influence the instruments of war very profoundly. Nor was the Navy, always a conservative service, in the van of advance; and in 1850 it was indeed still equipped, manned and administered on lines which differed but little from the 18th century. After twenty years of strife, which had left the nation with a debt of £900 millions, economy was of course the order of the day. By 1822 the strength of the Navy had fallen to 24,000 men, and its annual cost to £6½ millions. If financial stringency was unavoidable, the choking of the flag lists was not; and the consequences of there being no retirement scheme for senior officers were serious—the more so because the period was one of far-reaching change. In 1850, nearly all admirals were septuagenarians, and it was perhaps too much to look to them for the energy and mental suppleness needed to meet the challenge of the new era then dawning. Thus it is hardly surprising that, when war broke out with Russia in 1854, all the accumulated neglects of the previous forty years came home to roost. If the Navy was then found wanting to a lesser extent than the Army it is perhaps chiefly because the inefficiency of the latter plumbed unbelievable depths.

The Crimean War could not be conducted on the basis of a mainly maritime strategy for the simple reason that Russia was impervious to the pressure of blockade, and even the loss of her Black Sea and Baltic fleets would not have proved an irremediable disaster.

She could only be attacked by amphibious power, and it was in trying to exploit our overwhelming maritime superiority for such purposes that naval deficiencies were grievously exposed. For example the British contingent of the expeditionary force to the Crimea never totalled more than about 30,000 men (less than Bonaparte had carried to Egypt in 1798); yet the transport of the troops was carried out in so 'bungling and foolhardy a manner',[1] that very long delays ensued before the troops could be landed in the chosen theatre. In planning the operation no consideration was given to the possibility, nay desirability, of achieving surprise; and the support given by the fleet after the Army had disembarked had little effect on the outcome. We seemed to have forgotten what Lord St. Vincent had remarked on more than fifty years earlier—namely that 'shells thrown from ships are impotent weapons, and will be laughed at when the first consternation is over'.[2] For the ineffectiveness of naval gunfire against substantially built fortifications, such as those at Sevastopol, had to be demonstrated all over again—as indeed it often has since. The most useful lessons derived from the Black Sea campaign were that the organisation and administration of the Navy were completely out of date, and that sailing ships-of-the-line had ceased to be of any practical value for fighting. In 1855 a new conjunct expedition was sent into the Sea of Azov, where the fleet penetrated right up to the Don estuary, and another to the mouth of the Dneiper. These operations were certainly far better conducted than the initial expedition to the Crimea, and by aggravating Russian supply problems probably contributed to their withdrawal from Sevastopol in September. But the destruction of the Black Sea fleet was more the result of the land campaign than of anything done by the Allied navies.

Much less well known than the Black Sea naval operations in the Crimean War are those carried out in the Baltic, the White Sea and in the Far East. Each summer we sent a substantial fleet into the

[1] Laird Clowes, *The Royal Navy, a History* (Sampson, Low, Marston & Co., 1901), Vol. VI, p. 404.
[2] Quoted Richmond, *Statesmen and Sea Power*, p. 210 (O.U.P., 1946).

Baltic, and lesser forces to the far north and the Sea of Japan. In 1854, Admiral Napier, whose age and timidity made him ill-suited to high command, missed a chance to attack the Russian Baltic fleet, which thereafter ensconced itself behind the forts of Kronstadt; and in the following year, though we had complete control of the Gulf of Finland, the many bombardments and small landings produced insignificant results. Nor did the blockade of Archangel and Murmansk, and of the seaports of the Maritime Provinces of Siberia, have appreciable influence on the war. It was undoubtedly the case that the British public was disappointed over the performance of the Navy in the Crimean War. Although too much was probably looked for by those who did not understand, to quote Sir Julian Corbett, 'how impotent [sea power] is of itself to decide a war against great continental states, how tedious is the pressure of naval action unless it be nicely co-ordinated with military and diplomatic pressure ',[1] it none the less remains true that the inefficient condition of the fleet, its indifferent leadership, and the antiquated state of its supply organisation together lost all chance of quick successes. *Punch* probably expressed the disappointment felt over the Navy's poor showing fairly accurately when it asked its readers to solve the riddle ' What is the difference between the fleet in the Baltic and the fleet in the Black Sea?' The answer provided was that ' The fleet in the Baltic was expected to do everything and did nothing: the fleet in the Black Sea was expected to do nothing and did it '. Finally we should remember how, in spite of all the efforts of the Allied navies around the enemy's coasts, and the suffering of the troops sent to the Crimea, the heart of Russia remained quite untouched by the war, and peace came largely because the Allies had little idea what to do next.

The Declaration of Paris which followed the signature of the peace treaty in March, 1856, had far-reaching consequences for Britain, since she then abandoned the right to stop the carriage of contraband goods in neutral bottoms in time of war, accepting

[1] *England in the Seven Years' War* (Longmans, Green, 1907).

instead the oft-repeated argument of the continental states that the nationality of the ship covered her cargo. This was the very claim against which both the Pitts and, less than half a century earlier, Fox, Canning and Castlereagh had all stood firm; and it is indeed difficult to understand why such long experience should have been disregarded. It was true that the same declaration abolished privateering; but it should not have required very great vision to foresee that the privateer working under a Letter of Marque would in a future war be replaced by the warship or armed merchant raider, cruising under her national colours, or in disguise, for precisely the same purpose as the privateer. But another 60 years were to elapse before the full consequences of our short-sighted action were brought home to us.

Though the British people and government showed no very marked interest in naval affairs during the years immediately following the end of the Crimean War, the Admiralty did set about remedying the worst of the inefficiencies which the conflict had exposed. Among the more important reforms then introduced was the establishment of naval reserves; for it had been shown all too clearly that a fleet which lacked them could not expand quickly if a sudden emergency arose. The R.N.R. and R.N.V.R., which were to perform such signal service for their country in the wars of the next century, both have their origin in the recommendations of a Royal Commission of 1859. Thus, after some three centuries of improvisation, did we accept the principle that adequate and trained reserves of seamen form an essential element in maritime strategy.

In the early 1860s, British strategy was again directed against France, for the expansionist policy of Napoleon III in North Africa was causing concern. After about 1868, however, it became clear that the rising tension between France and Germany made it unlikely that the former would challenge our sea supremacy, and interest in the Royal Navy thereupon declined sharply until 1884, when agitation in the Press drew attention to the poor condition of the fleet. For the next fifteen years British eyes were once more focused on the intentions of France and Russia—especially in the Mediterranean; and when in 1882 the formation of the Triple Alliance by Germany, Italy and Austria caused France and Russia to draw more closely together, serious apprehensions were aroused in London. This grouping of the major European powers provides the background to the Naval Defence Act of 1889, and to the establishment of the 'Two Power Standard', by which we meant equality with the combined navies of France and Russia; but such a policy was in fact nothing new for Britain. It merely signified a return to that of the 18th century, when it had been the two Bourbon powers (France and Spain) that had threatened our security.

The acceptance of the Two Power Standard marked the founding of the modern Navy; but its birth was accompanied by an upsurge of Chauvinism of an intensity that now seems astonishing. It was the time when a large proportion of the British people could approve the boast ' We've got the ships, we've got the men, we've got the money too . . .'; and they bought approvingly dozens of editions of Henry Newbolt's *Admirals All*, in which he arrogantly urged them to ' Stand by to reckon up your battleships. Ten, twenty, thirty, there they go . . .' Such an attitude of mind cannot have assisted the healthy assimilation of the technological changes which were pressing on the service from all sides; and there was in fact hardly any study of the impact of the new weapons on strategy and tactics. Against France the strategy was to be close blockade of her bases; but with the object of keeping her fleets bottled up in Brest and Toulon—not with the purpose of fighting them if they came out, as Nelson had always aimed to do. There was much discussion on whether, in the event of war with France and Russia, we could continue to use the Mediterranean sea routes and the Suez Canal, which had been opened in 1869. But no clear strategy was framed, and the final decision was to concentrate the fleet at Gibraltar and wait upon events. Nor was any study of the problem of commerce protection in the age of steam undertaken before the turn of the century, and the accepted view merely was that cruisers should be sent out to 'dog, hunt down and destroy' raiders. Though we knew that one school of thought in France—that of the 'jeune école'—strongly favoured the guerre de course, rightly believing that Britain's vulnerability to that form of attack had been greatly increased by the industrialisation of the country, we never even considered the desirability of reverting to the ancient strategy of convoy and escort. Nor was any consideration given to the consequences which the Declaration of Paris was bound to exert on our ability to apply economic pressure against enemy countries. Indeed the agitation in the 1890s in favour of what was called the 'Freedom of the Seas'—which Corbett has stigmatised as 'one of those ringing phrases which haunt the ear and continue to confuse the judgment'—weighted the scales against what had been a primary consideration in British strategy ever since the 17th century.

Invasion was a recurrent bogey during the latter half of the 19th century. In 1859, Palmerston had declared that 'steam has bridged the Channel', and the government thereupon spent £10 million on building fortifications around our southern naval bases. They may still be seen, performing their only useful service as children's playgrounds in the approaches to Portsmouth and Plymouth. However in the 1880s the 'Blue Water School' entered the field with a strong restatement of the principle that, as long as our fleet controlled the narrow seas, invasion was not a practicable operation of war; and gradually that view gained ground. But from 1888-92 the Admiralty and War Office were at loggerheads over the invasion issue, the soldiers declaring that the fleet might be lured away, in which event 100,000 men could, so they declared, easily land and capture London; and the arguments were to continue well into the next century. As to amphibious warfare, one does find at this period of antagonism towards France a broad realisation of its merits in some quarters. For example in 1897, Field-Marshal Wolseley, the Commander-in-Chief of the Army, wrote that, 'we want to make

our power what it must be to be offensive; namely amphibious '.[1]
But he added the qualification that ' we have still got to convince
the Navy that they can't win a war by themselves '; and the Navy
at this period was indeed behaving as though it could. Co-operation
between the services was ' irregular, uncertain and impeded by
formality ', and their two departments were on little better than
speaking terms.[2] No special training for amphibious warfare was
undertaken, and when a need arose to land troops quickly it was
very commonly done by forming a Naval Brigade. Though the
sailors employed on such undertakings in India, China and South
America showed admirable adaptability and enterprise, one does
rather wonder whether it would not have been better for the Navy
to have joined hands with the Army in creating an integrated organisation of specialists in that form of warfare, drawn from both services.
But it was to take two world wars to prove the need beyond all
argument: and as the 19th century drew to a close there was no sign
at all of either service stepping out of the watertight compartments
of Whitehall within which they had so firmly immured themselves.

The appearance of Mahan's *Influence of Sea Power on History* in
1890, has already been mentioned; and that book, together with the
same author's later works on maritime war and strategy, exerted a
profound influence—especially in the United States and in Germany.
In Britain the interest they aroused was neither so immediate nor so
widespread. Certainly Mahan's cogently argued theses did not lead
to the establishment of institutions such as Staff and War Colleges,
where the principles he propounded could be analysed in relation to
contemporary political, economic and technical developments, and
so assist in formulating sound strategy. Rather did his gift for
gripping narrative, his plangent rhetoric, and his genius for creating
an image by a simple, telling phrase (such as ' those far-distant,
storm-beaten ships upon which the Grand Army never looked '[3]),
cause his British readers too often to remember the phrase and forget

[1] Maurice and Arthur, *Wolseley*, pp. 205-6. (Doubleday, Page & Co., N.Y., 1924.)
[2] A. J. Marder, *British Naval Policy 1880-1905*, p. 79 (Putnam, 1940).
[3] *The Influence of Sea Power on the French Revolution and Empire* (1892), Vol. II, p. 118.

the reasoning, often accompanied by cautious and discretionary qualifications which lay behind it.

In the realm of training and tactics there was little advance in the last half of the 19th century. There were a few innovators, such as Sir George Tryon; and it was a misfortune that he lost his life when his flagship the *Victoria* was rammed and sunk by his second-in-command in 1893. In general the fleet's training remained more appropriate to the era of masts and yards than of steam: more attention was paid to the smartness and appearance of ships than to their fighting efficiency (there are well-authenticated cases of practice ammunition being jettisoned rather than risk damage to paint-work by firing it). And the ending of the long era of dependence on the wind for propulsion had been used, not to win the tactical freedom which it made possible, but to impose a higher degree of rigidity than ever before.

In part the weaknesses of the late Victorian navy can confidently be attributed to the excessive and uncritical adulation which it received from the British public, and in part to the consequences of almost a century of undisputed supremacy. The officers of the service were of course a microcosm of contemporary society; and in that society the privileges of wealth and birth had as yet been little touched by the cold winds of reform. It is difficult not to feel that the authoritarian attitude and outlook of many senior officers of the period was a factor in the too slow adaptation of the service to the vast changes brought about by the Industrial Revolution. For example the submarine became a practical weapon of war in the 1890s, with France leading the world in development of them. Yet the Royal Navy was very slow to visualise the vast changes in strategy and tactics which underwater warfare would impose on the fleets of the world. Not until 1901 did the Admiralty place an order for the construction of our first submarines.

An interesting point with a very up-to-date ring about it, is that in the 1890s one finds the suggestion being put forward that the destructive power of the new weapons and explosives had made war impossible, and that the mere possession of the instruments of destruction would have a deterrent effect on aggressors. No less a person than Lord Rosebery spoke about the peace-making influence of great armaments, and a similar line of thought appeared in books and Press articles in France as well as England as the 19th century drew to a close.

That raises the question of the broad influence of British sea power on world affairs from the end of the Napoleonic War to the turn of the century. In the first place the Royal Navy undoubtedly provided the chain which linked together all the scattered territories of our colonial Empire; while in the field of foreign policy it was repeatedly used as the instrument whereby the British Government made its views effectively known. Thus when revolt broke out in Spain in 1823, and Louis XVIII obtained a mandate to crush the revolution, we used our sea power to make it plain that we would not allow the Spanish colonies in the western hemisphere to become subject to France. That act of high policy gave birth to the Monroe Doctrine, which was in fact, though never acknowledged by the nation which propounded it, always underwritten by the Royal Navy. Again it was the Navy that was used during Palmerston's two terms as Foreign Secretary (1830-41 and 1846-51) to 'rescue Turkey from Russia and the highway to India from France'.[1] Then, when relations with Germany became very strained at the time of the Boer War, British sea power was probably the chief restraint on the Kaiser's interventionist purposes. Thus it seems true to say that because in the 19th century British influence was applied by *visible* instruments, and because the governments of the day did not hesitate to use them, our sea power did in general act as a deterrent against aggression. Furthermore the same instruments were constantly employed on the wholly creditable duties of suppressing slavery and piracy; and in the revolts of dependent states, such as Greece and the Spanish South American colonies, they were nearly always used in support of the peoples who were

[1] Dictionary of National Biography.

striving to gain their freedom. But British sea power was not, of course, mainly, let alone wholly, directed to such altruistic purposes; and throughout the century its most constant function probably was the nourishment and extension of our overseas trade. If the methods sometimes used (notably in the Opium War of 1839-42) would nowadays be regarded as shocking, one has to remember that the public conscience was not then nearly so tender.

The last of the series of recurrent crises with France arose in 1898 over the Fashoda incident. But eight years earlier the young Emperor William of Germany had dispensed with the services of Bismarck, the pilot who had guided the destiny of Prussia and then of Germany for the previous thirty years; and very soon the reckless utterances of the Emperor began to cause concern. In 1897 Tirpitz was appointed Secretary of State with the object of building up a Navy which, to Britain, seemed so unnecessary a possession that it could only have one purpose; and the German Navy Law of June 1900, whereby she proposed to double her battleship strength, hastened a complete shift of our foreign policy. The challenge implicit in the German naval programmes may be taken to mark the dividing line between the second and third phases of the development of Britain's maritime strategy.

III

From the beginning of the
Twentieth Century to
the end of the
First German
War

At the beginning of the 20th century the Royal Navy still enjoyed the uncritical confidence of the British people; but in fact the service suffered from serious weaknesses in almost every direction. Many of its ships and weapons were obsolete, the fleet was undermanned, and the legacy of authoritarianism bequeathed by the Victorian era was still a characteristic of many of its senior officers. In 1904, however, Admiral Sir John Fisher became First Sea Lord, and during the next six years his dynamic energy and ruthless methods made themselves felt in every direction. This is not the place to discuss the Fisher reforms in any detail, nor to ponder the character of that remarkable man. But we should note that, in the teeth of powerful opposition, he scrapped over 150 obsolete ships, he improved the readiness of the reserve fleet by introducing nucleus crews for its ships, he completely overhauled the system of entering and training officers, he redistributed our strength with the emphasis on the threat from Germany, and by the design of the all-big-gun *Dreadnought*, launched in 1906, he rendered all earlier battleships obsolete. In the long uphill struggle against prejudice and orthodoxy, Fisher made many enemies and, inevitably, some mistakes. The worst consequence of his ' ruthless, relentless and remorseless ' methods was that he split the service into two factions—those who were ' in the Fishpond ' and those who were not; and many years were to pass before the schism was healed. In retrospect it seems to-day that most of his reforms were timely, if not overdue; but Churchill, who was First Lord from October, 1911, until the disastrous quarrel with Fisher in May, 1915, probably erred on the side of generosity in assessing them as high as nine-tenths right.[1] What is certain is that the fleet which fought the 1914-18 war was to a very great extent Fisher's creation. In many instances his foresight was to prove un-cannily accurate—for example over the influence of the submarine, and the certainty that it would be used in an unrestricted *guerre de course*: over the magnitude of the revolution which airborne weapons would bring about: and over the need for large numbers of combined operations craft—'amphibian hippopotami' as he called them.[2] In the creation of a body of specialists in the new fields of engineering and technology he was far ahead of the majority of his contemporaries; and his outlook towards the welfare of the lower deck was not to achieve complete acceptance until half a century later. But there were, for all his undoubted genius, serious defects in his character, and gaps in his intellectual equipment. As to the former, the excessive emphasis—even violence—with which he always expressed himself led to clashes with the politicians and with the soldiers which certainly did not help to prepare the country for the war he so clearly foresaw; and he was so strong an individualist that he would not use a Staff properly, nor sit down to argue amicably on strategic issues to which there was obviously more than one answer. His mistrust of staff work was perhaps the weakness which was to have the most serious consequences; for the approach of most senior officers to their profession was still thoroughly un-intellectual. Churchill has written that when he came to the Admiralty in 1911 he 'found that there was no moment in the career and training of a naval officer when he was obliged to read a single book about naval war, or even pass the most rudimentary examination in naval history'[3]; and when in 1912 he organised the Naval War Staff 'to be the means of sifting, developing and applying the results of history and experience . . . to be tireless and unceasing in its action, applied continuously to the scientific and

[1] *The World Crisis*, Vol. 1, p. 74 (Thornton Butterworth, 1923).
[2] Letter to G. Lambert, 21st Dec., 1917. Quoted Marder, *Fear God and Dread Nought*, Vol. 11, p. 493 (Cape, 1956).
[3] *The World Crisis*, Vol. I, p. 93.

speculative study of naval strategy and preparation ',[1] his hopes were largely frustrated by the individualism of the old Admiral who was soon to return to the Admiralty as his principal naval colleague. Furthermore Fisher's sceptical attitude towards history (though he was perfectly capable of using it when it suited his book to do so) caused him to see strategic issues in too simplified a form. There is, for example, a good deal more to amphibious warfare than to declare that ' the British Army is a projectile to be fired by the Navy '[2]; and by the same token his lack of interest in tactics made him completely blind to the consequences cf the very rigid fleet instructions then in force. Yet it seems certain that, but for the Fisher reforms, the Navy would have been as ill prepared to fight Germany in 1914 as it had been to fight Russia in 1854. Two examples will suffice to illustrate the complacency and stubborn conservatism of the service early in the present century. In 1902, Admiral Sir Arthur Wilson, who was to succeed Fisher as First Sea Lord eight years later, declared that submarines were ' underhand, unfair and damned un-English '[3]; and in 1907 the Admiralty refused to take up the Wrights' original patents for flying machines because it considered them ' of no particular value '.

The attempt to establish a common doctrine between the services and to arrive at an agreed strategy in the event of war with Germany was an uphill struggle, and the arguments were protracted and acrimonious—to no small extent because of Fisher's intractability. Thus in 1904 the Committee of Imperial Defence was founded ' to obtain and collate for the Cabinet all the information and advice for shaping national policy in war '; but, largely because of the opposition of the Admiralty, which resented what it called ' meddling ' in its own affairs, the committee was for a long time impotent to fulfil its functions. Lord Esher did not exaggerate when, in 1909, he wrote that the C.I.D.'s work ' was treated as the amiable aber-

[1] *Statement on the Navy Estimates*, 1912-13 (Cmd. 6106).
[2] Letter to King Edward VII, 4th October, 1907. Marder, *Fear God and Dread Nought*, Vol. II, p. 143 (Cape, 1956).
[3] Quoted Marder, *From the Dreadnought to Scapa Flow, the Royal Navy in the Fisher Era, 1904-1919*, Vol I (O.U.P., 1961).

rations of a few well-meaning but harmless strategists '[1]; and, for all his admiration of Admiral Fisher, in the same year he told Mr. Balfour that ' there is a good deal of truth in Haldane's contention that the weak point in our national armour just now is, not the material and personnel of the Navy, but the Board of Admiralty, and its want of modern ideas, and inefficient organisation '.[2] Happily by 1912, largely thanks to the work of a very able Marine officer called Hankey who had joined the C.I.D. secretariat, the committee's status had won a fair measure of recognition.

The principal strategic issues which had to be resolved in the first decade of the present century were the perennial problems of invasion, of commerce protection and of amphibious warfare. As to the first, the clash of the 1890s between the ' Blue Water School ' of sailors, who held that as long as we controlled the narrow seas and our fleet was intact, invasion was not a practicable operation of war, and the ' Bolt from the Blue ' school of soldiers, who considered that the fleet might be lured away and a substantial enemy force landed, was renewed with even greater acrimony. In 1905, however, Mr. Balfour's Cabinet decided that, provided that the Navy was efficient, ' invasion . . . is not an eventuality we need consider '.[3] On the question of commerce protection, in 1912, Fisher, who was then out of office, foretold that the submarine would be used to attack merchantmen; but Churchill and Asquith disagreed, and the Prime Minister refused to circulate the Admiral's paper. The official view was that we would only have to deal with German cruisers and armed merchant raiders; and that hunting operations by our detached squadrons would suffice to restrict their depredations and bring them to book. No suggestion was made that convoy might be necessary, but in 1913 steps were taken to arm our merchantmen with anti-submarine guns. Thus Mahan's view, that the *guerre de course* could not by itself be decisive was ac-

[1] To M. V. Brett, 29th Dec., 1909. *Journals and Letters of Reginald, Viscount Esher*, Vol. II p. 430 (Nicholson and Watson, 1934).
[2] To A. J. Balfour, 24th December, 1909. Ibid. pp. 428-9.
[3] Speech in House of Commons on May 11th, 1905. (Hansard, Vol. 146.)

cepted; but his warning that the convoy system 'when properly systematised and applied' would have more success than hunting for raiders was ignored[1]—surely a classic example of the misuse of historical study.

In the field of offensive strategy our object was to bring the enemy fleet to action; and the assumption seems to have been that it would fall in with our wishes in that respect. German commerce was to be swept off the seas and oceans, and a blockade of their naval bases was to be established. In 1904 the Admiralty had accepted that the mine and submarine had between them made close blockade impracticable; but the possibility of employing such a form was none the less resurrected seven years later. By that time the advent of the military aircraft had—at any rate in the eyes of the more far-sighted officers—increased the impracticability of close blockade; and the 1914 War Plans actually provided for an open blockade of the enemy's coast and bases. Churchill, however, was dissatisfied with what he regarded as a passive and purely defensive strategy, and pressed for an immediate offensive—'a grand drive' as he called it. But the Admiralty's War Staff was, quite understandably, unable to visualise how such an offensive was to be instituted. As Richmond, then serving as Assistant Director of Operations, put it 'merely to steam about at sea is not taking the offensive'.[2] Incidentally we may here note how in 1939 Churchill again produced exactly the same argument, and in his memoirs has himself told how he 'could not rest content with the policy of "convoy and blockade" '.[3] In that conflict it was Admiral Pound, the sorely-tried First Sea Lord, who echoed Richmond's earlier remark when he wrote that 'it is only politicians who imagine that ships are not earning their keep unless they are rushing madly about the ocean'.[4] And in 1939, as in 1914, Churchill's conception of

---

[1] *The Influence of Sea Power on the French Revolution and Empire*, Vol. II, p. 217 (Sampson Low, Marston, 1892).
[2] Marder, *From the Dreadnought to Scapa Flow*, Vol. I (O.U.P., 1961).
[3] *The Second World War*, Vol. I, pp. 362-3 (Cassell, 1948).
[4] Letter to Admiral Sir Andrew Cunningham, 28th December, 1942 (Lord Cunningham's papers).

offensive naval strategy, which pre-supposed that the enemy would provide the necessary targets, quickly proved fallacious.

Apart from the measures to be taken against Germany's own merchant shipping, the application of economic pressure by stopping her flow of imports received little consideration in the 1914 war plans; and we seem to have forgotten that in every conflict since the 16th century the chief difficulty had been to control the shipment of contraband in neutral bottoms.[1] This had led gradually to the establishment of a Maritime Code, on whose maintenance our statesmen of the Seven Years' and Napoleonic wars had, as we have seen, always firmly insisted. But the code was intensely unpopular with neutral nations, because it restricted the vast profits which they have always made out of wars; and it had been one of the chief causes of America entering the struggle against us in 1812.[2] The consequences of our signing the Declaration of Paris in 1856 have already been discussed. Here we may remark that this imprudent act seems to have been based on the belief that the introduction of steam had made attacks on shipping easier, and that it would therefore be to our benefit to restrict or abolish the *guerre de course* in all its forms. But it took singularly little cognizance of all the accumulated experience of the wars of the 17th and 18th centuries. Towards the end of the 19th century a considerable agitation had taken place to extend still farther the principle accepted in Paris, under the grandiloquent title of ' the Freedom of the Seas ': and again the British government had made no firm stand—or indeed any stand at all—on the matter of belligerent rights. Then the London Conference of 1908 tried to establish a new code regarding the carriage of contraband goods in war. Astonishingly, it was the British representative who proposed that contraband should be entirely abolished. Fortunately the suggestion was turned down: but, instead, definitions of what were called ' Conditional contraband ', ' Unconditional contraband ' and ' free goods ' were established. The unreality of such legalistic processes is well illus-

[1] See pp. 52 and 75.   [2] See p. 86.

trated by the fact that aircraft and metal ores were classed as 'free goods'. Though we did not in fact ratify the Declaration of London, the influence of the policies put forward at the 1856 and 1908 conferences was so great that in neither of the German wars of this century did we actually declare a blockade of the enemy countries. We thus entered the first of them with one of the principal weapons of a maritime strategy grievously blunted. Nor was the magnitude of our error long in revealing itself—as we shall see later.

It was of course the Entente Cordiale with France of April, 1904, which necessitated a fundamental reassessment of British strategy, and brought a renewal of the ancient clash between the 'continental' and the 'maritime' or 'amphibious' school: and Fisher, who once expressed the view that 'any ass could be a general', and refused to reveal naval plans to the War Office, did not make it easy to arrive at an agreed strategy. The probability is however that French military thought, addicted as it was to '*la grande guerre*' on the continent, would in any case have prevailed. For their view was supported by prominent statesmen such as Grey and Haldane: and Foch had great influence with General Sir Henry Wilson, the Director of Military Operations. By the time that Sir Julian Corbett's cogently argued *Principles of Maritime Strategy* appeared in 1911, the case had already been settled in favour of the 'continentals', and his work attracted little attention until in the 1920s, the spotlight of historical research began to be focused on the lost opportunities and strategic errors of the 1914-18 war.

Throughout the long pre-1914 controversy between the 'Maritime' and the 'Continental' schools the primary purpose urged by Admirals Fisher and A. K. Wilson and others of their way of thinking was that a landing should be made in strength on the Pomeranian coast, only some 90 miles from Berlin. In addition they wished to carry out pin-pricking raids at many points on the enemy's coastline —as had been done in the Seven Years' War at the instigation of the elder Pitt. But the War Office declared that 'this class of operation (i.e. coastal raids) possibly had some value a century ago, but now that land communications are excellent they are doomed to failure '[1]—an *obiter dictum* which took as little account of historical experience as it did of the arguments in favour of such measures. One of the reasons behind Churchill's appointment as First Lord was the government's desire to make the continental strategy, which he had accepted, more palatable to the Navy—a purpose in which he was so successful that by 1914 all plans for amphibious projects had been discarded. Nor was there any revival of interest in such undertakings until Fisher returned to Whitehall as First Sea Lord in 1914, in succession to Prince Louis of Battenberg. It is thus true to say that the strategy employed in the opening phase of the 1914-18 war was the product of the period when Churchill was First Lord. But we may here note that, before the war had been in progress many months, he transferred his allegiance from the Continental to the Maritime school by becoming the principal advocate of the expedition to Gallipoli: and it is ironical that Fisher, who had only a few years earlier been arguing with all his usual force for amphibious enterprises, should have fallen out with his First Lord over the first important one to be mounted.

To turn to the realm of tactics, in 1914, the rigid line of battle, controlled by a centralised command system held undisputed sway; and Fisher, Wilson, Jellicoe (Fisher's choice to command the Grand Fleet), and Beatty were all champions of the line. The Fighting Instructions of the period, which comprised a substantial volume of some 100 foolscap pages, were called the Grand Fleet Battle Orders, and were issued over Jellicoe's signature in September, 1914. They endeavoured to lay down in precise detail the action which was to be taken to meet every eventuality, and allowed practically no initiative to juniors. As Richmond pointed out later, such a code ministered to two common weaknesses; it made it easy for officers to escape the anxieties of personal responsibility, and it eliminated

[1] Marder, *From the Dreadnought to Scapa Flow*, Vol. I (O.U.P., 1961).

the need for original thinking.[1] The virtually unchallenged acceptance of this reversion to the tactical principles of the mid-18th century can probably be attributed chiefly to the ascendancy of the material school over what may be called the historical school, which was so marked a phenomenon of the late 19th and early 20th centuries.

The unimaginative tactical training of the fleet and the inhibition of initiative imposed by the Battle Orders were not, unfortunately, the only handicaps under which the Royal Navy laboured in 1914. For the prolonged pre-war arguments over whether Scapa, Rosyth or Cromarty should be the fleet's main base resulted, when the choice finally fell on Scapa, in that anchorage being totally undefended at the outbreak of war; and a fleet which has to work from an ill-defended base cannot carry out its functions properly. Secondly, although their full extent was not to be realised until after the Battle of Jutland, there were serious defects in our armour-piercing shell and in the magazine protection of our ships. The former reduced the effectiveness of our own gunnery as greatly as the latter increased the vulnerability of our ships to the enemy's. Furthermore no training in anti-submarine warfare had been undertaken, we had no mining policy, and the few mines we possessed were almost useless: none of our minesweepers were properly fitted out, and we had no anti-aircraft weapons at all. These deficiencies probably all stemmed from the pace of material advance set by Fisher, and from the lack of a properly organised Naval Staff.

The Royal Navy, did, however, possess two solid advantages over its adversaries. The first lay in its superior numerical strength; for whereas in 1914 we possessed 31 modern capital ships and another 16 were building, Germany had only 18 such vessels, with 10 more under construction. In pre-Dreadnoughts and in other classes of ship, such as cruisers and destroyers, the British superiority was also substantial; but this was to a considerable extent offset by the

[1] *The Service Mind* (Nineteenth Century, 1933).

world-wide nature of the Royal Navy's responsibility for commerce protection. It is indeed a commonplace of history that a small number of enemy raiders will engage the attention of a vastly greater number of defending cruisers. Secondly the Royal Navy undoubtedly possessed a moral advantage over its adversaries—partly arising from the high confidence it felt in its own capacity, deriving from its long tradition of success, and partly from its familiarity, bred of long periods of sea time, with the fickle element on which it had to work.

In addition to the advantage of our naval superiority, British strategy again benefited, as in our earlier wars with Holland and France, from the geographical situation of these islands. Enemy ships were only able to escape from the North Sea either by way of the narrow, tide-swept, and closely guarded waters of the English Channel, or by the long route round the north of Scotland, which was always patrolled and covered by our main fleet.[1] Furthermore we were blessed with the possession of fine harbours in the Orkneys and on the east coast of Scotland—exactly where they were needed. In the German wars of this century they played the same vital part that Plymouth and other harbours in the west country had played in the wars against France and Spain in the 18th century. Geography has always had a profound influence on strategy, and Britain has been singularly fortunate in the benefits she has fortuitously derived from it.

On the outbreak of war British sea power was quickly successful in sweeping German shipping off the oceans. But to stop the carriage of contraband goods directly or indirectly to Germany in neutral bottoms proved a very thorny problem, and the exercise of belligerent rights soon involved us in trouble with neutral nations. As

---

[1] See for example Admiral Sir John Fisher to Hon. Seymour Fortescue, 14th April, 1906. 'It is so very peculiar that Providence has arranged England as a sort of huge breakwater against German commerce, which must all move either one side of the breakwater through the Straits of Dover, or on the other side of the breakwater [round] the north of Scotland'. (A. J. Marder, *Fear God and Dread Nought*, Vol. II, p. 72 (Cape, 1956)). The memoirs of Admiral Karl Dönitz (*Ten Years and Twenty Days*, Weidenfeld and Nicolson, 1959) show that the enemy fully realised the extent of the handicap imposed on him by geography in the war of 1939-45.

Corbett had remarked about the Seven Years' War ' every step towards gaining command of the sea tends to turn neutral powers into enemies '[1]; for goods which should have been declared contraband on the outbreak of war began to flow into enemy ports in huge quantities, to the very great profit of the neutral nations— especially of the United States, whose favourable balance of trade increased from 690 million dollars in 1913 to 3,000 million dollars in 1916.[2] Though we always had to move cautiously to avoid giving excessive offence to neutral susceptibilities, we gradually extended the contraband list by a series of no less than eight Orders in Council, thus repeating the measures we had adopted against Napoleon's Continental System in 1806-07.[3] We also took steps to enforce our orders by such measures as rationing neutral countries' imports, by requiring shippers to certify the true destination of cargoes before we would allow them through, by ' black-listing ' firms suspected of trading with the enemy, and by refusing bunkers to ships whose owners would not comply with our rules. But it took about two years for the slow pressure of our economic blockade to take effect; and it is hard not to conclude that, had we been able to exert our ancient belligerent rights from the very beginning, the conflict would have been considerably shortened. Not until the war was over did we discover the tremendous impact of our blockade on the German economy.

The gradual tightening of our blockade led inevitably to counter-measures by the enemy, and it is therefore to the *guerre de course* that we must next turn. Initially it was waged by the German cruisers which were on foreign stations when war broke out. But disguised raiders soon joined in and, as in earlier wars, we found it very difficult to catch and sink those elusive enemies. Though they forced on us a vast dispersal of effort, and caused considerable dis-organisation to the flow of our shipping by their sudden appearances in remote waters, the actual losses they inflicted never came near to

[1] *England in the Seven Years' War*, Vol. II, p. 5.
[2] *Encyclopedia Britannica*, 1946 Ed., Vol. 22, p. 836.
[3] See pp. 82-83.

endangering our economy. The well-led and efficient German Asiatic Squadron from Tsingtao achieved an unpleasant success by trapping and sinking two weak and ill-equipped armoured cruisers off Coronel on the south-west coast of Chile on 1st November, 1914. But as soon as news of that action was received the Admiralty rushed two battle cruisers out to the Falkland Islands; and that brilliant piece of anticipation led, if somewhat luckily, to the destruction of Von Spee's Squadron five weeks after Coronel. The Battle of the Falkland Islands virtually marked the end of what we may call the Cruiser Period of the *guerre de course*. In the meanwhile, however, enemy submarines had, as Fisher had foretold, joined in the attack on our merchant shipping, though at first adhering to the rules of 'visit and search' laid down by international law. But submarines cannot wage war effectively under such restrictions; and, just as we sought to increase the pressure of our blockade without causing mortal offence to neutrals, so did the Germans seek ways and means of improving the effectiveness of their submarines without arousing similar antagonisms. It is, however, certain that in furthering such purposes our methods were altogether more skilful and subtle than the enemy's. In 1915 Allied losses of merchant shipping totalled only 1.3 million tons; but nearly 400 ships of over 1 million tons were sunk by U-boats—a clear indication of which enemy was the most dangerous. The following year produced a drastic change for the worse: for our total losses rose to 2.3 million tons, and the proportion sunk by U-boats (actually 964 ships of nearly 2 million tons) was even greater than in 1915. The government and the Admiralty were by this time seriously worried; but before we consider the most critical months of the U-boat campaign, and discuss the means whereby the threat was finally surmounted, we must review the work of the main fleets from the beginning of the war up to 1916.

In the Mediterranean responsibility for maritime control was shared with the French Navy, whose particular care was the transport of their troops from North Africa to metropolitan France. But just after the declaration of war we suffered a serious set-back when the German battle cruiser *Goeben* and light cruiser *Breslau*, which sailed from Messina on 6th August, gave our greatly superior forces the slip and reached the shelter of the Bosporus in safety. It now seems that the main responsibility for this untoward incident, which led to the usual search for scapegoats, must be placed on the Admiralty; for they sent the C-in-C a whole series of signals which were certainly confusing and in some respects contradictory. Thus on 30th July he was told to assist in guarding the French transports, but was not to engage superior enemy forces. Three days later he was given detailed instructions to shadow the *Goeben* with two battle cruisers, and watch the Adriatic with cruisers and destroyers. On the day war was declared against Germany he was told to respect Italian neutrality rigidly, and was not to allow any of his ships within six miles of that country's coast—which entirely precluded his using the Straits of Messina. The final blunder came on 8th August when the Admiralty signalled to 'commence hostilities against Austria', although war had not actually been declared: and that caused the C-in-C to abandon the pursuit of the *Goeben* and concentrate at Malta in accordance with the War Orders. The despatch of this last message arose through a clerical error; but the earlier ones, dealing with the disposition and movements of the fleet, were undoubtedly initiated by Churchill, the First Lord. The consequences show very clearly the danger of trying to control fleet movements from a remote headquarters, and how far preferable it is to signal the broad intentions of the government, and also the Intelligence available at headquarters, and then to leave it to the man-on-the-spot to put the intentions into effect. It is beyond doubt that the safe arrival of the *Goeben* and *Breslau* at Constantinople had a profound effect on the whole war. For when Turkey joined the Central European powers at the end of October, 1914, the western Allies were almost completely cut off from Russia; and it was chiefly the need to restore communications with Russia that led to the costly Dardanelles and Mesopotamian campaigns.

In our home waters a clash between light forces in the Heligoland Bight on 28th August, 1914, seemed to promise that our fleet
would successfully assert the clear superiority which it possessed;
but that impression was to some extent offset by a U-boat sinking
in rapid succession three elderly cruisers, which were patrolling off
the Dutch coast with no destroyer screen on 22nd September.
Plainly the threat of the submarines against surface ships had to be
taken seriously, and henceforth it had far-reaching influence on the
strategy and tactics of the Grand Fleet. In December, 1914, the
Germans started to make lightning raids and bombardments against
open towns on the east coast. They actually inflicted little damage
and caused few casualties and, in the light of what the British people
were to endure by way of bombardment a quarter of a century
later, the public outcry caused by the raids does now seem exaggerated. The most important effect on our strategy was that heavy
pressure was applied on the Admiralty to bring a part of the Grand
Fleet to a more southerly base than Scapa—a proposal which the
cautious Jellicoe resisted on the grounds that to divide our strength
in such a manner might give the enemy the opportunity to trap and
overwhelm one part before the other could come to its support.
Yet it is a fact that ships based on Rosyth had a much better chance
of intercepting the German raiding squadrons in the North Sea; and
in 1918 we did finally transfer our main strength to that base.

We saw earlier how on the outbreak of hostilities we had, because of the complete ascendancy gained by the Continental school,
made no serious preparations for amphibious warfare. Yet the war
was only a few weeks old when the ancient needs arose yet again,
and in urgent form. In September, 1914, there took place on the
Continent the ' race for the sea ', with both sides' armies extending
their northern flank towards the Channel—the Germans with the
object of gaining the ports on the coasts of Belgium and north-
west France, and the Allies with the object of frustrating such a
purpose. To hold up German progress every effort was made to
stiffen the Belgian defence of Antwerp—the key port which, ever

since the days of the Spanish Armada, has played so great a part in British strategy; and after a visit by Mr. Churchill early in October, we rushed across a hastily formed and ill-equipped Royal Naval Division, consisting mostly of reservists. Such eleventh-hour improvisations are, of course, foredoomed, and the Admiralty's claim that the Naval Division's influence in the general situation was 'powerful and helpful' now seems to have been purely rhetorical.[1] It lost over half its strength, though many of its men did escape into Holland, where they were interned for the rest of the war.

A few weeks after the survivors of the Naval Division had been taken off from Ostend we carried out a small combined operation at Tanga in German East Africa. Troops from India were landed successfully, but their training for such an enterprise quickly proved as inadequate as their equipment was deficient, a complete rout ensued and we had to re-embark them hastily. Antwerp and Tanga marked the limits of our attempts to exploit our command at sea by the traditional amphibious enterprises until the Dardanelles expedition of April, 1915—to which we will return shortly.

In January, 1915, a strong German force set out on another raid across the North Sea with the object of bombarding our east coast ports. This time it was intercepted by Beatty's battle cruisers off the Dogger Bank. In the chase action that followed, the British flagship, the *Lion*, was seriously damaged and a breakdown of tactical control then ensued. Beatty, though out of the fight, continued to make signals; but they were difficult to read in the other ships, and were capable of more than one interpretation. His second-in-command who, under a more flexible system would surely have felt free to press on against the enemy, interpreted the messages as meaning that he was to finish off the damaged and lagging armoured cruiser *Blücher*. He therefore broke off from pursuing the main German force, and Hipper's three battle cruisers were allowed to proceed on their homeward way unmolested. Though

[1] Corbett, *Naval Operations*, Vol. I, p. 201 (Longmans, Green, 1920).

it was not unfair that the chief blame for the enemy's escape should have been laid on the second-in-command, Beatty's attempts to maintain control from a distance were surely misjudged. And neither he nor anyone else seems to have realised that a misunderstanding such as arose on this occasion would have been impossible had our system of tactical control been more flexible. Furthermore the optimistic claims of damage inflicted on the enemy battle cruisers (which actually received only three hits as against the 14 scored on the *Lion* and *Tiger*) concealed the fact that the German gunnery had proved superior to our own. The narrow escape of an important part of the High Seas Fleet did, however, cause the Kaiser to refuse to accept such risks again, with the result that for the next fifteen months its ships were kept in harbour, and priority was given to the U-boat campaign. Thus did the Germans accept that the attempt to gain command at sea had failed, and turn to the *guerre de course*—exactly as Louis XIV, Louis XV and Napoleon had done before them. So far our strategy of naval blockade had once again proved itself. But the issue still to be settled was whether the replacement of sail by steam, and the advent of the submarine as the primary weapon of commerce destruction, had so increased the vulnerability of a mercantile nation that the principle enunciated by Mahan, to the effect that the *guerre de course* could not by itself achieve a decision, was still valid.

In fact, however, the settlement of that issue was deferred for another two years; since the Germans soon reverted to the attempt to dispute our command at sea with their High Seas Fleet. This arose partly because neutral reactions to submarine attacks on merchant shipping were so strong that they did not yet dare to take the ultimate risk of starting unrestricted warfare, and partly from the appointment of Admiral Scheer, a vigorous and capable leader, to command of the German fleet early in 1916. A raid against Lowestoft in April held out promise that Scheer's plan to use his reconnaissance Zeppelins to gain early knowledge of our movements, to lure Jellicoe over a U-boat trap, and finally to fling his whole strength against one part of the Grand Fleet, could be brought to fruition. Thus was the stage set for the only fleet action of the war.

By the evening of 30th May, 1916, unusual activity in the German bases led the Admiralty to expect a full scale sortie. The Grand Fleet at Scapa and Cromarty, now consisting of 29 battle-ships, and Beatty's six battle cruisers at Rosyth, which had just been reinforced by the four new *Queen Elizabeths* of the 5th Battle Squadron—the most powerful squadron afloat—promptly prepared for sea. By the following morning the two greatest arrays of fighting ships ever seen were converging towards a point off the north-west corner of Denmark. But neither the German nor the British C-in-C yet had any idea that his adversary's main force was at sea. In fact as late as noon on 31st May, the Admiralty told Jellicoe that the German fleet flagship was still in the Jade river. This totally false deduction was based on our wireless interception service having reported that the German flagship's call sign (DK) was being used by a shore station at Wilhelmshaven. Nor was this by any means the only instance where the intelligence produced by the Admiralty's brilliantly manned cryptographic section (called Room OB 40) was misapplied by the Operations Staff.

We cannot here follow the events of that fateful summer's day in the North Sea in detail. But it is necessary to understand how it happened that, although a decisive victory was within our grasp at more than one critical moment, the opportunities were not seized, and the German fleet, though shaken and a good deal battered, finally reached port in safety. In the first phase Beatty's six battle cruisers engaged Hipper's five, but magazine explosions soon caused the loss of two of our ships. It is virtually certain that these disasters, and the loss of a third battle cruiser later in the day, arose from lack of magazine protection against flash produced by explosions in the vicinity. German ships had actually suffered from a similar defect; but the experiences of the *Seydlitz*, which was nearly lost in the Dogger Bank fight, had caused this to be eliminated before Jutland.

The battle cruiser action, besides revealing structural defects in our ships, was unsatisfactory from a tactical point of view; for errors in signalling by Beatty's flagship produced confusion in the distribution of gunfire, and the shooting by his ships was again shown to be markedly less accurate than the enemy's. Only when the four *Queen Elizabeths* came into action—rather belatedly, for Beatty had not kept them in close support of his lighter armed battle cruisers—did Hipper begin to feel the weight of our numerical superiority. Meanwhile the presence of the whole of Scheer's High Seas Fleet had been reported by a scouting cruiser, and Beatty's primary duty was to keep Jellicoe, his C-in-C, who was hastening down from the north, fully informed regarding the enemy's position and course. This duty Beatty did not fulfil until almost the last moment, when urgent appeals for information reached him from the C-in-C. It thus came to pass that Jellicoe approached the critical point at which he had to deploy his battle squadrons from their cruising formation into line of battle without knowing exactly where his adversary was. Throughout the day enemy reporting proved one of the weakest links in British training.

Rivers of ink have been spilt in argument over the alternative deployments open to Jellicoe. Here it must suffice to say that at 6.15 p.m. he ordered his *port* wing column to lead ahead and the other five columns to turn and form astern of it. This placed a barrier of battleships right across the line of advance of the German fleet, on to whose leading ships a hail of fire was soon directed. Only one manoeuvre could extricate the Germans from their predicament, and Scheer therefore promptly ordered the ' battle turn away together ' which he had conceived and rehearsed to meet just such an eventuality. With the enemy's leading ships damaged and their formation thrown into disarray the advantage thus swung heavily in the British favour. It was at this moment that an arduous pursuit, with each of Jellicoe's powerful battle squadrons acting more or less independently, might well have turned an advantage into a decisive victory. Jellicoe however gave no such order—nor had his subordinate admirals been trained to expect so high a degree of initiative to be allowed them. Instead the Commander-in-Chief kept all his squadrons under his own strict control, he only turned gradually in the enemy's direction, and when German destroyers appeared to threaten him with torpedoes he actually turned away from the enemy.

Scheer, however, had to break through to the east if he was to reach his base in safety, and his return in that direction half an hour later gave Jellicoe a second chance. Again the German fleet came under a storm of fire, again Scheer had to execute a hasty ' turn away together ', and again Jellicoe not only forebore to press his retreating adversary, but turned away in face of the torpedo threat. None the less by nightfall the whole mighty Grand Fleet still lay between the High Seas Fleet and its home bases, and a decision might therefore yet be gained at daylight on 1st June. But whereas the British policy was at this time not to seek action during the hours of darkness, and little training in night fighting had therefore been carried out, the Germans had prepared themselves for such an eventuality with all their usual thoroughness.

Throughout the night Jellicoe steered to the south with his destroyer flotillas disposed astern of the battle squadrons: and between 11 p.m. on 31st May and the early hours of the following morning the entire High Seas Fleet passed across his wake to safety. There were many fierce close-range encounters between light forces, and the 5th Battle Squadron actually had Scheer's battleships in sight at one moment: but not one enemy report reached Jellicoe. Furthermore, although during the night deciphered enemy signals gave the Admiralty's Operations Division absolutely firm intelligence regarding Scheer's intentions, Jellicoe was given no indication of the reliability of the information passed to him: and one message of vital importance was not passed at all.[1] Though it is true that by about 11 p.m. Jellicoe himself might have deduced that Scheer was making his way home by the Horns Reef passage, the

---

[1] This was the German signal ordering ' all T.B.D. flotillas to be assembled by 4 a.m. at Horns Reef '. It was sent at 10.32 p.m. (G.M.T.) and the decipher was handed to the Operations Division at 11.15 p.m.

greater share of the responsibility for the High Seas Fleet's escape must surely lie with those in Whitehall who denied him the full knowledge that was in their hands, and with the ships at sea which failed to report their contacts with the enemy.

Daylight on 1st June thus found the Grand Fleet's lookouts scanning an empty sea, what time Scheer's battered ships were creeping into the safety of their harbours. British losses in ships and men had been far the heavier, which lent some support to the enemy's claims of a victory; but in his heart Scheer must have known that the chief factor in his escape from an almost desperate situation had been mismanagement on our part. One must not, however, judge the actions of the British senior officers too harshly: for the real fault lay in the tactical system under which they worked; and the relevant orders, including Jellicoe's intention to turn away in face of a torpedo threat, had been accepted and approved by the Admiralty.

It is worth considering what the consequences of a decisive British victory on 31st May, 1916, might have been. In the first place the strategic influence of the High Seas Fleet, which can be detected in every single sphere and aspect of the war, would have disappeared. It would no longer have forced us to hold great strength in readiness to deal with it, so preventing us from allocating adequate forces to other urgent purposes. Thus it was impossible to provide enough destroyers for escort duty while keeping the Grand Fleet immediately ready for battle. Secondly, it was the High Seas Fleet's command of the Heligoland Bight that kept the Kattegat closed, so inhibiting offensive operations in the Baltic in support of Russia; and, thirdly, it was the power behind the submarine campaign. Had it been destroyed not only would our command of the North Sea have become virtually complete, but communications with Russia would have become very much easier. Control of the Baltic would have enabled our blockade of Germany to be greatly tightened, and might even have made possible the amphibious assault on the Pomeranian coast, which Fisher had advocated early in the war; and adequate light forces could certainly have been released to afford proper protection to mercantile convoys well before the opening of the unrestricted submarine campaign. In sum it is impossible not to conclude that the strategic influence of a decisive victory in the North Sea would have been profound in every direction. And just as in several of our earlier conflicts, but especially in the War of American Independence (1775-83),[1] a heavy price was exacted for our failure to destroy the enemy's main fleets, so did the failure to exploit the opportunities which undoubtedly arose during the Battle of Jutland contribute to the continuation of the deadlock in France and Flanders, and to the carnage of the land battles of 1917 by which we tried to break it.

In the enemy's camp the most important outcome of the Battle of Jutland was that it hastened the movement towards unrestricted U-boat warfare; since Scheer and the Kaiser agreed that, ' even if further operations by the High Seas Fleet take a favourable course and we are able to inflict serious damage on the enemy, nevertheless there can be no doubt that even the most successful outcome of a fleet action will not *force* England to make peace '.[2] The Germans therefore now concentrated their effort on the *guerre de course* as the only alternative remaining open to them.

In spite of the realistic attitude of the Germans to their future prospects in the North Sea it was not long before the High Seas Fleet was out again. For on the following 18th August, Scheer took his full available strength to sea with the object of bombarding Sunderland, and of trapping our ships with the large number of U-boats he had disposed on the flanks of his intended course. This time Scheer took very elaborate precautions to avoid being surprised by the Grand Fleet; but the Admiralty was none the less again able to give Jellicoe warning of the sortie, and early on the 19th

[1] See pp. 60-62.
[2] Admiral Scheer's report (Gg. 5068.0) on the Battle of Jutland dated 4th July, 1916, and the Kaiser's MSS. comments thereon. (Admy. captured German archives).

it seemed that another fleet action was imminent. The weather however turned very hazy, and although the two sides' scouting forces approached to within about 30 miles of each other neither had accurate knowledge of the other's position. When Scheer received a report of strong British forces to the south of him (which was actually incorrect) he abandoned the bombardment and turned for home. Apart from submarine attacks the day produced no contacts, and by nightfall the two fleets were again widely separated. Bearing in mind that the defects in our ship construction and in our shell design, revealed at Jutland, had not yet been corrected, Jellicoe's caution on this occasion can be easily understood. Nor had he altered the principles on which he exercised tactical control of the fleet since that battle.

To return to the subject of amphibious enterprises, towards the end of 1914, discussions took place in the War Council on ways and means of breaking the deadlock in France, and of taking some of the weight of German military might off Russia; but the Baltic operation favoured by Churchill and Fisher encountered very strong opposition from the War Office, and never even reached the stage of preliminary planning. It was, however, Kitchener, the C.I.G.S., who first raised the question of a naval demonstration off the Dardanelles; but he flatly refused to countenance the Admiralty's proposal for a large scale amphibious expedition to be mounted from Marseilles. Early in January, 1915, Churchill asked the admiral in command of our Eastern Mediterranean squadron, whether it was practicable to force the Straits by warships alone. When he replied that they ' could not be rushed but might well be forced by extended operations with a large number of ships ' he was told to prepare a plan.[1] On 13th January, the War Council approved that the ' Admiralty should prepare for a naval expedition in February to bombard and take the Gallipoli peninsula with Constantinople as its objective '[2]—a most extraordinary proposal,

---

[1] Corbett, *Naval Operations*, Vol. II, p. 64 (Longmans, Green, 1921).
[2] Churchill, *The World Crisis*, Vol. II, p. 111 (Thornton Butterworth, 1923).

since how could a purely naval force take Gallipoli? And, as we had
discovered in 1807, when Admiral Duckworth's fleet was sent
through the Dardanelles in an endeavour to coerce Turkey into
making peace with Russia,[1] what could a naval force alone do if it
did reach Constantinople? Fisher, the First Sea Lord, next turned
against the plan, on account of the weakening of our strength in
home waters which it would entail. But Churchill argued him into
acquiescence, and on 28th January, 1915 (four days after the Dogger
Bank action), the decision was taken to go ahead.[2] If the strategic
purpose of using our sea power to attack the enemy at a remote but
vital point on his long continental perimeter was sound, the plan to
do so with naval forces only must surely be open to criticism. The
first bombardment took place on 19th February, 1915 and, although
it did not silence the forts, a few sailors and marines did in fact land
soon afterwards—as had happened in 1807. They met scarcely any
opposition on the Gallipoli peninsula. The Turks however soon
recovered, drove out the landing parties, and then our troubles
really began—especially over sweeping the Straits clear of mines.
In mid-March Admiral de Robeck, who had recently taken over
the naval command from his ailing predecessor, renewed the attack.
But three old battleships were lost on mines, and that caused
apprehension far beyond the value of the ships. Thus the second
naval attempt was even less successful than the first. Yet it is
likely that, even at that date, quite small military forces could have
seized and held the Gallipoli peninsula—had they been available.
Fisher now declared, quite correctly, that it was ' futile ' to continue without soldiers. ' Somebody ' he said, ' will have to land at
Gallipoli some time or other '[3]—a view which had in fact been
expressed by Admiral Jackson, the head of the Admiralty War
Staff, at the very beginning of the discussions on the project. There

[1] See p. 83.   [2] Churchill, *Op. Cit.* pp. 163-6.
[3] Note to Lloyd George, quoted Moorehead *Gallipoli*, p. 97 (Hamish Hamilton, 1956).
See also Lord Fisher to Sir John Jellicoe, 15th March, 1915, ' Things are going badly at the
Dardanelles. We want military co-operation, as pointed out by me in January last, but it was
ignored by everyone. Now we are held up for want of soldiers! ' Marder, *Fear God and
Dread Nought*, Vol. III, p. 165 (Cape, 1959).

now ensued a prolonged argument on whether troops should be sent from England (against Kitchener's wishes) or from Egypt.

A few days after the second naval bombardment de Robeck reported that his fleet could not force the Straits alone. Though Churchill wished to order him to attack again, Fisher and his naval colleagues on the Board of Admiralty strongly opposed the idea. It should however be mentioned that Commodore Keyes, a forceful and energetic officer who was serving as Chief of Staff to de Robeck, always held that the Navy could have accomplished such a purpose early in April.

Meanwhile orders had been given to embark a military expeditionary force of some 75,000 men in Egypt. But we were so ill-prepared for a large-scale amphibious undertaking that the embarkation and transport of the troops produced appalling muddle and confusion. None the less landings were successfully carried out on Cape Helles, the tip of the Gallipoli peninsula, on 25th April—though at a heavy cost in lives. For the enemy, having had ample warning of our intentions, had greatly strengthened his defences, and the Turkish troops resisted most stubbornly. On 9th May de Robeck, under heavy pressure from Keyes, agreed unenthusiastically to renew the naval attack. But the quarrel between Fisher and Churchill over the despatch of more warships to the Dardanelles was now moving to a climax. At Fisher's instance the reinforcements were refused, and the order to renew the naval attacks on the Straits was rescinded. Churchill however continued to press his views, and on 15th May, Fisher suddenly disappeared from the Admiralty, leaving behind him an abrupt note resigning his office. Churchill has—perhaps too magnanimously—attributed this astonishing act on the old admiral's part to a nervous breakdown—'hysteria not conspiracy' he wrote 'is the true explanation of his action'.[1] Be that as it may it was, from the country's point of view, hardly a happy moment for a major upheaval in the government and the Admiralty. A few days later Balfour replaced Churchill as

[1] *Great Contemporaries.* Essay on Lord Fisher (Collins' Fontana Ed., 1959), p. 280.

First Lord, Sir Henry Jackson became First Sea Lord, and Fisher thereafter played no significant part in the affairs of the service on which his influence had been so profound.

The next decision by the government was the belated one that the Gallipoli campaign should be prosecuted more vigorously, and strong naval and military reinforcements were therefore ordered out. But five fierce and costly battles fought on Cape Helles in June and July did nothing to break the stalemate. Then on the night of 6th-7th August, we successfully landed 20,000 troops in Suvla Bay on the west coast of the peninsula, well behind the enemy lines on Cape Helles. Complete surprise was achieved, and once again a decision was within our grasp. Unfortunately the soldiers were ill-trained, and their elderly leader, General Stopford, totally failed to seize the chance. The new beach-head was soon as completely contained by the enemy as the old ones, and the stalemate continued unbroken. In October Germany attacked Serbia in strength, and the War Council had to face the alternative of supporting her by sending an expedition to Salonika or of continuing the struggle on Gallipoli. It was Kitchener who first raised the question of evacuating our forces from the peninsula; but the tussle between those who favoured withdrawal and those who wished to fight on, of whom Keyes was the most determined and resourceful, was prolonged. Finally evacuation was decided on, and in December the 83,000 men in the Anzac and Suvla beach-heads were gradually reduced until, on the night of 19th-20th, the last were safely removed. Evacuation of Cape Helles was yet more hazardous. Yet by the early hours of 9th January, 1916, all the 35,000 men involved were, contrary to the predictions of the pessimists, successfully taken off. So ended a campaign which had lasted 259 days, to which we and our Allies had finally been forced to commit half a million men, and in which we suffered 250,000 casualties. Though a Royal Commission was set up in 1916 to investigate the failure, and in its reports criticised the whole strategy on which the undertaking was based,[1]

[1] Cmd. 8490 (First report) and 8502 (Supplement to First Report), H.M.S.O., 1917.

recent historical research, and above all the experiences of another war, have brought about a complete change of opinion. To-day the use of sea power to strike the enemy unexpectedly, in a theatre of our own choosing, has once again become a widely accepted strategic principle; and enemy records have revealed how narrow was the margin by which we failed on Gallipoli, and how great would have been the rewards of success. It has moreover become plain that the basic causes of the failure were identical to those which had ruined so many earlier British amphibious enterprises—namely the lack of clear strategic direction by the home authorities, and of careful and co-ordinated inter-service planning: the failure to establish a sound command structure for the execution of the undertaking: inadequate preparation for the transport of troops and equipment by sea: irresolute leadership by the naval and military commanders on the spot: and, lastly, lack of training in the difficult and hazardous task of carrying out an assault from the sea. The possibility of achieving surprise at the first attempt was sacrificed when the decision to try and force the straits with warships only was taken. And when the Suvla landing did achieve surprise, it was the failure of the military commanders to seize the opportunity which caused the loss of all its benefits. The truth was that the long ascendancy of the continental school of strategy had left us totally unprepared to exploit the greatest advantage of our overwhelming sea power. But the long-term results of the Dardanelles failure were yet more far-reaching; for it discredited the whole conception of amphibious strategy, and made it certain that no more such enterprises would be considered for the remainder of the war. Thus was the stage set for the long-drawn campaigns of attrition in France and Flanders, culminating in the costly struggle around Ypres in 1917; and a quarter of a century was to elapse before amphibious warfare came to regain its rightful place in British strategy.

To return to our home waters, in December, 1916, Jellicoe became First Sea Lord in succession to Sir Henry Jackson, and Beatty took over the Grand Fleet. But the new C-in-C, though he un-

doubtedly desired to adopt a more forceful strategy, did not
fundamentally alter the tactical system by which the fleet was
controlled; and he was still plagued by the technical defects which
reduced the offensive power of his fleet, and also made his ships
vulnerable in defence. Furthermore the rising intensity of the
submarine campaign necessitated the diversion of resources to cope
with that menace. It thus came to pass that for about a year the
situation in the North Sea was not far removed from a stalemate
which the Admiralty and the C-in-C could find no way to break.
In the southern area, however, the Germans were steadily extending
their control by sowing minefields to guard the approaches to
Heligoland Bight, and were regularly sweeping the mines which
we were laying in the same waters. The German minelaying and
sweeping operations were always covered by substantial light forces,
with heavy units hovering in the background. It was these forces
that Beatty finally decided to attack. But before his plan was ready
we suffered an unpleasant setback far to the north.

For many months convoys had been running on a regular cycle
between the Shetland Islands and Bergen in Norway, and there had
been no enemy attempts to interfere with them. It seems that the
high degree of immunity the convoys had so far enjoyed had lulled
us into a false sense of security; for when on 17th October, 1917,
two German cruisers suddenly attacked a convoy, only two small
destroyers were present to protect the merchantmen. They were
easily overwhelmed, nine out of the twelve ships in the convoy were
sunk, and the attacking force made its way safely back to Germany
across 500 miles of sea—in spite of more than 80 British warships
being out on patrol.

Exactly a month later Beatty gave orders to carry out his long-
cherished plan to attack the enemy minesweepers and their covering
warships on the fringes of the Heligoland Bight. The forces allocated
were very substantial, including the 1st Battle Cruiser Squadron of
five ships and the two fast 15-inch heavy cruisers of the *Glorious*
class, which marked the climax of Lord Fisher's policy that ' speed is

armour'; while a squadron of six modern battleships was to cover the operation. At the outset it seemed that the plan would achieve its purpose admirably; for our various squadrons reached their positions undetected on 17th November, and a weakly protected enemy mine-sweeping force was surprised. But it very soon became apparent that poor staff work had deprived us of a valuable success; since the senior officers of the squadron detailed to penetrate into the Bight had not been given the full details of the minefields and the German swept channels which were in the C-in-C's possession. Thus the admiral in command of the cruiser force was handicapped by lack of information about the dangers ahead of him, and when the enemies he first encountered retired to the east he did not even pursue at full speed. The action was finally broken off with almost nothing accomplished—and the feeling of disappointment in the fleet was widespread. As so often before an inquiry was ordered: but the Admiralty seems to have been reluctant to probe the matter deeply, and no blame was attributed to anyone. Next, on the night of December 11th-12th, the Germans made another lightning raid, this time with destroyers, on our North Sea convoys. While some attacked the east coast shipping, others found a Norwegian convoy which was again only lightly protected. The entire convoy of six merchantmen and one of the two escorts were sunk, and once more the enemy striking forces regained their bases in safety. In considering the causes of these disasters it must, however, be remembered that whereas the Germans, by choosing their moments skilfully, could strike sudden blows at many points spread over a wide area, it was extraordinarily difficult for us to give each of our numerous convoys strong protection throughout their passages. Indeed the initiative in that type of hit and run raid was bound to rest with the enemy.

In order to improve the cover for our North Sea convoys and increase the chances of intercepting German raiding forces, in April, 1918, the main base of the Grand Fleet was shifted from Scapa to Rosyth in the Firth of Forth; and the last sortie by the High Seas

Fleet actually took place ten days later. Scheer, profiting by the experiences of the earlier attacks on our Norwegian convoys, had made an ambitious plan to use his main strength to catch and over-whelm our covering forces before the main fleet could come to their support. He took the utmost precautions to conceal his intentions, and actually got to sea unreported on 22nd April. It was only when an accident in the battle cruiser *Moltke* caused Admiral Hipper, commander of the 1st German Scouting Group, to break wireless silence on 24th that the Admiralty realised that a dangerous situation was developing, and ordered the Grand Fleet to sea; and by that time the main German force was off south-west Norway. Scheer actually retraced his steps soon afterwards, and although it is true that at the time he might have reached our Norwegian convoy route he would actually have found the sea empty, the implications of his totally unheralded approach to one of our most sensitive points were extremely serious.

We left the U-boat campaign at the end of 1916, at the time when we were suffering serious losses, and the Germans were still hesitating over starting unrestricted warfare on merchant shipping. On 1st February, 1917, they finally took the plunge, declaring that they would sink at sight ships of no matter what nationality sailing to and from Allied ports. It quickly became apparent that we were facing the most serious crisis of the war. In the *single month* of April, 1917, the U-boats sank 354 ships totalling 835,000 tons—a rate of loss which, if continued, was bound to bring disaster to the Allied cause. What, one may ask, had the Admiralty been doing through-out the two-year period of warning they had received? The answer is that a great variety of anti-submarine measures had been tried— patrolled lanes for shipping, minelaying, sweeps and searches by light forces and aircraft, and fitting out the much-advertised ' Q-ships '. But none of them had achieved significant success, and a reversion to the historic strategy of convoy and escort had been firmly rejected as being ineffective and impracticable. From the out-break of war to the end of January, 1917, the Germans lost only 52

U-boats from *all* causes; and we now know that as many as eight of those losses were caused by accidents, while Allied efforts may have had no hand in the destruction of eight others. That leaves no more than 36 which can be attributed to all our various counter-measures during 28 months of war: no very great recompense for the $3\frac{1}{4}$ million tons of merchant shipping which the U-boats had destroyed in the same period. Thus even before the start of un-restricted submarine warfare there was ample evidence that the tide was flowing strongly in the German favour, and that all was not well with out anti-submarine strategy. Yet as late as January, 1917, the Admiralty had told the War Council that ' a system of several ships sailing in company as a convoy is not recommended in any area where submarine attack is a possibility. . . . It is evident that the larger the number of ships forming a convoy, the greater [is] the chance of a submarine being able to attack successfully, and the greater the difficulty of the escort in preventing such an attack '[1]; and in support of those dogmatic statements they produced an array of equally dogmatic arguments about the difficulties of organising a convoy system and the ineffectiveness of such a measure if it was introduced. No account at all was taken of historical experience, and no attempt was made to apply scientific or mathematical analysis to those aspects of the problem which undoubtedly could have yielded to such an approach.[2] Fortunately for the country only a few weeks after Jellicoe had presented these ill-considered recommendations, Sir Maurice Hankey, the Secretary of the War Cabinet and Committee of Imperial Defence, produced a paper challenging the entire basis of the Admiralty's arguments.[3] And at about the same time a junior officer in the Admiralty's anti-sub-marine department proved that the official statistics of our ship-ping losses, which were compared with the weekly arrivals and

[1] Quoted Churchill, *The World Crisis*, Vol. IV, Part II, p. 364. See also Beaverbrook, *Men and Power* (Hutchinson, 1956), p. 152.

[2] See Churchill's criticism of the official history's account of the convoy controversy in *Thoughts and Adventures* (Thornton Butterworth, 1932), pp. 123-138.

[3] The paper, dated 11th February, 1917, is reproduced in Newbolt, *Naval Operations*, Vol. V, pp. 11-14 (Longmans, Green, 1931).

clearances of ships in British ports—so including all coastal traffic—were wholly misleading. Armed with this information Lloyd George, the Prime Minister, went over to the Admiralty on 30th April and successfully imposed his desire that convoy should be introduced. Jellicoe had actually accepted that view a few days earlier; but the change of front came too late to restore the government's confidence in the professional advice tendered by the Board of Admiralty. The First Lord, Carson, was replaced, and at the end of the year Jellicoe was in effect dismissed from the post of First Sea Lord. The consequences of the upheaval provoked by the Prime Minister were soon felt. The first ocean convoy sailed from Gibraltar in May, and three months later the strategy was being widely applied.

In the Mediterranean as well losses to enemy submarines, which worked from the Austrian bases at the head of the Adriatic, were extremely serious in 1917. In that theatre the problems of shipping protection were immensely complicated by the difficulty of achieving a unified command to control the British, French, Italian and Japanese forces involved. But the strategy of establishing patrolled shipping lanes again proved ineffective, as did the attempt to block the exit from the Adriatic by establishing a net and mine barrage across the Straits of Otranto. In May, 1917, a Mediterranean convoy organisation was however created, and in the following July a satisfactory unification of the various naval commands concerned was at last achieved. As in the home theatre shipping losses at once declined, and successful attacks on U-boats by convoy escorts soon rose sharply. By September, 1917, our world-wide shipping losses had dropped to less than half the April total, and our counter-measures were proving much more effective. It was without doubt the work of the convoy escorts, which sank 24 U-boats between August, 1917, and the end of the war, and the be-lated arrival of an efficient mine, which were chiefly responsible for the drastic reversal of the previous wholly unfavourable trends in the *guerre de course*. Yet in 1917 we lost 2,439 merchantmen of over

5½ million tons through submarine attacks. If ever there was a case in which a service staff should have accepted historical experience as a guide it was in the application of convoy strategy to the conditions produced by the unrestricted U-boat campaign. But its final acceptance in the summer of 1917 was by no means the end of the story. The American Navy was at first as unwilling as the British to adopt such measures; and, as we shall see later, all the old arguments against convoy were resurrected during the uneasy peace of the 1930s[1]. There is much justice in Churchill's bitter comment that ' the reluctance of all the naval chiefs in every Allied country to adopt convoys finds its counterpart only in the reluctance of the military chiefs of all the armies, Allied and enemy, to comprehend the significance of the tank. In both cases these means of salvation were forced upon them from outside and below '.[2]

We must now glance at the influence of the Admiralty's miscalculations regarding the U-boat war on the struggle in France and Flanders. In 1917 Jellicoe, who seems to have become extremely pessimistic in outlook,[3] several times told the War Council and Sir Douglas Haig that unless the Army could capture the Flanders bases (Ostend and Zeebrugge) from which some of the U-boats were working we should lose the war; and that ominous forecast undoubtedly influenced Haig's decision to continue the Third Battle of Ypres into the autumn of that year. Yet Jellicoe's views were based on a wholly false premise. In the first place only two flotillas of the smaller (520-ton) U-boats were stationed in Flanders, and had we threatened their bases from the landward side they would merely have moved east to the bases from which the larger High Seas Fleet U-boats were working. There might have been some decline in attacks on our Channel shipping: but the campaign

---

[1] See pp. 152-3.   [2] *Thoughts and Adventures* (Thornton Butterworth, 1932), p. 138.
[3] Jellicoe had long been one of Fisher's chief protégés, and it was Fisher who selected him for command of the Grand Fleet in war. Yet the war was not many months old before Fisher was complaining about Jellicoe's caution and pessimism. See his letters to Churchill of 20th June, 1915, to C. P. Scott of 19th February, 1916 and to E. G. Pretyman of 27th December, 1916 (A. J. Marder, *Fear God and Dread Nought*, Vol. III, pp. 134, 316 and 408 respectively).

as a whole would have been little affected, and it is very hard to understand how the First Sea Lord could have expressed such false conclusions. Secondly, apart from the introduction of convoy, which the Admiralty were at the time opposing, a far more effective and far less costly means of putting the Flanders bases out of action than struggling towards them overland through the mud of the inundated country around Ypres was available—namely by assault from the sea. The first proposals for combined operations to be mounted against the Flanders bases were actually made in 1916,[1] but were turned down because of the insatiable demands of the land campaign in France. In May, 1917, the idea of blocking Zeebrugge was raised by Commodore Tyrwhitt, the commander of the Harwich Force; but his proposal suffered the same fate as the earlier one. On 1st January, 1918, however, Rear-Admiral Keyes one of the few men to emerge from the Dardanelles failure with enhanced reputation,[2] took over the Dover command, and very soon made his influence felt in two directions. His first task was to make the Dover mine barrage effective; for U-boats were still passing to and from the Atlantic by way of the English Channel at the rate of about 30 a month with very little hindrance and few losses. In this purpose he was much assisted by the belated arrival of efficient mines—which his predecessor had always lacked; and successful passages by U-boats soon showed a marked decline. But Keyes had also turned his mind to the problem of cutting off the U-boat base at Bruges from the canal exits at Zeebrugge and Ostend; and his fiery energy was such that by March, 1918, he had made a plan and trained an assault force. The first sortie on 11th April was frustrated by unfavourable winds, and the plan was then very nearly abandoned. Keyes however persuaded the First Sea Lord, now Admiral Wemyss, to let him try again, and the attack actually took place on the night of 22nd-23rd April. As a feat of arms the storming of the Zeebrugge mole, and the penetration into the harbour by the blockships, is unlikely ever to be surpassed. Yet the truth was

[1] By Admiral Sir Lewis Bayly, commander at Queenstown.   [2] See p. 124.

that, for all the gallantry displayed, the Zeebrugge canal entrance was only partially blocked, while the attempt at Ostend was a total failure—as was the repetition of it on 10th May. We now know that German U-boat movements in and out of the Flanders bases were hardly impeded at all. But the attacks on Zeebrugge and Ostend did cast a ray of light through the gloom of a very difficult period for Britain: since it was in that same month that Haig issued his famous ' backs to the wall ' order to the troops in France and Flanders. In retrospect it seems clear that nothing short of a full-scale combined operation could have achieved our purpose against such strongly defended targets. And after more than three years of war we still had no inter-service organisation for planning such enterprises, nor any specially trained men; while the equipment provided was all of an extemporised nature. Furthermore the results of the attacks on Zeebrugge and Ostend certainly appear to lend support to the old lesson, that only rarely has a purely naval attack on an enemy stronghold achieved success. Lastly by the time the attacks were actually carried out we were, thanks to the introduction of convoy, well on the way towards defeating the U-boats.

One other measure taken by the Allies against the U-boats demands brief attention. In September, 1917, Jellicoe as First Sea Lord had proposed the laying of a new minefield across the North Sea from the Shetlands to the limit of Norwegian territorial waters near Bergen. The proposal was accepted, and the Americans energetically set about producing very large numbers of mines, whose efficiency was soon shown to be of a low order. Laying began in March, 1918, and over 70,000 mines were finally placed in the barrage. Yet even had a purely defensive measure such as this been a sound strategic conception, the existence of the gap off the Norwegian coast, of which U-boats were bound to take advantage, was certain to vitiate its effectiveness. In fact we now know that it achieved only very slight results. U-boat passages in and out from the Atlantic were little affected, and no more than two of them came to grief in the barrage. Furthermore even if the ready acceptance of the original proposal can, at any rate in part, be explained by the fact that, at the time, the convoy strategy had not yet fully proved itself, its execution was continued long after the success of the ancient principle was beyond all doubt. Indeed the whole idea of the Northern Barrage underlines the lack of the Admiralty's faith in the strategy of convoy and escort; and the records prove that it was the American Admiral Sims, who commanded the U.S. Navy's contingent which came across in 1917 to join the Grand Fleet, who first realised the unsoundness and wastefulness of embarking on such a project what time we had ready to hand, and were indeed at last beginning to apply, the only counter-measure which could produce the desired results.[1] Yet proposals very similar to the Northern Barrage of 1918 were not only revived but carried out in the Second World War: and the results were again almost negligible.

Throughout the years of endurance for Britain and France our economic blockade of the central European powers had been slowly but steadily tightening. And the entry of the United States into the war on 6th April, 1917, enabled us to extend and strengthen our world-wide control of merchant shipping and cargoes until it became a stranglehold. Of all the measures adopted by the Allies to bring about the enemy's downfall it now seems that the blockade was the most lethal. By the spring of 1918 shortage of food was inflicting the most severe hardships on the German and Austrian people, and the difficulty of obtaining raw materials was affecting their fighting services. Meanwhile the stream of American soldiers crossing the Atlantic to replace the terrible losses suffered by Britain and France at Gallipoli, on the Somme, at Verdun and in the long battles of attrition around Ypres was becoming a flood; and once the dangerous German offensive of March, 1918, had been stopped the outcome of the war was no longer in doubt. As early

[1] See Newbolt, *Naval Operations*, Vol. V, p. 133. 'Admiral Sims must be given the credit of being the first naval expert in high position who had the insight to realise that the remedy for which the Allies were still seeking had actually been found.'

as July and August, 1917, there had been serious disorders in the
High Seas Fleet, arising partly from political influences, and partly
from genuine grievances over the inadequacy of the rations and the
severity of the discipline imposed on the warships' 'crews. The
disaffection was, however, quelled by a combination of conciliation
and firmness; and, as we have already seen, the German fleet so far
recovered its morale as to carry out several vigorously conducted
sorties in the autumn of that year. But the seeds of discontent, if
temporarily suppressed, still remained dormant; and with the
success of the Russian Revolution the political agitation for the
overthrow of the existing régime in Germany found increasing
support. Finally on 29th October, 1918, the men of the once proud
High Seas Fleet broke into open mutiny when orders were received
to prepare for a final desperate sortie. That led directly to the
surrender of a navy which could, with some reason, claim that it had
never suffered a major defeat in battle. Of all the factors which led
to that climax the steady application of our blockade was undoubtedly the greatest.

In this brief survey of the naval war of 1914-18, developments in
aviation have so far received scant attention; and that has been
because the aircraft's influence on strategy, which is our main concern, was not considerable. None the less as the war progressed
signs were not lacking that the steadily improving performance of
aircraft did justify the claims of the early pioneers that they were
capable of playing an important part in naval warfare, and would
in the future exert a profound influence. Thus it will be logical to
conclude with some account of the work of the naval air arm in the
1914-18 war, in which one may see the genesis of the far-reaching
strategic changes brought about by air power in the second struggle
with Germany.

The Royal Naval Air Service, which grew out of the original
Naval Wing of the Royal Flying Corps, was officially recognised
on 1st July, 1914, at which date its personnel numbered some 800
officers and men, and it possessed about 100 seaplanes, aeroplanes

and airships. On the outbreak of war the R.N.A.S. was, rather curiously, made responsible for home defence—the reason being that the greater part of the R.F.C. had gone to France. The first seaplane carrier had already been built, and several more were ordered in 1914. But the seaplane did not prove a very successful offensive aircraft, and by the following year we realised that the future lay with aircraft capable of taking off from a ship's deck.

In the early stages of air developments the chief functions of naval aircraft were recognised to be reconnaissance for the fleet, and spotting for the big ships' gunfire. But many offensive sorties were carried out against targets such as German Zeppelin hangars, and the long-range strike rôle of aircraft was certainly not ignored by the Royal Navy. Thus in the Gallipoli campaign naval aircraft performed a wide variety of duties, including the first torpedo attacks on enemy ships, with considerable success. In 1916, the R.F.C. took over responsibility for home defence, and the Naval Air Service then concentrated on intercepting raiding Zeppelins at sea, on spotting for bombardments of the Belgian coast, on anti-U-boat work, and on strikes at special targets in enemy territory. By 1917, development of aircraft carriers was proceeding apace, several conversions were in hand, and one ship (the *Hermes*) had been specially designed for the purpose. The first successful deck landing took place on 3rd August of that year. But a lack of co-ordination in the various aspects of air warfare at sea and on land had meanwhile become apparent; while the unconventional approach to their work of the early pioneers, and their unorthodox attitude towards authority, did not always smooth the workings of administrative machinery. To regularise the present position, and establish the lines of future development, in October, 1917, the government appointed a committee under the chairmanship of General Smuts; and that body recommended the creation of a third service to take over all aviation activities. In consequence on 1st April, 1918, the R.N. Air Service's 67,000 officers and men, with nearly 3,000 aircraft, 103 airships and 126 air stations were taken over by the newly-formed Royal Air Force. There can, of course, be no doubt that the formation of the third service was a wise decision; but where the Smuts Committee now seems to have erred was in the failure to realise that a strong case existed for the continued separate development of specialised naval aviation. It is likely that the vociferations of the extreme propagandists of air power, led by the Italian General Douhet, influenced the recommendations of the Smuts committee; yet their meek acceptance by the Admiralty none the less seems very puzzling. Nor were many months to pass before the Navy realised the magnitude of the error then committed; and a long and often acrimonious struggle over the control of naval aviation ensued. It was not finally resolved until 1937, when the Admiralty regained full control of what it should never have surrendered. No doubt there was excessive conservatism towards naval aviation in some quarters during the 1914-18 war—and especially among the powerful school which placed its faith in the big gun as the sole arbiter of defeat or victory at sea. But by 1917, it should surely have been clear that the capabilities of shipborne aircraft had reached a stage where it was essential that the service which employed them should control development and training—as it controlled the design and construction of the ships from which they would work.

Looking back to-day at the events of the naval war of 1914-18, and surveying the use then made of our sea power, it is hard not to feel a sense of disappointment similar to, if less acute than that which had been so prevalent after the Crimean War. For we did not emerge with a tale of victories in any way comparable with those which had decided our earlier struggles against continental dictatorships. None of the clashes with the German Navy—not even the Falkland Islands battle—produced a result which can stand alongside La Hogue or Quiberon Bay, the Nile or Trafalgar. Nor was there any instance of an overseas conjunct expedition, or a major land campaign in a remote but vital theatre, receiving support from the sea such as made the expedition to Quebec of 1759 so brilliantly successful, and finally enabled Wellington to gain his great victories in the Peninsular campaign of 1812-14. The sense of disappointment stems from our present realisation that favourable strategic opportunities certainly were lost; and that can surely be attributed to the fact that, with the exception of Churchill, none of the nation's political leaders appreciated the possibilities inherent in a maritime strategy, and no soldier of prominence gave more than belated and reluctant support to the amphibious concept of war. In reviewing the strategic shortcomings of the British governments of those days one must, however, remember that they had no Chiefs of Staff Committee to present the consistent and agreed views of the heads of the fighting services.[1] But one cannot attribute the sense of disappointment over the Royal Navy's accomplishments entirely to the defective organisation for the higher direction of the war; since failings and weaknesses were revealed in the service's own professional field, and responsibility for them can be placed nowhere else than at its own door. No doubt the causes of the failings were complex; but one of them, and perhaps the chief one, was that the far-reaching technical changes which took place during the latter half of the 19th century had so profound an impact on every aspect of naval warfare that material progress became the predominant influence—to the almost complete exclusion of what one may call the historical and theoretical aspects of naval education and training. And when Fisher turned his fiery energy to the modernisation of the Navy early in the 20th century, the pace of technical advance was still further accelerated, thus frustrating the efforts of those like Churchill and, among naval men, Richmond who saw the need for an intellectual approach to strategic problems, and for the formation of a properly organised and trained naval staff. It seems beyond doubt that indifferent staff work was responsible for at any

[1] The Chiefs of Staff Committee was set up as a result of the Salisbury Report of 1923, and the first meeting took place on 17th July of that year.

rate a share of the Gallipoli muddles, for the indecisiveness of Jutland, and still more for the false views propogated by the Admiralty with regard to the adoption of the escort-of-convoy strategy in face of the U-boat menace. The schisms produced in the Navy by Fisher's drastic methods took a long time to heal, and internal disunity in a fighting service must surely militate against efficient staff work and sound planning. The fact that between 1910, when war with Germany was recognised to be likely, and 1918, the office of First Sea Lord changed hands no less than six times suggests that all was not well both in the upper hierarchy of the service and in the relations between the admirals and political leaders.[1] Moreover frequent changes in the senior member of the Board of Admiralty must surely break the continuity of thought which is so essential to consistent and careful planning. In passing we may remark that between 1939-1945 there was only one change of First Sea Lord, and that came about only through the illness and death of Sir Dudley Pound. If one can trace too many signs of disunity in the naval service between 1910 and 1918 one can find scarcely any examples of inter-service unity. Soldiers and sailors were almost chronically at loggerheads over strategic issues, and the relations between both of them and the civil government often left much to be desired. The bitter disagreements between ' the frocks and the brass ' were certainly not entirely the fault of the service men. Lloyd George's devious methods, and his capacity for intrigue, were such that antagonisms were bound to be generated between Downing Street and Whitehall. But it is none the less true that over such issues as the need to call a halt to the holocaust in France by adopting a more flexible strategy, and over the introduction of convoy, Lloyd

---

[1] The following officers became 1st Sea Lord on the dates shown:
25th Jan., 1910   Admiral of the Fleet Sir Arthur K. Wilson.
 5th Dec., 1911   Admiral Sir Francis C. B. Bridgeman.
 9th Dec., 1912   Admiral Prince Louis of Battenberg.
30th Oct., 1914   Admiral of the Fleet Lord Fisher of Kilverstone.
27th May, 1915   Admiral Sir Henry B. Jackson.
 4th Dec., 1916   Admiral Sir John R. Jellicoe.
10th Jan., 1918   Admiral Sir Rosslyn E. Wemyss.

George now seems to have had a large share of the right on his side. There is irony in the fact that it was the Prime Minister's stand against Haig and Robertson, and his plain threat of drastic action, that brought about one of the rare instances of unity between the admirals and generals.

It was probably inevitable that the first phase of the conflict with the Central European powers should have been fought mainly on the basis of a continental strategy; for we could hardly have left the French to face the German onslaught alone. But when their initial drive had been decisively checked, and the land campaign in the west had lapsed into a state of stalemate, a more determined search should surely have been made for a way out of the strategic impasse. It is difficult not to feel that, had the attack on Gallipoli been planned, organised and carried out on an inter-service basis with such an object in view it might have contributed a good deal to providing the solution. Even after it had failed there still remained the possibility of wearing down the weaker partners of the central alliance—and in particular the Austrian Empire—by adopting an imaginative strategy in Italy and the Adriatic. Indeed Lloyd George struggled hard to break the deadlock in the west by giving more support to the Italian campaign; but our military leaders were too firmly wedded to the war of attrition in the west. It is, of course, impossible to prove that greater emphasis on the maritime or 'peripheral' possibilities would have brought victory more economically. But when one considers the appalling cost in human life and material resources of the long struggle in France and Flanders, and remembers the overwhelming preponderance which we all the time possessed at sea, it is difficult to accept that we made the best possible use of our sea power.

As to the fighting record of the Royal Navy itself, enough has already been said about the rigidity of our tactical system to explain the failure of our main fleet to achieve any striking success. It is indeed in exploits such as the penetration by our submarines into the Baltic and the Sea of Marmara, in the Zeebrugge raid, in the work of the Q-ships and the flotilla craft of the Dover Patrol that one can see that the old spirit certainly was not dead. But individual efforts can avail but little when the organisation for the strategic direction of a war is defective, and the staff work which should visualise, create and exploit opportunities for decision leaves much to be desired. Another quarter of a century was, however, to elapse before we and our American Allies were to prove conclusively that a predominantly maritime strategy could still bring vast benefits at relatively small cost—notwithstanding the far-reaching nature of the changes in warfare wrought by man's conquest of the air. And in the second struggle against Germany the Royal Navy itself was to recapture the confidence in performance and execution, derived from firm direction and wise leadership, which had proved the source of so much of its strength in earlier struggles against continental conquerors.

IV

Uneasy interlude

1918-39

The first German war proved that the emasculation of our ancient maritime rights, which started with the Declaration of Paris of 1856, had been an exceedingly expensive error. For the conflict had undoubtedly been prolonged by the slowness with which we were able to restore those rights and apply the full pressure of which our sea power was capable. Furthermore the advantages which we had expected to gain from the abolition of privateering had proved entirely illusory, and the international agreements governing the use of submarines in the *guerre de course* had been shown to be worthless. In 1919, the Lloyd George government actually restored the situation to what it had been a century previously by rejecting out of hand the oft-pressed argument of continental states for ' the Freedom of the Seas '—a doctrine which, in time of war, is bound to operate wholly unfavourably towards a mercantile state, but which had been included in President Wilson's famous ' Fourteen Points '.

So far so good. Yet hardly was the ink dry on the treaty of peace before the victorious nations embarked on a whole series of diplomatic negotiations which in the sum resulted in Britain sacrificing her ancient maritime supremacy, and accepting the limitation of her naval armaments to a ratio agreed between the major powers. One has to view the decisions of the Washington Conference of 1921-22, and the Five Power Naval Treaty which grew out of it, in the light of the hopes then entertained that the League of Nations would prove an effective organisation for the preservation of peace. But it is none the less plain that the naval treaty gravely weakened British security; and because it was linked with complicated rules governing the displacement of major warships and the calibre of their primary armaments, it produced for the Admiralty a large crop of difficult technical problems. Moreover under pressure from the United States, which had never liked the Anglo-Japanese Alliance of 1905, we agreed to replace it by a Four Power Treaty which included the U.S.A. and France. This fundamentally altered our position in the western Pacific, where our commercial interests were extremely valuable. And so we set our feet on a novel path, marked by few signposts in history, and which soon appeared to be leading us into an increasingly sombre future. The financial stringency of the 1920s was moreover so severe that the Admiralty had to wage an unceasing struggle to prevent the whole Royal Navy lapsing into obsolescence. Few new ships were laid down, and we, in common with other nations, felt obliged to design those that were built up to the top limits of displacement and weapon calibre permitted by the treaties. Thus a great deal of valuable experience gained with earlier classes of ships and weapons was sacrificed to the need to conform to arbitrary standards agreed around a conference table. We very soon found that our designs of, for example, 10,000-ton cruisers armed with 8-inch guns had little to commend them. As long as the Naval Limitation Treaty of 1922 remained valid—and it did not expire until 1936—there was little that the Admiralty could do by way of replacing our rapidly ageing fleet with ships which really did meet our needs; and only very gradually could money be found even to modernise a proportion of the older ships. True we still possessed the world-wide chain of naval bases, which was a legacy of the 18th and 19th centuries; and we were well aware of the great part which efficient bases must play in maritime strategy. But when money for ship-building is hard to come by no Board of Admiralty is likely to allot a high proportion of its vote to the equipment and defence of bases. It is indeed no exaggeration to say that by 1930 neither at home nor abroad did we possess a single base which was capable of meeting the needs of the squadrons which would, in time of war, depend on them. Even the decision to build a modern base at Singapore was so beset by political vacillations that progress was exceedingly slow. Furthermore in spite of the rise of Japan, and the rapid worsening of our relations with that country, we could not return to the two-ocean Navy which had been necessary to deal with the Bourbon alliance of the 18th century, or to the Two Power Standard which we had established in the face of the Franco-Russian threat in the 19th. Thus we were never able to base a proper fleet in the Far East, and in such conditions Singapore was, in Richmond's words, ' like a sentry box without a sentry '[1] The final weakness in the policy of the 1920s was that it was bound to leave us with a quite inadequate force of cruisers and flotilla vessels to protect our commerce. For the Treaty of London of 1930 extended the limitations imposed at Washington to those classes of ship and to submarines, taking no account of all of the abundant experience which had proved that ' a scattered and divided trade ' required ' a very large force to furnish it with adequate security '.[2]

Nor did the rise to power of Adolf Hitler in Germany, the denunciation of the Washington Treaty by Japan in 1934, and the increasing intransigence of Fascist Italy awaken the British people to their peril. Instead, their traditional reliance on a navy which could take on all comers was replaced by a vague belief in the League of Nations and in the Locarno Pact for the abolition of war—a belief which was fostered by a great deal of idealistic but highly misleading ' peace ' propaganda. Then, in 1935, we committed the crowning folly of signing an agreement permitting Germany to build a navy one third as large as our own, and allowing her to increase the agreed figure of 60 per cent of our strength in submarines up to 100 per cent if *she* judged it necessary. In 1935, Mussolini's designs on Abyssinia produced a grave crisis, and it was largely the somewhat exaggerated reports received in London with regard to the weak state of the Mediterranean Fleet that inhibited

---

[1] *Statesmen and Sea Power*, p. 221 (O.U.P., 1946).
[2] Report to the Admiralty by Admiral Pellew in 1810. Quoted Richmond, *Statesmen and Sea Power*, p. 291.

strong action by the British Government, and allowed the Italian bluff to succeed. Meanwhile a campaign was being conducted in this country, in France, and above all in the United States in favour of the abolition of blockade and of the right of a belligerent to interfere with neutral cargoes in time of war. But the American Neutrality Act of 1935 did ease our problem in some respects, since the United States thereby virtually abandoned the neutral rights for which they had gone to war with us in 1812.[1]

Not until 1937 did the British Government embark on a modest measure of rearmament; and, as the clouds over Europe darkened, our weakness in every single element of maritime power—in fighting ships, in merchant shipping (in which our proportion of the world's tonnage had dropped from 41 per cent in 1914 to 26 per cent in 1938, due largely to the competition of heavily subsidised foreign ships), and in properly defended bases—was causing grave anxiety to men of understanding in maritime affairs. Finally, only a few months before the outbreak of hostilities, we surrendered unconditionally the right to the two naval bases in Eire (Lough Swilly and Berehaven) which had been reserved to us by the terms of the settlement of 1922. That conciliatory but incredibly myopic act was to increase greatly the difficulty of providing adequate protection to our convoys in the Western Approaches. The only glimmer of light which penetrated the sombre scene in 1939 was cast by the high professional efficiency of the ships we had in service, and by the fact that our belligerent rights remained more or less where they had stood in 1918.

Throughout what Churchill has aptly called ' the locust years ' the Admiralty fought a continuous uphill struggle to give the service for which it was responsible the best weapons and equipment which could be provided within the limits imposed by the international treaties already referred to and the funds allotted by Parliament; while the commanders-in-chief of our main fleets at home and in the Mediterranean trained their ships with the object of eliminating

[1] See pp. 86-7.

such of the weaknesses revealed by the previous conflict as lay within their scope and capacity. Thus great emphasis was laid on efficiency in night fighting—in which we had not shown up well at Jutland; and in the Mediterranean the strategic and tactical problems involved in the operation of carrier-borne aircraft were continuously investigated. The big gun was, however, still regarded as the principal arbiter in naval warfare; while the duties of carrier-borne aircraft were laid down as reconnaissance for the fleet, spotting for its gunfire, attacks on a retreating enemy in order to slow him down and so enable the big guns to decide the issue and, lastly, providing anti-submarine protection for the fleet. Trade protection was still regarded as being chiefly a matter of locating enemy surface raiders and bringing them to book. Nor were any exercises carried out to investigate the problems of using aircraft as well as flotilla vessels to defend mercantile convoys against submarine attacks. Co-operation with the shore-based aircraft of the Royal Air Force was based on the priorities established for ship-borne aircraft, and none of the former received any training in anti-submarine tactics, in the defence of convoys, or in attacks on enemy merchant shipping.

As international tension increased in 1937-38, plans were framed for a war with Germany and Italy, and discussions took place between the Admiralty and Air Ministry on the thorny question of the part to be played by the shore-based aircraft of the R.A.F.'s Coastal Command. As to the war plans, it is interesting to compare them with those made before the first German war. This time there was no conflict between the ' Blue Water ' and the ' Bolt from the Blue ' schools on the invasion question[1]; and it was tacitly accepted that as long as we held command of our home waters invasion need not be seriously considered. This corresponded to the decision of Mr. Balfour's government of 1905. Equally there was no repetition of the clash between the ' Continental ' and ' Maritime ' schools on the strategy to be adopted in Europe. In fact the war plans made no mention at all of the possible need to carry out amphibious

[1] See p. 104

enterprises. The inter-service body which had recently been set up to study and develop that form of warfare (the Inter-Service Training and Development Centre) was actually closed on the outbreak of war—on the grounds that 'there would be no combined operations in this war ';[1] and we started the struggle entirely committed to a continental strategy in support of the French. In part this arose from the experiences of the previous conflict, in particular from recollections of the Gallipoli failure, and in part from the views expressed by the extreme protagonists of air power to the effect that the new instruments of war had made assaults from the sea on a hostile coast impossibly hazardous.

An entirely new form of 'continental' strategy had, however, arisen in between the wars. It was based on the belief that air power had rendered all earlier strategic conceptions obsolete, and would by itself break the enemy's power of resistance. Partly through the assiduity with which that doctrine was propagated, and partly because the actual effects of air bombing were much overestimated before the war, it came to pass that 'strategic bombing' was always given priority over maritime needs and purposes. Though we will return to the subject when we review its consequences later,[2] we may here note that this was probably the biggest error made by us in the realm of strategy in the war of 1939-45. For when the time came to turn to the offensive, it was shortage of shipping that cramped and restricted every single Allied plan and purpose; and the vast losses incurred during the first four years simply could not be replaced.

The acceptance in 1939 of a predominantly continental strategy meant that the first duty placed on the Royal Navy was once again the safe transport of the British Expeditionary Force to France. The naval war plans also aimed, as in the previous struggle, to sweep enemy merchant shipping off the seas and oceans of the world, and then to establish a blockade of Germany. Contraband control

[1] See L. E. H. Maund, *Assault from the Sea*, pp. 19-21 (Methuen, 1949).
[2] See p. 180.

stations were to be established at home and overseas: neutral ships intercepted at sea would be directed into them, and they would not be allowed to complete their journeys unless or until we were satisfied that their cargoes were not destined for enemy countries. Thus did we rapidly reassert the belligerent rights upon which British statesmen had repeatedly insisted since the time of the elder Pitt, but which had been blunted by our acceptance of the Declaration of Paris. The main instrument for enforcing the blockade which, because of the restrictions to which we had agreed in 1856, was never actually declared, was to be a Northern Patrol of cruisers. Supported by the main Home Fleet, they would guard the passages from the North Sea out into the Atlantic. Our blockade measures and contraband control at once proved effective; very few German ships slipped through, and neutrals soon began to call voluntarily in order to get their cargoes cleared. True there were certain leaks: we could not stop enemy traffic in the Baltic, some supplies soon began to reach Germany through the Pacific and Black Sea ports of Russia; and, as we were anxious to keep Italy neutral, we several times relaxed the full stringency of our measures in respect of her shipping. But in the sum German overseas trade was reduced to a trickle, and the effectiveness of our world-wide maritime power as the principal instrument of blockade was shown to be unaffected by modern developments.

With regard to the Mediterranean, the war plans stated that the French Navy would be responsible for the western basin, and our own fleet, which would be based on Alexandria by virtue of the Anglo-Egyptian treaty of 1936, for the eastern basin. There it would be well placed to cover the Suez Canal and the overland routes to the oil fields of Iraq and Persia, as well as the sea routes to India and the Far East; and it would also immediately sever the communications of all the Italian forces which had been laboriously assembled in East Africa, but which had always been hostages to British sea power—once we chose to assert it. The British Mediterranean fleet was, however, a good deal handicapped by the inadequacies of its base organisation in Egypt, which had been extemporised somewhat hurriedly when the government accepted the views of the Army and Air Force that Malta could not be defended against Italian air power.

When the war plans were being framed the defence of our merchant shipping and the question whether it should be ordered into convoy were the most lengthily debated points. The Air Staff's opinion was that ships massed in convoy would offer the enemy easier targets than single ships—which was actually one of the arguments against convoy which had been discredited during the previous struggle. Fortunately in 1937, the two Services had agreed that convoy should be adopted—but only if the enemy resumed unrestricted U-boat warfare. This hesitant approach to the adoption of the convoy strategy is most surprising, since the abundant evidence of its effectiveness available in history had been convincingly re-affirmed as lately as 1917. But the decision to convoy—though made conditional on the enemy's method of waging war—did enable the Admiralty to create the necessary world-wide shipping control organisation; and by 1939 those measures were well advanced. This did not, of course, mean that all ships could be ordered into convoy as soon as war was declared: since there were some 9,500 British merchantmen (21¼ million tons) scattered all over the world, cargoes already loaded had to be delivered to their destinations, and it would have been very uneconomical to interrupt shipping movements wholesale while awaiting the organisation of convoys. But it did enable the Naval Control Service Officers, who were the representatives in overseas ports of the Trade Division of the Naval Staff, to institute the necessary measures, and the operational authorities at home and abroad to organise the escort forces. The first mercantile convoys actually sailed within a few days of the outbreak of hostilities; but it was perhaps fortunate for Britain that a U-boat sank the liner *Athenia* on the day war broke out—actually in contradiction of Hitler's orders: for that act removed the last lingering doubts regarding the need to adopt convoy. The Admiralty, however, at first regarded surface raiders as a more serious threat than the submarine. The war plans therefore provided for air and warship patrols in the North Sea, and for cruiser patrols in the focal areas of our shipping overseas, to intercept the raiders. The North Sea air patrols were thus made the primary responsibility of Coastal Command, while anti-submarine co-operation with the Navy was placed second in its duties. But the short endurance of the aircraft then in service, combined with the difficult weather conditions generally encountered in the North Sea, soon made it clear that the patrols provided no sure means of gaining warning of enemy warship movements. And as none of the aircrews had received any training in anti-submarine warfare, and the bombs provided to them were completely useless, they played no effective part in the first phase of the struggle against the U-boats.

The war plans also provided for laying a minefield to bar the Dover Straits to enemy submarines, and for a barrier to be laid off our east coast to hinder enemy incursions against the convoys sailing between the Thames and Firth of Forth. We may here note that the Dover barrage, which was only made really effective towards the end of the earlier struggle, this time fulfilled its purpose admirably.

Thus, after an interval of just over two decades, did the British maritime services prepare for the renewal of the struggle with Germany. Though the assets which they possessed and the weaknesses from which they suffered will be discussed later, we may remark that, as had been the case in 1914, it was in the human field that they were strongest. Indeed, as so often before, the quality and experience of the long service officers and men of the Royal Navy, and the sturdy imperturbability of the Merchant Navy crews, whose 'elusive corporate discipline is the peculiar tradition of their service ',[1] were again to rise above the serious difficulties produced by the inadequate, and in some respects faulty equipment provided to them. Furthermore all the senior officers flying their flags in our fleets and squadrons, as well as the majority of captains of our major

[1] R. H. Thornton, *British Shipping*, p. 50 (C.U.P., 2nd Ed., 1959).

warships and masters of our merchantmen, had served in the previous conflict. Though they may not have realised the extent to which airborne instruments were to influence every aspect of maritime war, their earlier experiences made them confident of their capacity to deal with the many problems which were bound to arise. And they were inspired by traditions which had been gradually built up during the past three centuries.

V

The struggle with
Germany renewed—
the defensive phase
1939-41

We saw earlier how no preparations for amphibious warfare had been included in the 1939 War Plans.[1] However, Mr. Churchill had not been many days back at his old desk in the First Lord's room before he began to press for a naval expedition to the Baltic very similar to that which he and Lord Fisher had considered in the early days of the previous war. As, however, air power had greatly enhanced the risks of what was bound in any case to be a hazardous undertaking, in January, 1940, he reluctantly agreed to the plan being shelved. Though this operation (called 'Catherine') was never intended to be a full-scale amphibious enterprise, and one may feel that it was fortunate that it was overtaken by events, Churchill was undoubtedly right to seek ways and means of attacking the enemy at an unexpected point.

From the beginning of the war until the spring of 1941 we could only convoy merchantmen a few hundred miles out into the Atlantic, after which they dispersed and proceeded independently to their destinations. The need for fuelling bases as far to the west as possible at once became apparent, and it was now that the lack of bases in Eire was grievously felt.[2] New bases were finally developed at Belfast and Londonderry in Northern Ireland; but that took time, and in the meanwhile our escorts had to break off from their convoys with enough fuel in hand to reach a British port.

In the early months our convoy strategy was further vitiated by pressure to employ our slender force of flotilla vessels on hunts and sweeps, instead of on escort duty. In part this undoubtedly arose from Mr. Churchill's desire to adopt what he regarded as more

[1] See pp. 149-50.   [2] See p. 148.

'offensive' measures than convoy.[1] But some naval authorities were prone to the same error—forgetting that as recently as the 1914-18 war hunting operations had proved singularly ineffective, and that because enemy raiders (be they submarines, aircraft or surface ships) are certain to be drawn to the convoys, opportunities for the escorts to strike back are bound to arise. The result was that our convoy escorts were too often depleted in order to form hunting groups, that merchantmen were lost in convoy because of the weakness of the escorts, and that opportunities to counter-attack the U-boats were sacrificed. The hunting strategy was even carried so far as to employ our few and precious aircraft carriers on such duties. The only result was that one of them—the *Courageous* —was torpedoed and sunk by a U-boat. Though the carriers were then withdrawn, the fallacy of the hunting group proved very enduring, and it was not until 1941 that we really concentrated on providing the strongest possible escort to our convoys.

In the initial phase of the *guerre de course* the Germans were bound to hold the initiative—for they had sent out two pocket-battleships and 39 U-boats (their whole available strength) well before war was declared; and many of our merchantmen were still sailing independently. Thus in the first four months of the war we lost about ¾ million tons of shipping—over half of which was sunk by U-boats. But we exacted a heavy toll from those enemies, and the broad results of this phase were by no means wholly unfavour-able to our cause. The Germans did, however, score a success with their magnetic mine, which caught us by surprise—for all that we had manufactured mines of that type, and actually laid a few of them towards the end of the previous struggle. Yet in 1939 we had no sweepers capable of dealing with them. For a time the situation was serious—especially on the east coast and in the Thames estuary; but new sweeps were quickly produced, and by the spring of 1940 we had mastered the threat. The magnetic mine initiated the long

[1] See for example *The Second World War*, Vol. I (1st Ed.), pp. 362-3:—'I always sought to rupture this defensive obsession by searching for forms of counter-offensive. . . . I could not rest content with the policy of "convoy and blockade".'

battle of wits between enemy mine designers and our sweep designers. As the war progressed many other varieties of mine, with almost infinite variations in fuses and delay mechanisms, were produced. But none of them, except perhaps the pressure-operated mine first used in 1944, caused us such serious trouble as the early magnetic mine. The lesson we did learn was that the modern mine was a very potent instrument of blockade, and that large numbers of sweepers, capable of dealing with all its variations were needed to keep the shallow inshore channels and the approaches to our ports open.

Enemy bombing attacks on our merchant ships were at first not very effective. But we were desperately short of anti-aircraft weapons, and it took time to arrange with the R.A.F., which had had not been asked before the war to accept any responsibility for the defence of coastal shipping, for fighter protection. Gradually, however, the passage of coastal convoys was made a joint Navy-Air Force responsibility, and the combined defences kept the short-range bombers of the Luftwaffe in check. After the enemy had acquired air bases in Norway and western France in 1940, a new threat from the air developed; for long-range bombers were then able to reach our convoys to the west of Ireland, and for a time they inflicted considerable losses. Again emergency measures, such as fitting merchantmen with a single Hurricane fighter, which could be catapulted into the air, had to be taken; and again it was the joint work of the two services involved that overcame the threat. We were, moreover, always helped by the lack of co-operation between the Luftwaffe and the German Navy: for it completely inhibited the development by the enemy of an effective joint air-sea strategy. Undoubtedly Marshal Göring's megalomania, and the bad blood that existed between him and Admiral Raeder, were the chief factors in bringing us this unlooked-for benefit.

By 1940 we realised that the convoy strategy could only be made really effective if the merchantmen carried along with them their own air defence, as well as the normal anti-submarine protection:

but the full requirements could only be met by providing escort carriers, of which we had none. It was the end of 1941 before the first ship of that new class entered service.

On the broad oceans German surface raiders caused us a good deal of trouble by their sudden appearances and disappearances. Yet the losses they inflicted never approached those caused by the U-boat, the bomber and the mine. And in December, 1939, the River Plate Battle showed that, once our cruisers had found such an enemy, he would not easily escape from their clutches. Unfortunately our shortage of cruisers was so acute that the Admiralty had to employ armed merchantmen as substitutes; and they were very soon shown to be far too weak to deal with the powerful disguised raiders which the Germans sent out. In addition to patrolling the focal areas and putting as much shipping as possible into convoy, the Admiralty adopted the strategy of seeking the enemy's secret fuelling rendez-vous, and then striking at the raider supply ships. This was in effect an extension of the principle enunciated by Mahan that ' When ... the enemy confines himself to commerce destroying ... then the true military policy is to stamp out the nest where they [i.e. raiders] swarm '.[1] In 1941, we caught no less than ten German supply ships in the Atlantic, and that drastically curtailed the raiders' operations. Though the last disguised raider was not accounted for until October 1943, they did not cause us serious concern after the end of 1941.

The first phase of the renewed conflict with Germany thus re-moved a good many pre-war misapprehensions. Firstly the convoy system had proved itself once again to be the linchpin of our strategy; but the defence of convoys, on the broad oceans as well as in coastal waters, had to be treated as a joint Navy-Air Force responsibility. Secondly the great potentialities of the aircraft in anti-submarine warfare and in convoy defence had become as plain as the fact that in the war plans the priorities of the duties laid down for them had in some respects been wrongly assessed. But it would take time to provide the right types of aircraft and weapons for anti-submarine

[1] *The Influence of Sea Power on the French Revolution and Empire*, Vol. II, p. 252.

work: and the training of aircrews to make their tactics really effective was hampered by the long-lasting belief that to sink an enemy submarine was quite a simple matter. Moreover our pre-war failure to carry out any joint sea-air anti-submarine training had an unhappy legacy in delaying the introduction of airborne depth charges until the spring of 1941. Minesweeping had, as in the 1914-18 war, become an unceasing burden; and the shortage of long-range escort vessels was proving as acute as it had been in every one of Britain's earlier maritime wars. Steps were in hand to extend their range, notably by fuelling from a tanker in the convoy; but again the need had not been fully foreseen, and it took time to provide the necessary equipment. In spite of the serious difficulties and weaknesses which had been revealed, neither the surface raiders, the U-boats, the mines nor the bombers had gained the enemy a clear and lasting advantage; and our successes against all of them had been reasonably satisfactory in relation to the losses we had suffered. Thus after six months of a war for which we had, as usual, been ill-prepared, it seemed as though the defensive strategy to which we were inevitably committed would gain us time to place our economy on a war footing and to muster our resources; that the silent pressure of our sea power would, as so often before, gradually reduce the enemy's war potential; and that the combined effects of those influences would ultimately enable us and our French Allies to turn to the offensive. Hitler, however, was not the man to allow such processes to develop to his disadvantage, and the events of the spring and summer of 1940 transformed the strategic situation in a manner wholly unfavourable to Britain.

It was the natural reluctance of a democratically elected government to take strong steps against a weak neutral country that gave the Germans the initiative in the Norwegian campaign; and the half-hearted action we did take to tighten our blockade by stopping the German traffic through the 'Inner Leads' merely served to convince the Germans of the need to strike quickly. Yet a more accurate appreciation of the intelligence which was available might at

least have prevented us being tactically as well as strategically surprised. For the Home Fleet did not leave Scapa until 12 hours after
the northward movement of the enemy forces had been reported,
and we failed to intercept any of them before they had landed their
troops. However, in the various clashes with the German Navy that
followed, and especially in the two battles of Narvik (10th and 13th
April, 1940), we inflicted such losses and damage that at the end of
the campaign the enemy had hardly any major warships fit for
action.

As soon as the German intention became clear, the demand arose
to carry troops to Norway; and two separate expeditions were
embarked with the object of recapturing Trondheim and Narvik.
But the haste with which men and equipment were assembled, the
lack of special craft for combined operations, and above all the
impossibility of providing air cover to the expeditions, foredoomed them to failure; and the Trondheim forces very soon had
to be brought home again in a series of hazardous evacuations. The
Narvik operations were much more prolonged, and we finally had
25,000 troops committed to the recapture of a place garrisoned by
no more than 2,000 Germans. Such is the price of failure to intercept an enemy expedition while it is at sea. Finally when we did
capture Narvik at the end of May, we had immediately to evacuate
it, because Hitler's offensive in the west was making such threatening
progress that we could obviously not continue to support an overseas expedition in the far north. Although we brought nearly all
the soldiers home again safely, we lost another of our fleet carriers,
the *Glorious*, when the two German battle cruisers caught her by
surprise while she was ferrying home the R.A.F. fighters which had
been so laboriously carried to Narvik. But the returning troop
convoys were so lightly covered, because of the other very heavy
commitments then falling on the fleet, that we were fortunate to
escape a worse disaster.

The Norwegian campaign drove home several hard lessons. The
first was that the Navy had to admit that it could not work effectively

in coastal waters where the enemy held command of the air: and the second was that the special craft needed for combined operations could not be extemporised, nor could trained men be produced at short notice. The mobility of our Air Forces, on which the defence of the troops on shore and of the ships which supplied and supported them so greatly depended, was plainly inadequate; and lastly, but perhaps most important of all, an integrated command organisation was once again shown to be essential to success in such undertakings.

In terms of strategy the Germans accomplished an important gain. By seizing the eastern hinge on which the invisible barrier of our sea power rested in the North Sea, they forced it far back to the west. Happily in Iceland a new hinge existed on which the barrier could be rehung, and in May, 1940, we occupied that island; but it possessed, of course, no developed naval or air bases suitable for our purposes. None the less Iceland did enable us to maintain our hold over the northern passages to the Atlantic; and because our mid-ocean escorts could use its harbours for refuelling, we were able greatly to extend the zone over which we could give the convoy proper protection. In fact it seems true to say that, in the struggle for control of the north Atlantic, what we gained in Iceland was in the end more valuable than what the enemy gained in Norway. When, however, we started to run convoys to the Arctic ports of Russia in 1941, possession of the Norwegian bases off the flank of the route brought the Germans a great advantage. Such is the un-changing influence of geography on strategy.

The story of the campaign in the Low Countries and France in the summer of 1940 is too well known to require recapitulation: but it is worth recalling how our sea power was used. First to carry naval and military contingents to many continental ports with the object of evacuating shipping, rescuing important personages, denying vital supplies such as oil to the enemy, and bringing home particularly valuable commodities such as gold and diamonds. Secondly small garrisons were thrown into Boulogne and Calais with the object of holding up the German advance against our en-

circled expeditionary force; and, finally, there came the astonishing
climax of Dunkirk, from which over 338,000 Allied soldiers were
rescued in the course of nine days and nights of unceasing toil, in
which ships and craft of every conceivable type took part. It should,
however, be remarked that it was the conventional instruments of
sea power, and especially the destroyers and troop-carrying vessels,
that brought home the great majority of our soldiers. The popular
idea that yachts and pleasure craft, manned by volunteers, rescued
the British Expeditionary Force is a travesty of what actually
occurred. In terms of strategy it was not only the rescue of the
fighting men that was important: for the effect on neutral opinion,
especially in the United States, was profound. And although we had
suffered a severe defeat on land, the German armies were, for the
first time, robbed of the full fruits of their victory. Much less well
known than Dunkirk, but in many ways an even more convincing
demonstration of the resolute employment of sea power, was the
subsequent rescue of 192,000 more soldiers from ports stretching
from the mouth of the Seine right down to the Spanish frontier,
and from those on the Mediterranean coast as well. However, the
complete withdrawal from Europe not only left the enemy in possession of the Channel ports, for which such long and costly struggles
had been waged in the 1914-18 war, but also those on the Biscay
coast of France, which had not been held by an adversary since
1815; and from those bases German surface, submarine and aircraft
raiders were able to reach much farther out into the Atlantic. In
consequence the English Channel was now closed to our shipping
except for coastal convoys, all ocean traffic had to come in and out
round the north of Ireland, our east-west convoys had to take the
northern route across the Atlantic, while those bound to the south
had to make a big detour to keep as far as possible from the enemy's
newly-won bases. All these changes lengthened the convoys' voyages, and so slowed the turn-round of our shipping.

While the crisis in northern Europe was at its height urgent
action had to be taken to replace lost French maritime power in the

Mediterranean. In June, 1940, the Admiralty therefore formed a new fleet based on Gibraltar, and reinforcements were also sent to the eastern Mediterranean and Red Sea to meet the threat from Italy. Most of these ships were transferred from the Home Fleet which, as so often in the past, acted as the strategic reserve of our sea power. Taken together they provided a classic example of a maritime concentration—of 'force massed and handled in skilful combination' as Mahan put it.[1] But the shift of numerical strength caused by France dropping out and Italy coming in was so heavily in the Axis countries' favour that the Admiralty considered whether we should withdraw from the Mediterranean altogether, as we had done at the crisis of 1796.[2] However, the Prime Minister's firmness of purpose, and Admiral Cunningham's confidence in the capacity of his own fleet to deal with the greatly superior Italian Navy, caused the proposal to be quickly dropped. In the western basin the first task placed upon the new fleet was the distasteful one of trying to ensure that the French warships in African bases should not fall into German hands, and that led to the attacks on Oran and Dakar early in July. Pre-emptive measures of that nature had, of course, often been ordered in earlier wars, the best-known instances probably being our attacks on the Danish fleet in Copenhagen in 1801 and again in 1807;[3] but they are bound to arouse violent hostility in the nation against which they are taken, and can only be justified by the seriousness of the emergency—and by success in execution. To the British Government the crisis of 1940, certainly seemed to justify strong measures: yet there none the less remain doubts whether, had time been allowed for negotiation, our object could not have been attained peaceably. For at Alexandria Admiral Cunningham did succeed in achieving the immobilisation of the French ships which had joined his fleet without resort to force. Moreover at Oran we were only partially successful, while at Dakar we failed completely. Where Churchill, who bore a particular responsibility

---

[1] *Sea Power in its Relation to the War o* 1812.   [2] See p. 69.
[3] See pp. 75 and 82-3.

for what was done, perhaps judged the effects accurately was in the attitude of neutral nations, and especially the United States, to our display of resolution. It helped to remove any doubts regarding the British will and capacity to fight on. Nor was the action against the French fleet the only courageous decision taken at this time. For the reinforcements sent to both ends of the Mediterranean left our Home Fleet very weak at a moment when invasion was plainly threatened; and the despatch of more troops to the Middle East reduced our home defence forces temporarily to a level at which it was problematical whether, if the enemy succeeded in landing in any strength, we could contain his beach-head. The parallel between the moves ordered in 1940 and those of 1798, when the British Government reinforced the Mediterranean fleet in disregard of Bonaparte's invasion threat, was mentioned earlier.[1]

Unhappily in September, 1940, the government yielded to the common temptation of using our sea power to launch an amphibious enterprise prematurely, and for an insufficiently important purpose. Although in terms of strategy the possession of Dakar would have brought some benefits, as long as we had the use of Gibraltar and Freetown it could scarcely be classed as essential. None the less a substantial Anglo-French expedition was despatched: but the commanders were handicapped by very restrictive orders with regard to the use of force, and such instructions are bound to militate against speed and resolution in execution—two elements often shown to be essential to success in such undertakings. Furthermore all possibility of achieving surprise was sacrificed; and, having thus ignored several of the fundamental requirements for success in combined operations mentioned earlier,[2] it is not surprising that the expedition ended in fiasco. Indeed, apart from the questionable strategic soundness of the project, its clumsy execution earns for Dakar, 1940, a place alongside Cadiz, 1625, Cartagena, 1741, Walcheren, 1809, and all the other failures in amphibious enterprises with which British history is so liberally punctuated.

[1] See pp. 72-3.   [2] See pp. 28-9.

Far sounder in purpose than the Dakar expedition was the preparation at this time of an expedition to occupy some or all of the Spanish and Portuguese Atlantic islands in the event of the Germans invading Spain and depriving us of the use of Gibraltar. Though the forces never sailed, it is beyond doubt that, had we lost Gibraltar, only possession of those islands could have enabled us to maintain our command at sea in the central Atlantic and in the approaches to the Mediterranean from the west. In the Napoleonic War we twice found it necessary temporarily to occupy Madeira,[1] and it was in similar circumstances that our eyes turned again to the Atlantic islands in 1940. For possession of the Canaries and Azores would have had as great influence on control of the central Atlantic as Iceland had on the northern reaches of the same ocean, and Malta on the central Mediterranean.

In 1940, the defeat of the German invasion plan arose firstly from the failure of their attempt to gain command of the air over southern England, as the essential preliminary to putting their armies afloat, and secondly from the unimpaired and very evident control of the narrow seas which our light naval forces exercised. Though the Germans, and especially Marshal Göring, were reluctant to admit that air power alone could not command the seas sufficiently to produce the conditions in which invasion might succeed, they were finally forced to do so; and it detracts nothing from the credit due to those who won the Battle of Britain to point out that their victory was not the only factor in causing the enemy to abandon his intention. For it was the flotillas based on Harwich, Dover and Portsmouth which, by sweeping the narrow seas day after day and night after night, finally forced the Germans reluctantly to accept that they could not gain a sufficient measure of local maritime control to ensure that their slow-moving convoys could survive even a short sea passage. There is indeed truth in the suggestion that this silent victory was no less important than that won in the skies over southern England; yet because the Germans gave up

[1] See pp. 75 and 83.

without making the attempt it has attracted little attention. One may regret their decision the more because, had they put their plan to the test, it must surely have resulted in a British victory which, for its far-reaching strategic consequences, would have been comparable to La Hogue or Quiberon Bay. In sum the strategy that defeated the invasion threat of 1940 was, *mutatis mutandis*, identical to that which had been equally successful in 1588, in 1692, in 1759, 1798 and 1805. But in the latest instance air power joined with sea power in the traditional function of watching, blockading and attacking the enemy's assembly ports: while in the background lay the heavier forces (bomber aircraft as well as warships) instantly ready to force a decision should the invasion flotillas put to sea. Just as on 13th August, 1805, when Villeneuve turned south from Ferrol instead of north to Brest, Napoleon knew that his invasion plan had failed,[1] so by 17th September, 1940, when Hitler postponed operation 'Sealion' indefinitely, was the new continental conqueror forced to admit defeat.

In the Atlantic the 18 months which followed the withdrawal from Europe produced acute difficulties, not least because our flotillas had suffered such heavy losses off Norway and in the fighting in the narrow seas that our convoy escorts were reduced almost to vanishing point. In 1940 our merchant shipping losses had totalled nearly four million tons, to which the U-boats contributed almost half; and at the beginning of the following year the monthly sinkings were even heavier. By the middle of 1941, however, the new bases in Iceland and Newfoundland were sufficiently developed for us to be able to introduce continuous escort right across the Atlantic, and our escort groups were slowly gaining strength; while the German attack on Russia had resulted in the transfer of most of the Luftwaffe's forces to the east. The combined effect of these changes was to bring us a substantial easement in the Atlantic theatre, and from May to November, 1941, our losses declined sharply. That year, however, saw a powerful revival of commerce

[1] See p. 79.

raiding by German warships and disguised merchantmen. The chief threat came from the two fast and powerful battle-cruisers *Scharnhorst* and *Gneisenau*, which were loose in the north Atlantic from January to March, 1941: but the pocket battleship *Scheer* was working in the south at the same time the heavy cruiser *Hipper* carried out a brief foray, and no less than six disguised raiders were at sea as well. Our convoy system was, however, by this time far more widespread than in 1940, and the Admiralty was giving as many convoys as possible a battleship or heavy cruiser as ocean escort. No German warship or disguised raider ever successfully attacked a convoy which had such an escort, and the mere presence of a single battleship saved several convoys without a shot being fired. This arose because the enemies which approached them simply dared not risk incurring damage on the high seas when they were far from any base to which they could return for repairs. Indeed in both wars of this century the lack of overseas bases, and the fact that our sea power made it impossible for the Germans to acquire even temporary bases, was probably the greatest handicap under which their *guerre de course* laboured—as one sees very clearly from their repeated attempts to establish secret fuelling rendezvous in remote harbours. It thus happened that throughout the war nearly all the losses inflicted by enemy surface raiders were among merchantmen sailing independently, or those which had recently dispersed from escorted convoys.

When the German battle cruisers and the *Hipper* returned to Brest, whence they could easily threaten all our Atlantic convoys, we instituted what was in fact a blockade of that base—though in a different form from the long blockades conducted by Hawke, Cornwallis and Keith during the Seven Years' and Napoleonic Wars. In 1941 we did at first try to keep heavy ships cruising off Brest: but, as in earlier conflicts, we found this excessively exhausting to ships and men. Thenceforth the blockade was therefore conducted by submarines, by minelayers, and above all by the bombers of the Royal Air Force. The result was at least as successful as any of our earlier blockades; since the enemy squadron was not only kept in port from March, 1941, until February, 1942, but both battle cruisers suffered serious damage at the hands of the bombers. This was the first successful application of air power to this historic strategy; for the attempts against enemy warships in their home bases, made at the beginning of the war, had failed completely.

The climax to the German surface ship raiding came in May, 1941, with the sortie of the *Bismarck* and *Prinz Eugen*. The two battle cruisers from Brest were originally to have joined in, but the blockade of that base completely frustrated such a purpose. The long pursuit of the *Bismarck* and her consort began disastrously in the Denmark Strait in the early hours of 24th May, when in a few fatal minutes the *Hood* was blown up and the *Prince of Wales* damaged. This was the last occasion when a battle squadron was handled strictly according to the principles laid down in the 1939 issue of the Fighting Instructions, which stated that ' prior to deployment the Admiral will control the movements of the battle fleet as a whole '; and in their rigidity one may detect an echo of the 18th century Fighting Instructions, whose prolonged and cramping influence on British tactics was mentioned earlier.[1] The Admiral brought his squadron into action against the *Bismarck* from an unfavourable bearing, with his ships in close order and only half their armaments able to engage, thus sacrificing the greatest advantage the British squadron possessed—namely its heavier weight of broadsides. Three days of anxious search and pursuit followed the disaster in the Denmark Strait: but they ended triumphantly—and just in time. For when the fleeing enemy was caught he was only some 450 miles from the shelter of Brest, and the British ships were running short of fuel.

Several points of strategic interest arise from the chase of the *Bismarck*. The first concerns the very large number of major warships (two aircraft carriers, three battle cruisers, four battleships and eight heavy or light cruisers) which we had to deploy in order

[1] See pp. 46-7, 65 and 80-1.

to locate and shadow the enemy, and bring him to decisive action. This experience entirely confirmed that of earlier wars, in which a small number of raiders invariably forced on us a great dispersal of strength. Secondly one may admire the Admiralty's far-sighted action in calling the Gibraltar squadron north to the Bay of Biscay well before they were certain that the German warships were bound for Brest. For it was the torpedo-bombers of the *Ark Royal* which so slowed down the *Bismarck* that the Home Fleet battleships were able to bring her to action. This was a remarkable demonstration of the flexibility of sea power, since, only six days before she crippled the German battleship in the Atlantic, the carrier had been well inside the Mediterranean flying off Hurricanes to Malta. Finally we may remark the vital part played by shore-based reconnaissance aircraft, one of which re-sighted the *Bismarck* after she had been lost for more than 30 critical hours. Furthermore the patrol which that aircraft was ordered to fly was based on the personal conviction of Sir Frederick Bowhill, C-in-C, Coastal Command, who had served many years at sea before joining the R.A.F., that the enemy would not steer directly for Brest, but would set course to make a landfall at Cape Finisterre. If accurate reconnaissance and enemy reporting must ever play a vital part in maritime operations, and the long-range shore-based aircraft has shown itself to be an excellent instrument for carrying out that traditional function of the cruiser, knowledge of the sea and understanding of seamen's habits of mind can still produce singularly rewarding results.

Meanwhile in the Mediterranean Admiral Cunningham had rapidly established a marked ascendancy over the Italian Navy. By a series of successful actions, and by the rising offensive of our Malta-based forces against the Italian supply routes to Africa, he placed the entire overseas land forces of Italy in jeopardy. Then came General Wavell's sweeping victories on land in the early days of 1941; and all the time our control of the Indian Ocean and Red Sea was making it possible for troops carried from many different points of the compass to advance into and finally conquer the whole of the Italian East African empire. In fact not the least interesting strategic phenomenon of this phase is the far-spread extent of our seaborne troop movements. While Canadian soldiers were crossing the North Atlantic to Britain, a steady stream of reinforcements was leaving these shores in the monthly WS convoys for the Middle East, to which Australians and New Zealanders were also being carried from the remote Antipodes, and Indian and South African soldiers from their home countries. Indeed no period of the war, not even the time of the great seaborne offensives of later years, demonstrates better how the happy possessor of sea power can, in the words of Francis Bacon, ' take as much or as little of the war as he will '.[1]

The great successes of 1940–41 in the Mediterranean and Middle East brought Italy so near to collapse that her Axis partner had to intervene to save her, and it was the arrival of the Luftwaffe in Sicily and of about a score of Dönitz's U-boats in the Mediterranean that turned the tide temporarily against us. Between them they came so near to gaining control over the cross-Mediterranean sea routes that it was now our position in the Middle East that was imperilled. Thus can the loss or gain of control over disputed waters drastically affect the fate of distant land campaigns.

Meanwhile the British Government's decision to send troops to Greece had not only brought General Wavell's offensive to a halt, but had thrown a great additional strain on the fleet. Then the heavy losses suffered in the evacuation from Greece and Crete, mostly at the hands of the Luftwaffe, almost crippled our sea power. Judged solely from the strategic point of view (and ignoring the political implications) the decision to send an expeditionary force to Greece is surely open to criticism; for we had no hope of maintaining it in the face of German land and air superiority. Moreover by putting all the resources which could be spared from the Middle East into Crete we might well have gained as much from the possession of that

[1] Essay No. 29, *Of the true greatness of Kingdoms and Estates* (1625).

strategic island as we lost from the enemy's conquest of the Greek mainland; and it is a reasonable supposition that the resources wasted in Greece would have been sufficient to turn the tide in the close-run battle for Crete that followed our evacuation of the Peloponnese.

We have already remarked how Malta, because of its situation near the intersection of the north-south and east-west Mediterranean sea routes, held the key to control of the central basin. From January, 1941, until November, 1942, the enemy attempted, with varying persistence, to put it out of action by bombing; and in April, 1942, he came near to accomplishing that purpose—at any rate temporarily. The German and Italian authorities seem to have realised that a permanent solution could only be achieved by invasion, and they certainly planned to carry out such an undertaking. But a shift of priorities from Malta to the western desert, combined with the lack of a properly trained assault force, caused them to postpone the plan, and the opportunity was allowed to pass. Though the bombing inflicted serious damage on the island base, it soon showed remarkable powers of recovery: and enemy air power, acting in isolation from the other arms, thus failed to achieve a decision. The defence of the island, on the other hand, produced an outstanding example of a co-ordinated effort by the naval, air and military commanders and the civil authorities; and that, backed by courage, resource and improvisation, brought it through the months of crisis. Probably the greatest factor in that achievement was the development of the technique of flying R.A.F. fighters to the island from naval carriers. But all the stores, fuel and reinforcements had to be carried in by sea, sometimes in heavily-defended convoys, sometimes in single merchantmen, and often in fast warships; while submarines acted as emergency supply vessels throughout the long siege. If it was the fighter aircraft that defeated the Luftwaffe over Malta, as they had done over Britain, it was our sea power that kept them flying and the guns firing, and also fed the gallant island's people. However, the inter-service aspects of the defence of Malta reached far beyond the island itself, since our convoys from the east could not reach it unless the Army held the desert airfields in Libya. Thus the land, sea and air campaigns were inseparably intertwined, the fortunes of each depending on the other two; and it was by welding all three into a single strongly forged strategic weapon that we achieved our purpose of first defending Malta, and then turning it into an offensive base from which our sea and air forces could strike at the Axis communications to Africa.

Towards the end of 1941, when our sea services were already strained to the utmost to contain the ambitions of Germany and Italy and to nourish our Army in Africa, the increasingly hostile attitude of Japan produced a most difficult strategic problem. For by gaining the use of strategically placed bases on the coast of French Indo-China, and then invading Thailand, the threat to Malaya and the rich islands of the eastern Archipelago had become too plain to be ignored. Unfortunately the recent heavy losses suffered by the Royal Navy, especially in the Mediterranean, had destroyed all possibility of carrying out the Admiralty's original plan to send a properly balanced fleet to Singapore. The issue to be decided by the War Cabinet was, therefore, what should be done with such ships as could be spared for the Far East. The Admiralty wished to build up a force based on Ceylon, where it would be well placed to cover the Indian Ocean, and whence it could move to Singapore if developments demanded its presence and the risks appeared acceptable. But the Prime Minister and Foreign Secretary (Mr. Eden) considered that the arrival of a small squadron of fast and modern ships at the eastern base would deter Japan's aggressive designs, and the Admiralty finally, though reluctantly, yielded to their views. Thus early in December the *Prince of Wales* and *Repulse* arrived at Singapore, and Admiral Phillips at once set about the difficult task of trying to build an integrated fleet out of the heterogeneous collection of British, Dutch, Australian and New Zealand warships which might come under his command. He also tried to obtain the co-operation of the American Asiatic Fleet, which was based on the Philippines. But before such plans and purposes had made any progress Japan struck, and in the endeavour to intercept an invasion fleet bound for north-eastern Malaya both Phillips's big ships were sunk by a Japanese air striking force. This disaster put in train a process of disintegration which ended only with the complete elimination of Allied sea power from the whole South Pacific. The consequences were the loss of the whole of the vast and rich territories for which we were responsible, the development of a serious threat to Australia and New Zealand, and a cataclysmic decline in the prestige of the white races throughout the Far East. Basically all those results can be traced back to our failure to build a two-ocean Navy at the time when Japan's attitude towards us had completely changed in the 1920s; for without such a Navy, Singapore was useless. On the strategic plane it is of course clear that the despatch of Phillips's ships to so remote a theatre, without any air support, and with no hope of quick reinforcement, was completely unsound; and that the Admiralty's purpose of building up our strength in Ceylon—to which we actually reverted early in 1942— was greatly to be preferred. That certainly would not have saved Malaya and the East Indies. But because it was very difficult for the Japanese to conduct extended operations in the Bay of Bengal, it might have saved Rangoon and Burma; and it surely would have shortened the time needed to recover from the shock of the first Japanese onslaught. One can even visualise that, with some help from America, a decisive naval battle might then have been fought in the Indian Ocean in 1942. But the disaster off Malaya on 10th December, 1941, meant that the process of recovery was immensely retarded, and that the counter-offensive, when it came, was launched from the opposite direction. Lastly in this sorry tale we may note how the sweeping Japanese successes stemmed entirely from the carrier air power of their main fleets, and from their skill and efficiency in the techniques of amphibious warfare.

VI

The period of balance

1942-3

In the Atlantic the first consequence of the Japanese attack was to provide Dönitz with a golden opportunity to exploit American unpreparedness by sending his U-boats to attack shipping off their eastern seaboard, where it was still sailing in peacetime fashion. Unreadiness for war being endemic in democratically-governed countries one should not judge the Americans too harshly on that account. What did at the time arouse strong feelings in London, and still seems very hard to explain, was their reluctance to institute convoy; since for more than a year we had been giving them all our hard bought experience, and their ' observers ' had been present in all our fleets to study our methods at first hand. It was true that, with many of their best ships urgently needed in the Pacific, the forces they could allocate to trade protection were slender. But they continued to employ them on patrols and hunting long after the ineffectiveness of such practices had again been convincingly demonstrated. It seems likely that the repetition of this error derived from American acceptance of the hoary fallacy that patrols and hunting were ' offensive ', and so in some way superior to the ' defensive ' strategy of convoy and escort; but the cost was again extremely heavy. During the first six months of 1942, the U-boats sank 585 ships of over three million tons, about a third of which were destroyed in the western Atlantic by a very small number of enemies (never more than two dozen), who themselves suffered only slight losses. When in April, the Americans did begin to convoy shipping off their east coast the U-boats moved south to the Caribbean, and there too they reaped a rich harvest until the convoy system was made effective in July.

The most favourable developments in this unhappy period were, first, that the Americans did manage to make all anti-submarine air operations a naval responsibility: and, secondly, that in the middle of the year we came to an agreement to divide the Atlantic into British and American strategic areas. A 'Change of Operational Control' line was established in mid-ocean, and the responsibility for the defence of convoys was switched from London to Washington or vice versa as they crossed it.

In Britain the very heavy losses suffered all over the world at this time, and the fact that the strain on the Royal Navy was obviously becoming heavier than it could bear, caused the Admiralty to seek relief from the one direction where it seemed possible that some easement of the burden might be obtained—namely by transferring a proportion of the R.A.F.'s effort from bombing Germany to the struggle at sea. This led to a long controversy in the Chiefs of Staff Committee and the Cabinet. But in the outcome, although a slight shift of emphasis was agreed, the bombing of Germany continued to be given priority, and Coastal Command continued to be starved of the long-range aircraft which alone could provide really effective air escorts far out in mid-Atlantic. As an example of the comparative importance attached to the bombing campaign and the maritime war, when the much publicised 'Thousand bomber raids' on German cities were started in May, 1942, large numbers of Coastal Command aircraft were lent to Bomber Command; but the latter always strenuously resisted any suggestion of a re-allocation of strength in the opposite sense. Observing that losses in convoy were very rare when both sea and air escorts were present, that shortage of shipping was the controlling factor in all Allied strategic purposes almost to the end of the war, and that we now know that the bombing campaign did not produce anything like the results claimed at the time, nor did it have appreciable effects in U-boat production until late in 1944, it is difficult not to conclude that our priorities were wrong.

The critical situation at sea in 1942 also caused the old question of the control of shore-based maritime aircraft to be reopened. In the Atlantic the joint Navy-R.A.F. system, under which operational control was vested in the Admiralty, worked well—largely because of the sympathetic understanding that existed between the commanders involved; and the rejection of the proposal made by Lord Beaverbrook at the end of 1940 that the Admiralty should take over Coastal Command was probably justified. Equally the refusal of the suggestion, put forward early in 1943, that a Supreme Commander should be given authority over all services of all nationalities taking part in the Battle of the Atlantic was undoubtedly wise. But in operations where events moved very fast and the initiative rested with the enemy, as commonly occurred around our coasts, it was much more difficult to make the joint system, which always demanded frequent consultations between the naval and air authorities, work efficiently. For in such cases decisions had to be made swiftly, and concentration of effort at the critical time and place was essential to success. In February, 1942, the escape of the German Brest squadron up-Channel to Germany, which aroused widespread indignation at the time, may be attributed more to the lack of unified command than to any other single factor; and in the autumn of the following year, when the pocket-battleship *Lützow* made her way unscathed from Narvik to the Baltic, similar weaknesses were revealed. Although from the strategic point of view the removal of the Brest squadron from its commanding position on the flank of our Atlantic convoy routes was a favourable development, as was the return of the *Lützow* from north Norway, one may feel that the enemy should not have scored such tactical successes—the more so since in both cases the Admiralty had been able to give adequate warning of his probable intentions.

In our home waters the entry of Russia into the war in June, 1941, soon produced a change in the strategic responsibilities of the fleet. For its main functions were switched from the guardianship over the northern passages to the Atlantic to the stormy and ice-bound approaches to the Russian ports on the Barents and White Seas. The despatch of supplies to Russia by that difficult route was made necessary by the enemy's control over the Aegean which, together with Turkey's neutrality, barred the Dardanelles and the way to Russia's Black Sea ports: by the physical difficulty of sending supplies overland from the Persian Gulf, and by the command Japan held over the approaches to the harbours of the maritime provinces of Siberia. But use of the 2,000 mile long Arctic route was itself beset by grave strategic handicaps. Because the enemy possessed air and naval bases in north Norway and Finland right on its flank, little deviation from the direct course was possible. In summer the continuous daylight acted wholly in the enemy's favour: and, lastly, the shallow approaches to Murmansk and Archangel could easily be infested with mines. Thus do geography and meteorology, even in the era of man's extended mastery over the elements, still exert a profound influence on strategy.

From their beginning in September, 1941, until the early months of the following year the Arctic convoys actually ran smoothly, and losses were comparatively light—chiefly because the Germans did not at once realise how great a volume of supplies was reaching Russia by that route. When, however, early in 1942, Hitler became obsessed with the idea that we intended to invade Norway (a misconception that we were happy to encourage), and the importance of the traffic to the Russian Arctic ports had become plain to the Germans, they transferred all their most powerful warships to Norwegian bases, they greatly reinforced the Luftwaffe squadrons in the same country, and they sent two flotillas of U-boats to work in the Barents Sea. Thenceforth the enemy's strategic advantages began to tell. For we found it almost impossible to provide adequate heavy ship cover for the Arctic convoys so far from our home bases; and, as we still lacked escort carriers, it was also very difficult to defend the merchantmen against air attacks. In March, 1942, the *Tirpitz* made her first lunge at a convoy, and although she failed to find it, and narrowly escaped being brought to action by the Home Fleet, she got safely back to harbour. Though the Germans were, we now know, worried by this experience, and decided that in future they would not hazard the battleship when an encounter with our aircraft carriers might be expected, to the Admiralty the episode seemed to underline the heavy risks involved in these operations, which had recently cost us two valuable cruisers. They therefore proposed to suspend the convoys during the summer months; but the naval view had to give way to the heavy pressure exerted by President Roosevelt and Marshal Stalin in favour of continuing them. In July all our apprehensions were fulfilled by a serious disaster befalling an outward convoy (called PQ 17) after the Admiralty, believing that the *Tirpitz* was about to attack, had ordered it to scatter. This was a very unhappy example of the errors and misunderstandings which can so easily arise when a shore authority tries to exert direct control over an operation in progress a thousand miles away. Had the Admiralty merely signalled the intelligence in its possession, and left it to the senior officer on the spot to decide what action should be taken, it is beyond doubt that the convoy would have been kept together. As it was 21 merchantmen were sunk after the signal to scatter had been obeyed. Then the urgent need to fight a convoy through to Malta in August forced us to postpone the departure of the next one to Russia until September.

In the summer of 1942, Home Fleet ships were repeatedly switched between the Arctic and the Mediterranean; since the failure of attempts to supply Malta from the east in March and June had made it clear that the island's salvation depended on getting supplies through from the other direction. A hard-fought battle resulted in two of a six ship convoy from Gibraltar arriving safely in June, and in August the Admiralty therefore mounted an even larger operation. Again it resulted in a prolonged sea and air battle, and in heavy losses to our escorting warships. Though only five out of the fourteen merchantmen in the convoy made port, they were enough—if only just enough—to stave off disaster. Then the survivors of the Home Fleet ships involved returned to their British bases to prepare immediately for the September convoy to

Murmansk. Thus were the instruments of our sea power rapidly transferred from one critical point to another, in each case gaining a sufficient degree of maritime control to achieve the strategic purposes planned by the high authorities. We may also here note how maritime control is often only temporary and local, the naval forces carrying along with them from Gibraltar to Malta, from Iceland to Murmansk, or from Halifax to Liverpool, a sufficient measure of control to enable the merchantmen under their charge to pass through to their destinations. Once the naval forces have withdrawn it is quite probable that the enemy will regain a high degree of command over the disputed zone: but it will avail him little if it is wrested from him on the next occasion when we desire to use that particular stretch of salt water for our own purposes. Indeed it seems true to say that in the application of a maritime strategy the capacity to establish zones of control where and when they are needed may be fully as important as gaining a general 'command at sea'; and that such zones of control are fluid rather than fixed, moving forward as a particular operation progresses, and shifting to a flank if a threat develops from that direction. Moreover recent experiences suggest that the attempt to establish more permanent zones of control, notably in the case of the patrolled lanes for shipping introduced during the 1914-18 war, can prove a strategic error.[1] For permanent control can hardly be won until the opposing forces have been virtually eliminated: and in that case final victory will be near.

Our total expulsion from the continent in the summer of 1940 at once gave a new impetus to amphibious warfare, since it was plain that only by developing the capacity to land troops overseas could we hope some day to fight the German army on its own ground. Although Mr. Churchill at once created the post of Director of Combined Operations, the British services' preoccupation with the many far-flung responsibilities that pressed on them from all directions made the development of the necessary techniques a

[1] See pp. 129 and 131.

slow process. However, designs for the essential landing ships and craft were produced and tested in Britain; and the Americans, for all that they had seen little use for such vessels before they found themselves at war, finally put them into production on a very big scale. Initially the shortage of equipment and trained men limited the scope of amphibious enterprises to small scale raids on the enemy-held coasts. But such undertakings, for which ample historical precedent exists, can produce strategic benefits out of all proportion to the size of the forces employed. In the first place they force a wide dispersal of strength on the enemy, who must try to guard long stretches of coastline against sudden descents from the sea: and it is well known that sterile garrison duties of that nature have a very debilitating effect on the troops. Secondly the raids will give encouragement to friendly elements in occupied countries—thereby extending still farther the police duties forced on the enemy. Our early raids, which were on a small scale against limited objectives on the Norwegian and French coasts, were almost uniformly successful. But as equipment and training improved, and experience was gained, we raised our sights. Thus in March, 1942, a well-planned and brilliantly executed attack on St. Nazaire succeeded in putting the great Normandie lock out of action. This operation provides an example of how a very small amphibious force (only 620 men were involved) can sometimes achieve a success which has real strategic significance: for there was no other dock on the Atlantic coast capable of taking the *Tirpitz*. In August of the same year, however, a large scale raid on Dieppe was a costly failure, and in the following month we suffered an equally severe repulse in an attack on Tobruk. Both of those results can be attributed to causes similar to those which had brought disaster to amphibious undertakings in earlier wars. Thus the plan for the Dieppe operation was excessively complicated, its execution suffered from postponement and delay, and the decision to forgo preliminary bombardments was proved to be a serious tactical error; while in the attack on Tobruk, which was undertaken to relieve the pressure on the Army in the western desert, we pitted far too weak forces against a very strong position, and with quite inadequate preparation.

While the series of disasters suffered off Malaya and in the East Indies between December, 1941, and February, 1942, were still in progress the Admiralty had started the slow process of restoring our sea power by building up a new fleet based on Ceylon—the policy which they had wished to adopt in the previous autumn. Unfortunately the critical state of the Mediterranean campaigns, which were going very badly for us in the western desert and over Malta, and the heavy responsibilities falling on the Home Fleet in the Arctic and Atlantic, made it extraordinarily difficult to assemble a balanced and modern fleet for that theatre. Early in April, 1942, while the Eastern Fleet was still very weak, the Japanese sent their powerful carrier striking force to attack our bases in Ceylon, while other warships scoured the Bay of Bengal. Though we managed to clear the harbours of Ceylon before the blow fell, the Japanese caught and sank a number of detached warships, and also inflicted heavy losses on the unprotected merchantmen which they encountered off the east coast of India. Luckily they failed to find our main fleet, which was working from a secret base in the Maldive Islands. Its strength was, however, so plainly inadequate to face such powerful opposition that the Admiralty ordered it to withdraw to Kilindini in East Africa, whence it could at least cover the vital convoy route to the Middle East. The whole of the Indian Ocean now lay wide open to the Japanese. But, instead of pressing their advantage, their fleet returned to the Pacific to prepare for the grandiose plan of attacking the Hawaiian Islands. In consequence we gained a much-needed breathing space.

In between the successful attack on St. Nazaire and the failures against Dieppe and Tobruk, mentioned earlier, we mounted a combined operation with a wider strategic significance—namely to eliminate the possibility that the Japanese would repeat and extend their recent devastating raid into the Indian Ocean, with the object of gaining the use of bases in Vichy-French Madagascar, whence they could have severed our vital supply route up the east African coast to the Middle East. The troops and their equipment were sent out 9,000 miles from Britain, while warships from the Home Fleet, the Gibraltar squadron and the Eastern Fleet moved to concentrate with the assault convoy off Durban. Late in April, the carefully laid plan was put into execution, and within 48 hours of the first landings the base of Diego Suarez was in our hands. An interesting feature of the operation was that the air cover was provided entirely from carriers—an innovation which the U.S. Navy was to exploit to the full in the Pacific. Although the Japanese threat was in fact eliminated by the American Navy's victory off Midway just a month after the seizure of Madagascar, the strategic importance of the island fully justified the despatch of the expedition. And the acquisition of Diego Suarez did something to mitigate the serious lack of developed naval and air bases from which we suffered in the Indian Ocean. One may find in British history abundant parallels to the strategic purpose behind this undertaking: for the many expeditions to the West Indies in the 18th century were designed to deprive the French Navy of bases in that theatre, and the seizure of Mauritius in 1810 and of the Dutch East Indies in the following year had a similar object.[1]

By the spring of 1942, both Britain and America were devoting great attention to the technique of combined operations, and discussions on the strategic purpose of the first major undertaking in the European theatres were in progress. Though large-scale amphibious enterprises are the very essence of the offensive phase of a maritime strategy, the selection of the moment at which to launch the first of them is a matter demanding very nice judgment. The pre-requisite for success is the ability to establish a sufficiently firm degree of maritime control to ensure not only that the expedition can reach its destination in safety, but that the supplies and reinforcements essential to the rapid build-up of the assault forces arrive on time and unhindered. It is indeed always easier to fling an assault

[1] See pp. 45, 54 and 85.

force ashore than it is to build up its strength fast enough to defeat the inevitable counter-attack, and so enable it to turn to the offensive with the least possible delay. For whereas an initial landing can be effected with only a very temporary degree of maritime control, the steady reinforcement of an army put ashore in an overseas theatre demands a far more durable degree.

For almost exactly five months after Japan's entry into the war her main fleet, whose principal striking power rested in the hands of its highly trained carrier aircrews, had swept all before it—striking at Pearl Harbour, at Port Darwin in North Australia, and at our warships and mercantile traffic in the Indian Ocean with little hindrance, and inflicting enormous losses at trifling cost to itself; while their very efficient amphibious forces exploited the command at sea obtained by the main fleet to carry out a large number of successful combined operations, so acquiring control over vast and rich territories. But in May, 1942, in the Coral Sea battle, the Americans checked the Japanese fleet's victorious progress, and an expeditionary force bound for Port Moresby in New Guinea was in consequence turned back. This did not, however, at once curb Japanese ambitions, and soon afterwards they sent their main fleet east to try and win Midway Island as a stepping stone to the vital Hawaiian group. The Americans were, however, forewarned of their intention, and on 4th June, they inflicted a crushing defeat on the Japanese fleet, sinking all the four aircraft carriers present. Just as Trafalgar did not of itself bring victory in the Napoleonic War, the Battle of Midway did not decide the struggle in the Pacific. But it did make a final Allied victory certain—unless the Japanese managed to reverse the decision by a success of comparable importance. Such is the profound influence on strategy of a fleet action lasting only a few hours.

In August, 1942, important strategic developments took place in the south Pacific. In that theatre, after the complete expulsion of the Allies from Malaya and the Eastern Archipelago, the most urgent need was to establish new bases farther forward than those in Australia and New Zealand, where the Americans were building up their forces. Fiji, Nouméa in New Caledonia and an open anchorage in the northern New Hebrides were selected. But they were all quite undeveloped, and everything had to be carried to them across many thousands of miles of sea from the west coast ports of the United States. Indeed the great distances between bases was always the chief difficulty that had to be overcome in the Pacific theatre; since it produced acute problems in the field that the Americans called ' logistics ', and forced them to devote a very large tonnage of merchant shipping to maintain the newly-set-up bases, and to support the forces allocated first to defend them and then to mount the counter-offensive from them. Though the ancient problems of ' hygiene and supply ' were bound to exert a profound influence on the Pacific campaigns, the British contemporary view was that the American fighting services were extremely wasteful in the requisitioning and employment of mercantile tonnage—of which we were always woefully short. Though strenuously denied at the time our view has recently been substantiated by Professor S. E. Morison, the U.S. Navy's own historian;[1] and it is difficult not to feel that, in the important matter of the economical employment of merchant ships, the Americans had a good deal to learn from our own Admiralty and Ministry of War Transport. Furthermore it is a fact that on this issue the two principal maritime Allies never achieved a properly co-ordinated policy.

Before Allied plans and preparations to turn to the offensive in the Pacific had been carried very far, Japanese southward probes towards the vital reinforcement route from the United States to Australia and New Zealand presented so serious a threat that the Americans decided to strike back quickly. On 7th August, 1942, an expeditionary force mounted in New Zealand accordingly landed on Guadalcanal in the southern Solomons and that led to a prolonged period of very stubborn fighting on land, at sea and in the air for control of the waters around those islands. Gradually, though not

[1] See *The History of United States Naval Operations*, Vol. XV, p. 164 (Little, Brown, and Oxford U. P., 1960).

without suffering heavy losses, the Allies established a local superiority, and early in February, 1943, the Japanese withdrew from Guadalcanal. Then the fighting moved up the Solomon Islands chain
towards the main Japanese bastion at Rabaul in New Britain,
which barred the entry to the Philippine Sea from the south. It was
now that the Americans developed the 'island hopping strategy',
assaulting only those islands which were needed to provide them
with more advanced naval and air bases, and leaving the cut-off
garrisons on others to waste away for want of supplies. This
proved both effective and economical. While one American offensive was thus forcing its way directly up the Solomon Islands
towards Rabaul another, directed and controlled by General
MacArthur, was working to outflank the same position by gaining
control of the Papuan peninsula in New Guinea. By January, 1943,
that purpose had been accomplished, and MacArthur was ready to
make a succession of amphibious leaps to the key bases on the north
coast of New Guinea, and also to seize the off-shore islands which
were needed to complete the isolation of Rabaul. We will return
later to the fulfilment of those strategic purposes in 1943.

By the end of 1942, the victory of Midway and the many hard-
fought sea battles of the Solomons campaign had won for the
Americans such a clear superiority in the most important factor in
the prosecution of a maritime strategy—namely the strength and
skill of the main fleets—that it was possible for them to plan with
confidence the amphibious enterprises on which their offensive
strategy had to be based. The sweeping successes gained by the
Japanese during the early months of that year, when their main
fleets had established almost undisputed control of the South
Pacific, and the rapid decline in their fortunes a few months later,
provide as clear an example of the profound influence of the main
fleets on maritime war as can be found anywhere in all the long
annals of history. The benefits derived from the battles of Lagos
and Quiberon Bay in the Seven Years' War, and from Aboukir Bay
and Trafalgar in the Napoleonic War, were thus reproduced by

Midway and the sea fights of the Solomons campaign in the last war. For those victories won for the Allies a sufficiently firm measure of maritime control to enable expeditions to be sent far overseas to land in theatres of their own choice.

In the western theatres similar developments—namely our mastery over the Italian Navy in the Mediterranean and the destruction or containment of Germany's principal warships—produced similar strategic opportunities at about the same time. It was in July, 1942, that the British and American governments accepted the proposal which Mr. Churchill and his colleagues on the British Chiefs of Staff Committee had put forward at the Washington conference in the previous December, that the first Allied offensive should be an invasion of Algeria and Morocco, timed to coincide with a new British blow against the Axis forces in the western desert, and having as its object the final expulsion of the enemy from North Africa. This proposal was, however, only reluctantly accepted by the Americans, who had pressed for a cross-Channel operation, chiefly to take some of the weight off the Russians. It is in these discussions that one detects for the first time the difference between the British preference for a peripheral strategy, designed to strike a series of surprise blows on the perimeter of the enemy's defences, so weakening his war-making capacity and opening up a way into the heart of his territories, and the American belief in striking as directly as possible at the same objective. The British outlook was undoubtedly influenced by our experiences during the 1914-18 war, and especially by the costliness of the long struggles on the Somme and around Ypres. But there is no doubt at all that in 1942, we simply did not possess the trained men and equipment needed to provide a reasonable chance of success in a frontal attack on the French coast. Indeed it seems certain that, had we yielded to the American view, the failure at Dieppe would have been repeated on a very much larger scale.

Two other points of interest that arise in connection with the strategy of invading North Africa may be mentioned here. The first is that among Allies in war the nation that pays the piper by providing the majority of the forces for any undertaking will, in the ultimate issue, be entitled to call the strategic tune: and in the case in question the majority of the maritime forces came from the British Empire. Secondly the apparent inconsistency between the predominantly maritime strategy which the Americans adopted in the Pacific and their more continental outlook in the European theatre calls for explanation. It seems, however, probable that this arose mainly, if not entirely, from considerations of geography: for in the Pacific campaigns the decision depended on the possession of widely separated islands, and the strategy employed to gain control of them was therefore bound to be mainly maritime. In western Europe on the other hand the large enemy-occupied land mass plainly had to be assaulted sooner or later, and the Americans believed that the heaviest possible blow struck at that objective at the earliest possible time provided the best and the quickest road to victory. Furthermore our Allies were fully conscious of the vast resources of men and material that they could tap, and their ebullient energy and drive were untouched by the years of hardship and endurance to which the British people had been subjected. Thus the British preference for a peripheral approach to the final objective aroused their impatience, and they found it hard to appreciate the reasoning that lay behind the need to husband our strength and deploy it to gain the greatest advantage by the most economical means.

The plan for the North African landings provided for assault forces from Britain to be carried to Oran and Algiers, while others, which had assembled and trained in America, were to cross the Atlantic to land at three points on the Moroccan coast. But our shortage of merchant shipping and of naval forces was so acute that the Admiralty could only meet the needs of the overseas expedition by re-organising our entire Atlantic convoy system, by stripping the Home Fleet and our coastal convoys almost bare of flotilla vessels, and by holding back all reinforcements which had been destined for overseas theatres, and especially for the Eastern Fleet. To give only one example of what these measures entailed, the Sierra Leone and Gibraltar homeward convoys were temporarily stopped, and ships from South Africa were routed either by way of Trinidad or through the Straits of Magellan and the Panama Canal to New York, whence they would cross to Britain in normal North Atlantic convoys.

The outward movement of the expeditionary force from Britain actually started in mid-October, 1942, and by the end of that month a stream of convoys and of warships was heading south-west far out into the Atlantic, before turning east for Gibraltar. No losses at all were suffered while on passage in the Atlantic. But it was fortunate for us that the most favourably placed group of U-boats was fortuitously attracted to a homeward-bound mercantile convoy, with which it became heavily engaged just when the troopships bound for Oran and Algiers slipped through to Gibraltar. The enemy, though aware that some major enterprise was afoot, was completely in the dark regarding our true intentions, and the secrecy in which the expedition had been prepared, combined with our various deceptive ruses, enabled us to achieve complete surprise. The landings took place in the early hours of 8th November, while it was still dark: since military opinion held that a night assault would increase the likelihood of surprising the enemy, and that view was allowed to override the naval preference for making the approach and first landings in daylight. In fact the advantages expected to derive from assaulting in darkness did not fully material-ise, and were in any case outweighed by the errors in pilotage and confusion on the beaches which resulted. Not until 1944, by which time American experience in the Pacific had confirmed the merits of daylight assaults beyond argument, did the British Army agree to adopt the same practice.

Although in the North African landings a good deal did not go exactly according to plan, within 48 hours Algiers, Oran and Casablanca had all been won, and a few days later we carried assault forces farther east to occupy the ports of Bougie and Bone. Unfortunately we had decided that it was too risky to make a lunge direct by sea to Bizerta, which commanded the Mediterranean 'Narrows'; and the result was that the Germans won the race for Tunisia. Not until May, 1943, did the sea-supported advance of the Eighth Army from the east meet that of the First Army from the west; and our sea and air forces then blockaded the Tunisian coast so successfully that hardly any of the trapped Axis troops escaped.

Though one may feel that the success of the North African enterprise could have been exploited more vigorously, so bringing its full benefits earlier, it none the less transformed the strategic situation in the Mediterranean. In the first place it brought an immediate end to the long siege of Malta. Secondly, once we had won Tunisia, it enabled the through-Mediterranean sea route to be reopened, and that gained us a very large saving in mercantile tonnage, and a substantial economy in the deployment of our maritime forces; for the long route to the Middle East by the Cape of Good Hope, which for nearly three years had been the lifeline on which our entire position in the Middle East depended, could now be closed. Finally our land forces were now poised and ready to strike into Europe from the south—again at a time and place of our own choosing. Indeed it is no exaggeration to say that at one amphibious blow the prospects of the entire war in the west had changed out of all recognition.

While the land forces from Egypt and Algeria were battling their way towards each other in North Africa the struggle against the U-boats in the Atlantic was moving into a decisive phase. In March, 1943, British, American and Canadian naval representatives met in conference in Washington, and the proposal by the Americans that they should withdraw entirely from North Atlantic escort duty, which at first caused us some alarm, was finally accepted on condition that they took over greater responsibilities in the southern waters of the same ocean. Britain and Canada thereafter shared the full burden of North Atlantic escort duty, and a new command was

established at Halifax to control all movements to the west of the
'Change of Operational Control' line, which was moved to 47°
West. But before this reorganisation could take effect the battle
suddenly moved to a climax. In March we suffered such heavy
losses, especially in the 'air gap' south of Greenland which could as
yet be reached only occasionally from the bases in Iceland and Newfoundland, that it seemed possible that the convoy system—the
linchpin of our maritime strategy—was failing us. Happily in the
same month the Admiralty was able to fulfil a long desired purpose,
which our chronic shortage of flotilla vessels had so far made impossible, and five 'Atlantic Support Groups' joined in the fray.
Moreover included in them were the first escort carriers to enter
service since the prototype of that class had been sunk at the end of
1941. The Support Groups were controlled from the headquarters
of the Western Approaches Command at Liverpool, and as soon as a
threat appeared to be developing against a particular convoy one or
more of them was sent to reinforce its escort. In April, 1943, a
number of severe convoy battles produced no decisive advantage to
either side, but our shipping losses fell to less than half those suffered
in March; and in the following month the tide suddenly turned.
Firstly a slow outward convoy was fought through a concentration
of some thirty U-boats; and its escort, reinforced by two Support
Groups at critical moments, sank five enemies. The sea and air
escorts of several other convoys inflicted further losses, and towards
the end of the month a slow Halifax convoy arrived in Britain completely intact, the escorts having disposed of five more U-boats on
the way across. On 23rd May, silence suddenly fell on the Atlantic
battle ground, and although we could at first hardly believe it, the
Germans had actually withdrawn. They had, we now know, lost
33 U-boats in three weeks, and the toll taken during the whole
month of May, 1943, was 41. This was the first and greatest victory
over the most dangerous *guerre de course* ever waged against British
shipping; and to-day it is abundantly plain that it was won by the
hard-driven British and Canadian Atlantic escort vessels, by the

Support Groups which came to their help at need, by our few escort carriers, and by Coastal Command's tiny force of 'Very Long-Range' aircraft. After this defeat the Germans increasingly sent their U-boats far afield, to seek ill-protected targets in remote waters. But the success of such a strategy depended very largely on their ability to refuel the boats at sea, and, except in the Indian Ocean, the use of surface supply ships was now out of the question. They therefore equipped and sent out special supply submarines (called 'milch cows'); while we and the Americans concentrated on finding their secret fuelling rendezvous—exactly as we had done in the case of the surface raiders of the first period of the *guerre de course*.[1] For a time the distant U-boats did quite well, especially in the Indian Ocean, since it was impossible for us to be strong everywhere and all the time. But with the ever extending use of convoy, and the introduction in overseas theatres of the system for co-ordinating and controlling our sea and air anti-submarine forces that had proved itself in the Atlantic Battle, we gradually gained the upper hand over them.

In the summer of 1943, the big effort that Coastal Command had for a long time been putting into its patrols over the U-boats' transit routes across the Bay of Biscay at last reaped a rich reward. However, the short period of high success derived mainly from Dönitz's error in ordering his boats to stay on the surface *by day* to fight it out with our aircraft. During the 94 days (1st May–2nd August) that the order remained in force the air patrols sank 28 U-boats and damaged 22 others; but once the order had been rescinded their successes returned to the very moderate level at which they had stood before it was introduced. There is indeed no doubt at all that, taking the war as a whole, convoy air escorts were vastly more effective than patrols—just as surface ship escorts repeatedly proved greatly superior to hunting groups. In fact the ancient principle that the escort-of-convoy strategy provides the surest protection to the merchantmen, as well as the best chance of striking

[1] See p. 160

196

back at the enemy, was shown to be as fully applicable to the new instruments of war (the maritime aircraft) as to the older instruments (the surface escorts).

In the autumn of 1943, the Germans renewed the battle against our convoys in the North Atlantic and on the Gibraltar route in the hope that their new equipment, and especially the acoustic torpedo, would regain for them the initiative which they had lost in the previous spring. But such hopes were soon proved vain, and the U-boats were once more repulsed by the escorts with heavy losses.

In October, 1943, the prolonged negotiations on which we had been engaged with the Portuguese Government regarding the use of bases in the Azores at last bore fruit, and the despatch of air and naval forces to those strategic islands greatly improved our hold over the central Atlantic. Other air bases had meanwhile been developed by the Americans in French Morocco, in Brazil and on Ascension Island; while we had extended our system of bases down the west coast of Africa. Taken together these developments meant that a close watch could now be kept on the narrowest parts of the central and south Atlantic, and the passage of U-boats and blockade-runners through those waters thus became far more hazardous. The effects of these changes were soon felt: for in the summer and autumn of 1943, American escort carrier groups achieved great successes in the enemy's favourite fuelling area to the north-west of the Azores, sinking several of his precious ' milch cows '. Other losses were inflicted off Brazil, and in the south Atlantic we caught so many of the merchantmen in which the Japanese and Germans were trying to exchange particularly valuable cargoes that they abandoned the attempt to break through our blockade.

The crisis in the Atlantic in the spring of 1943, and the heavy responsibilities falling on the fleet in connection with the combined operations in the Mediterranean, caused us to stop the Arctic convoys temporarily; and before renewing them we were very anxious to put the *Tirpitz*, which was still lying in Altenfiord in north

Norway out of action. This was a difficult strategic problem: the battleship was out of range of heavy bombers stationed in Britain; experience had proved that to send our bombers to work from the very primitive Russian airfields in the far north was unlikely to produce the desired result; and the Home Fleet rarely possessed more than one carrier. Moreover quite apart from the difficulty of finding suitable weather, the strength of the German surface squadron and U-boat flotillas stationed in the north made it a hazardous business to send aircraft carriers into the Barents Sea. But history contains many examples of daring penetrations into enemy bases in order to attack a particularly important target; and indeed in 1941, the Italians had damaged two of our battleships in Alexandria by such means. Since that time we ourselves had developed a variety of submersible assault craft, by far the most promising of which was the four-man midget submarine. In the summer of 1943, we therefore made plans for a number of them to penetrate the defences of Altenfiord and make a surprise attack on the *Tirpitz* and *Scharnhorst*. On 22nd September, two of the six midget submarines which had set out from a Scottish base in tow of conventional submarines successfully attacked the *Tirpitz*, and damaged her severely. A few weeks later we restarted the Arctic convoys, and it was during the passage of the last one of the year that, on 26th December, the Home Fleet caught and sank the *Scharnhorst*, which had made a somewhat ill-judged foray against the strongly protected convoy. Thus by the end of 1943, the strategic situation in the far north had altered greatly in our favour; for the main fleet which the Germans had assembled to dispute control of those waters had been greatly weakened.

VII

═══════════════

The offensive phase

1944-5

At the Casablanca Conference in January, 1943, the British and American statesmen and heads of the services debated the strategic alternatives which might be adopted after the enemy had been cleared out of North Africa, and the British representatives had once more to convince their Allies that a cross-Channel expedition was not yet a practical proposition. The Americans having, albeit reluctantly, accepted our view on that issue, the choice for the next offensive lay between Sardinia and Sicily. The British at first expressed a preference for invading Sardinia, largely because the forces needed would be smaller, and so the expedition could be mounted earlier. However they finally yielded to the American opinion that Sicily offered the greater rewards, and that it was worth waiting an extra two months to reap them. To-day it certainly seems that the American choice was the better of the two. Assault forces were already assembling and training at many African bases from the Red Sea to Algeria, as well as in Britain and America. But differences of opinion among the soldiers regarding the strength in which we should attack, and the positions at which we should land prevented the final plan being approved until mid-May—which left very little time for the intricate convoy programme to be organised. In the end it was agreed that the British Eighth Army would be carried from the Middle East, from Tunisian ports and from Malta to three sectors at the south-east corner of Sicily, while a Canadian division would come from Britain to make the assault in the Eighth Army's fourth sector. The American Seventh Army, part of which embarked in the United States and part in North African ports, was to attack in three sectors on the south coast of Sicily a short distance to the west of the westernmost British sector. An interesting development was the introduction of ' shore to shore ' assaults, in which the troops would land directly from the vessels in which they had embarked at the assembly ports, instead of transferring from troopships to landing craft on arriving in the assault area. This proved a valuable innovation in a combined operation where the sea passages were fairly short. The movements started in late June, and by 8th July a stream of convoys, comprising some 2,500 ships and craft with over 130,000 British and American soldiers embarked, was moving towards Sicily. It is interesting to recall that in 255 B.C., the Carthaginian expedition embarked for Sicily in the harbours that were used by part of the invasion army of 1943, and landed on beaches a short distance west of the American assault area;[1] and that a similar strategy was adopted by the Arab invaders from Tunisia in the 9th century A.D. In the latter case the historical parallel to recent events is remarkably close. Having landed on the south coast of Sicily the Arabs captured Palermo in 831, then advanced to Messina, whence they crossed to the Italian mainland, established bases at Bari and Taranto, and threatened Naples and Rome. This campaign destroyed the Byzantine Empire's influence in Sicily and southern Italy as completely as the British-American invasion of 1943 destroyed Germany's hold over the same territories.[2]

The landings by the American Seventh and British Eighth Armies took place about three hours before dawn on 10th July, and were all successful. But it was perhaps fortunate that the enemy's initial resistance was slight; for some of the troops were put ashore in the wrong places, and a certain amount of confusion resulted on the beaches and in the offshore anchorages. Though we had progressed some way since the North African landings we had not yet reduced amphibious warfare to the fine art attained later. Furthermore in the invasion of Sicily the close air cover and support pro-

[1] See Polybius I. 38. (Trans. Loeb Classical Library.)
[2] See Bernard Lewis, *The Arabs in History*, pp. 116-7 (Hutchinson's University Library, 1950).

vided to the assault forces left something to be desired. Though losses among the shipping crowded in the offshore anchorages were in fact not at all severe—at any rate by comparison with the experiences which we had undergone earlier in the eastern Mediterranean—the American naval commander expressed strong views on the need to provide carrier aircraft which could be controlled directly from the Headquarters Ships. There was in fact a good deal to be said for this proposal, which was introduced in later Mediterranean combined operations, and was very widely applied by the Americans in the Pacific.

Though everything did not go perfectly in the invasion of Sicily, the quick capture of Syracuse and Augusta by the Eighth Army greatly eased the problem of building up our strength quickly; and within a fortnight of the first landings the Americans had swept right across Sicily to capture the important port of Palermo, whence they swung east to advance on Messina. Unfortunately the British Army had meanwhile been held up by German troops south of Catania, and at the end of the month General Montgomery therefore switched his effort from the direct advance up the coast towards Messina to pass westwards around the great massif of Mount Etna. This surprised the naval commanders, who expected to be called on to carry out new combined operations to cut the coastal road and railway to the north of Catania. But it was not until 16th August that any such project was executed, and by that time the retreating Germans had passed the point at which we landed. Between 3rd and 16th August, over 100,000 Axis soldiers, with large quantities of guns, vehicles, stores and ammunition were successfully transported, *mostly by day*, across the narrow and heavily defended Straits of Messina to the Italian mainland. Observing that we enjoyed virtually complete command of the sea and air at the time it is difficult not to feel that more could have been done to stop that large scale evacuation. Unfortunately the three services involved never made a joint plan to accomplish such a purpose, and the effort of the Navy and Air Force was too disjointed and intermittent to have much effect. It now seems clear that the chief requirements were to put the ports of embarkation, and especially Messina, out of action by heavy and repeated bombing, and to neutralise the many batteries which the enemy had mounted on both sides of the Straits sufficiently to enable light naval forces to gain command of the narrow passage. But in fact the Strategic Air Force was at the time attacking targets on the mainland of Italy, and it was 13th August before the Tactical Air Force's effort was directed to the evacuation traffic. The enemy commanders expressed astonishment that we had not made greater use of our overwhelming air superiority. Perhaps the chief lesson to be drawn from this experience is that to stop a determined enemy from moving troops across a narrow sea passage is as difficult an undertaking as an offensive combined operation, and demands just as much care in preparation and planning, as well as an equally high degree of collaboration between the services. Off Sicily in August, 1943, no such plans were made, and the essential unity of purpose was also lacking.

While the clearance of Sicily was in progress continuous discussions on the next strategic move were taking place between the British and American leaders. Though they were agreed that the Italian mainland should be invaded, it was not until the Quebec Conference opened in August, 1943, that the shape of future operations became clear enough to formulate detailed plans; and difficulties arose with the Americans over the retention in the Mediterranean of assault ships which had been earmarked for the Indian Ocean. If shortage of shipping was once again the chief trouble that beset our offensive strategy, we now began to experience the mistrust that many highly-placed Americans felt towards all our strategic purposes in the Mediterranean theatre. The final decision was that the British Eighth Army should be carried across the Messina Straits to invade the ' toe ' of Italy, while the Fifth Army carried out a new combined operation in the Gulf of Salerno some 30 miles to the south of Naples. The former movement proved easy, and the landings were virtually unopposed: but the Fifth Army, which consisted of one British and one American Corps, encountered a resolute and fully prepared enemy entrenched in a strong defensive position. The landings took place shortly before dawn on 9th September, and serious difficulties were encountered on the beaches—especially in the American sector. The advance inland was slow, and while our beach-head was still only a few miles deep the Germans launched a dangerous counter-attack, which threatened to drive a wedge between the British and American assault forces. This was the type of danger which must always arouse grave anxiety in a combined operation. For it is inevitable that, unless surprise is achieved, the enemy should be able to reinforce the defenders faster than the assault forces can be strengthened. Thanks, however, to the emergency measures taken to rush in more troops and strengthen the naval bombardment forces, by the 15th the dangerous advance had been halted, and thereafter the Allied build-up proceeded steadily. Though all ended happily, and on 1st October Allied troops entered Naples, the difficulties encountered off Salerno emphasised all the well-known hazards of an assault from the sea.

While the landings in Salerno Bay were actually in progress the armistice terms accepted by Italy came into force, and within the next few days the greater part of the Italian Navy passed into Allied control. This surrender, taken with the occupation of Taranto, Brindisi and other ports in southern Italy, and the un-opposed landings in Sardinia which soon followed, gave us a high degree of control over the whole Mediterranean except the Aegean, the Adriatic, the Gulf of Lyon and the Ligurian Sea. Though German bombers working from southern France, and their dwindling number of U-boats still forced us to provide strong escorts to our through-Mediterranean convoys, their attacks never came near to imperilling the Allied offensive on land.

Thus did we achieve the strategic purpose which had always stood first in the minds of Mr. Churchill and his colleagues on the British Chiefs of Staff Committee—to knock Fascist Italy out of the war. The Germans had, however, taken over control of some two-thirds of that unhappy country, and it was hardly to be expected that they would allow us to occupy the whole of it without fighting. What is beyond doubt is that every offensive step which led to the Italian surrender was based on our command of the sea, and that the Mediterranean campaigns as a whole provide a wonderful example of the successful application of a predominantly maritime strategy. Rarely in history can so much have been won at such small cost as from the successive seaborne assaults on North Africa, Sicily and the Italian mainland.

While the autumn of 1943 was producing such favourable developments in the central Mediterranean theatre, we suffered a series of unpleasant reverses in the Aegean. In the surrender of Italy Mr. Churchill, perhaps remembering the tragedy of the ill-conducted Gallipoli expedition of 1915, for which he had been the principal advocate, saw a chance to seize the islands which command the southern approach to the Dardanelles. He believed that, as the Italian garrisons probably would not fight, only small forces would be necessary: and that, if we were successful, Turkey might be persuaded to end her neutrality, thereby opening to us a much easier supply route to Russia than the long passage to Murmansk and Archangel, and outflanking the whole German position in the Balkan Peninsula. This was perhaps peripheral strategy carried to excess. But the Prime Minister's imagination was fired, he urged the Middle East Commanders, whose organisation was entirely independent from the Mediterranean commands under General Eisenhower, not to lose a moment, and to improvise the resources which they did not possess. It was, however, the large island of Rhodes that held the key to the Aegean, and as the Germans had quickly wrested control of it from the Italians, a major combined operation would be necessary to eject them from it; but the resources needed for such an undertaking did not exist in the Middle East. Though we thus had to leave Rhodes in enemy hands we went ahead and occupied Cos, Leros, and a few smaller islands off the coast of Asia Minor. However, command of the air over those waters rested in

German hands, and the warships which we sent to supply and support the island garrisons thus soon began to suffer heavy losses at the hands of the bombers. Though the difficulties always produced by trying to maintain land forces across seas which one does not adequately control soon began to mount, we did not accept the inevitable and withdraw while there was still time to extricate them. Then, early in October, German sea- and air-borne invasion forces landed on Cos, and within a few days they regained the island. None the less we continued to try and reinforce Leros; and in November, after we had again failed to intercept an enemy invasion convoy while it was at sea, we lost that island as well. Whether the strategic opportunity in the Aegean was in fact as great as Mr. Churchill visualised may be debatable. But there can be no doubt that, in deciding to go ahead when we knew that we could not win Rhodes, we accepted heavy risks. On the other hand we now know that, as so often in war, the margin by which the enemy won back the islands was actually very narrow; and it may well be that a quite modest diversion of air strength from the Italian theatre would have tilted the scales in our favour. This was, however, one of the occasions when the Navy and Army felt that the Air Forces were too bent on pursuing their own strategic purposes, instead of giving all possible support to the sister services. It is perhaps unfair for a naval historian to adjudicate on such an issue. Yet it is at least true that at the moment of crisis in the Aegean no less a person than the Chief of the Air Staff signalled to the Mediterranean Air Commander that 'Leros is more important than strategic objectives in southern France or north Italy'. But the Strategic Air Force came under General Eisenhower's command, and the intervention from London did not produce the desired effect. On the other hand it is certainly the case that every diversionary or peripheral undertaking always absorbs more resources than are at first envisaged; and the Aegean venture proved no exception in that respect. And, lastly, the wisdom of launching a series of amphibious undertakings without establishing a suitable command organisation, or ensuring that the resources of all three services were adequate, must surely be called in question.

At the time when we were undergoing these unpleasant setbacks in the Aegean the Americans' strategy was developing very favourably in the Pacific. For on 1st November, 1943, they landed on Bougainville in the northern Solomons, thus gaining the naval and air bases from which Rabaul could be effectively neutralised. This assault from the sea may be said to mark the end of the Solomons campaign, which had begun in August, 1942, and during which the Japanese Navy had undergone a severe process of attrition—especially in its air arm. Allied losses had also been heavy, but they had been more than replaced by the new ships and aircraft now pouring out of the American dockyards and factories. On 20th November, three weeks after the landings on Bougainville, the Central Pacific forces opened a new offensive, and successfully seized the Gilbert Islands. Next the Fast Carrier Task Force swept in strength 1,000 miles farther to the west, and carried out a series of devastating attacks on the enemy bases in the Marshall group, as a preliminary to the assault on those islands. On the last day of January, 1944, the Americans landed on Kwajalein in the Marshalls, and so punched a hole right in the centre of the ' defensive perimeter ' which the Japanese had hoped to hold. Meanwhile in the south the decision had been taken to by-pass Rabaul itself, which was strongly garrisoned. This, however, entailed finding an alternative naval base in which to build up the forces needed for the drive towards the Philippines from the south. MacArthur's choice fell on Manus in the Admiralty Islands, where there was a fine harbour; and at the end of February, 1944, he therefore made a surprise landing on that island. Then he was ready to leap farther west along the north coast of New Guinea to the Humboldt Bay area, which he assaulted in April; and to assist in that undertaking the main Fifth Fleet was switched temporarily from the Central to the South-West Pacific theatre. A month after the capture of the Humboldt Bay bases MacArthur seized islands off the north-west corner of New Guinea, and that accomplishment may be said to mark the end of the campaign which had begun with the landings on the Papuan peninsula at the eastern end of the same island in January, 1943. MacArthur was now ready to swing the direction of his seaborne offensive northwards to join hands in the Philippine Sea with the Central Pacific forces coming from the east. One must pay high tribute to the grandeur of the scale on which this strategic edifice was built, as well as to the skill in amphibious warfare which made its execution possible.

On the Japanese side several of their more serious strategic errors were now coming home to roost. In the first place the idea of holding a vast 'defensive perimeter', stretching from the Aleutian Islands in the far north to the Andaman Islands in the Indian Ocean, was completely unrealistic. For they did not possess the resources needed to accomplish such a purpose. Furthermore they had recklessly squandered one of their most valuable assets— namely their merchant shipping. Not until August, 1943, did they attempt to adopt the escort-of-convoy strategy—which they despised as a purely defensive measure; and the far-ranging American submarines were thus able to exact a heavy toll at small cost to themselves. By the end of 1943, the Japanese had lost nearly a third of their original 6 million tons of shipping, and in the following year their Merchant Navy was almost annihilated.

While the American-conceived Pacific strategy was thus developing very favourably, in the British sphere of responsibility in South-East Asia, where Admiral Mountbatten had been appointed Supreme Allied Commander in August 1943, there had been no comparable progress. True the Eastern Fleet had been reinforced, and had moved back from Kilindini in East Africa to Ceylon in September: but we had not been able to spare the combined operation vessels needed to mount an amphibious undertaking across the Bay of Bengal. Indeed all such projects in South-East Asia were repeatedly bedevilled by the demands of the European theatres; and it thus came to pass that the reconquest of Burma had finally to be carried out by means of a long and very arduous land campaign. One may regret this the more because, by the spring of

1944, the Eastern Fleet had so far re-established command of the Bay of Bengal that it was able to launch carrier air attacks firstly on targets in Sumatra, and then against the important naval base of Soerabaya in eastern Java. It is difficult not to feel that, had we been able to send Admiral Mountbatten the shipping and combined operations vessels he needed, the amphibious strategy which he and Mr. Churchill always favoured might well have proved as successful as in the American campaigns in the Solomons and New Guinea. No theatre suffered from the consequences of our chronic shortage of shipping as enduringly as the South-East Asia command.

The same deficiencies came to a head in the Mediterranean when, late in 1943, an assault from the sea at Anzio, some thirty miles south of Rome, was planned to divert German forces from the defence of the ' Gustav Line ', running along the Sangro and Garigliano rivers, which the Fifth and Eighth Armies were hoping to breach. This was an eminently sound use of amphibious power: but, unfortunately, the attacks on the main front failed to achieve their purpose, and the landing at Anzio was therefore cancelled by the Army Commander. However, within a few days of that decision being taken Mr. Churchill reopened the matter at a conference in Tunis, and it was finally decided to enlarge the assault force from one division to two. The object now became to draw off enemy forces from the main front, in the hope of helping our next offensive against the Gustav Line. But the collection of the necessary ships and craft to carry the enlarged assault force proved very difficult, and was finally only accomplished by recalling virtually all Admiral Mountbatten's combined operation vessels, and cancelling the attack on Rhodes by which we had hoped to restore the position lately lost in the Aegean.

The assault convoys for Anzio assembled in Naples Bay, and the landings took place in the early hours of 22nd January, 1944. Complete surprise was achieved, and within 24 hours over 36,000 men and 3,000 vehicles had been put ashore with insignificant losses. We now know that there was at the time almost nothing to prevent the soldiers driving right into Rome. But the American general in command did not seize the opportunity, the Germans reacted vigorously, and by the early days of February the assault force was contained. A long stalemate, throughout which the Allied navies had to keep the beach-head supplied at a very unfavourable time of year, and in face of every conceivable form of counter-action from the sea and air, now ensued. Not until the end of May did the troops landed at Anzio link up with the Fifth Army advancing from the south; and on 4th June—five months later than we had hoped— Allied troops entered Rome. It is, of course, impossible to prove that, had the assault force shown more vigour during the first few days the desired result would have been achieved much earlier: and it has indeed been argued that it would more probably have led to its extermination by the powerful reinforcements that the Germans diverted to the scene. Such risks are, however, endemic in amphibious warfare, and if we were not prepared to accept them there could be little point in launching the undertaking. Mr. Churchill, being its chief protagonist, was of course intensely disappointed that the ' wild cat ' he had expected to hurl on shore turned into ' a stranded whale ';[1] and the navies undoubtedly felt that the complete success of the initial landings had deserved a more profitable outcome. Whether it was strategically sound to persevere with the Anzio operation after the first offensive against the Gustav Line had failed will probably remain one of the most warmly-debated issues of the war: but the operation does at least provide an example of a faultlessly planned and executed assault from the sea.

During the first six months of 1944, we gradually extended our maritime control northwards up both the coasts of Italy. While the light naval forces deployed in the Adriatic conducted a vigorous offensive against the coastal traffic on which the German forces in the Balkans largely depended, and co-operated with the Yugoslav Partisans in many small harassing raids on enemy bases and communications, those working in the Ligurian Sea also kept up a

[1] *The Second World War*, Vol. V, p. 432 (Cassell, 1952).

heavy pressure against the convoys by which the Germans attempted to ship supplies to ports close up to the fighting front. In June, a mainly French assault force was carried from Corsica to seize Elba. But by the time the operation took place the Fifth Army's rapid advance to the 'Gothic Line' had taken it beyond the adjacent coast of the mainland, and the island was therefore no longer needed as an Allied advanced base.

Meanwhile nearly all the Mediterranean Fleet's larger warships and many combined operation vessels had been recalled to Britain to prepare for the invasion of Normandy; and it is to that great enterprise that we must next briefly turn. So much has been written about operation 'Neptune' (the naval side of 'Overlord', as the whole undertaking was called) that it would be redundant to attempt to describe it here. In terms of strategy its importance lies in the fact that it marked the climax of four years of struggle to establish a sufficient measure of maritime control to enable us to launch a cross-Channel assault with reasonable prospects of success. Every vehicle, every bomb and shell, and every ton of stores, had first to be carried across the Atlantic; and the records also show that between 1st January, 1942, and the end of the war nearly three million fighting men from America and Canada arrived safely in Britain, most of them in our special troopship convoys. Second in importance only to control of the Atlantic came the need to establish a clear ascendancy in the narrow seas: and in accomplishing that purpose the fighter and bomber aircraft of the Royal and United States Air Forces joined hands with the light naval forces deployed around our coasts. The German surface fleet in western Europe being by this time very weak, it was the U-boats, the bombers and the mines that presented the greatest threat to the invasion fleet: and very careful plans were made to deal with each of them. Thanks to this, and to the enormous numerical superiority which we possessed at sea and in the air, the U-boats and bombers never proved a serious menace; but the new pressure-operated 'oyster' mine, which we were unable to sweep, did cause some anxiety.

Apart from the 1,213 warships, the great majority of which came from the British Empire, over 4,000 combined operation vessels were allocated to the undertaking; and in addition every branch of the sea and harbour services of the British Merchant Navy, from large liners serving as Infantry Landing Ships down to small coasters, tugs and cargo lighters, was represented. Indeed one of the most interesting aspects of operation 'Neptune' is the demonstration of the fundamental unity of all the maritime services that it provides; each class of ship provided some essential element, and in return received what was essential to it from the other classes. But to organise this very diverse Armada into an integrated fleet in which each officer and man thoroughly understood his task, was probably the most intricate piece of staff work that has ever been demanded; and it is indeed as a feat of organisation and planning, rather than a fighting victory, that the undertaking deserves chiefly to be remembered. Bearing in mind the scope and complexity of the invasion of Normandy as finally carried out, it is difficult not to conclude that we were entirely right to resist American pressure to launch a cross-Channel operation earlier. Moreover until 1944 we had not established a sufficient measure of air superiority over north-west France to offer a reasonable chance of success: and, as we had experienced in Norway and Greece early in the war, and had recently been sharply reminded in the Aegean, to send troops overseas without adequate air support was to offer them as hostages to fortune.

It thus came to pass that by June, 1944, we had met all the fundamental requirements for a large-scale amphibious assault. The objects of the expedition had been clearly laid down by the British and American governments, the plans had been most carefully framed, secrecy had been sedulously preserved, and the men taking part had been adequately trained. In the complete success achieved by the initial assaults we reaped the reward for all the care and attention given to those ancient and traditional needs.

Two other points merit attention here, even though they fall somewhat outside the realm of strategy. The first is that the initial landings were timed to take place between half an hour and two hours (according to the height of the tide in different sectors) *after sunrise*; thus reversing the policy adopted in all the previous Mediterranean amphibious operations, in which the British Army's preference for night assaults had been allowed to overrule the naval preference for making the final approach and the landing in daylight.[1] It seems indeed that the achievement of surprise, which is so important in amphibious operations, depends more on the attention given to deceiving the enemy, on defeating his reconnaissance, and on preserving the utmost secrecy regarding the invaders' true intentions, than on concealing the actual approach of the assault force under the shield of darkness. Secondly we may note the great emphasis placed on preliminary bombardments from the sea in the Normandy plan, and also the manner in which heavy-gunned warships acted as mobile artillery whenever their fire was called for by the Army. Against heavily protected coast defences the naval bombardments were more successful in neutralising the enemy guns than in actually destroying them: which confirmed the limitations of naval gunfire so often experienced in the past, when warships have been pitted against land fortifications. But against unprotected enemy guns, and still more against ' targets of opportunity ', such as concentrations of enemy vehicles, the naval fire proved extremely effective, and the soldiers made full use of the advantage of having it immediately available at call. By contrast to the accuracy of the naval guns, the preliminary bombing, though unquestionably awe-inspiring, accomplished disappointing results: since too many bombs fell wide of their targets.

Once the assault divisions were ashore, and the follow-up convoys were running smoothly, the Navy's chief responsibilities became the rapid construction of the artificial harbours, the protection of the crowded anchorages in Seine Bay against penetration by enemy U-boats and torpedo craft, and the provision of long and

[1] See p. 193.

close-range fire support to the Army. In fact the greatest danger experienced during the build-up period came—not from the enemy, but from an exceptionally violent storm which blew up on 19th June and lasted for three days: which may serve as a reminder that, no matter how great the technical advance in equipment may be, in amphibious undertakings the weather can still prove a major hazard, against which it is impossible to be completely insured. Thus the ancient art of seamanship can still prove of critical value—as indeed it did during the great gale of June, 1944.

Because the supply of an army over open beaches is at the best a slow and uncertain process, which may at any time be subject to unforeseen difficulties and delays, the early capture of a major port is a strategic requirement of first importance in any large-scale amphibious enterprise. In the Normandy invasion the American Army was therefore given the task of seizing Cherbourg as quickly as possible; and that was accomplished on 26th June. But German demolitions had been so thoroughly carried out that another three weeks elapsed before the port was any use to us. Thus the great trouble taken to ensure that supply over the beaches was as efficient as possible justified itself; and, in spite of the havoc wrought by the gale, the Army's plans and purposes were never held up for want of supplies or reinforcements. By the middle of June, four days before the great gale broke, half a million soldiers and 77,000 vehicles had been landed, and the millionth Allied soldier stepped ashore in France on 5th July—almost exactly a month after the first one had done so.

The original Allied intention had been to make a large scale assault on the south coast of France as near as possible to the date of the Normandy invasion. But because that proposal meant transferring substantial forces from the Italian campaign it had never held any appeal to Mr. Churchill, who wished to break into the Po valley and then strike across the Adriatic to the Istrian peninsula, whence he considered that a way could be opened to the Danube valley and the heart of central Europe. This time, however, the Americans were adamant and, as they were to provide by far the greatest share of the forces, we had to give way. The assault did not actually take place until 15th August—nearly six weeks after the Normandy landings. Little resistance was encountered, and the American Army was soon advancing fast to the north and east, while French troops swung west to capture Toulon and Marseilles. Though argument still continues regarding whether the landing in southern France was the best of the strategic alternatives open to us, it did fulfil the urgent need to capture and open up another major port, and it virtually ended the naval campaign in the western Mediterranean. But it probably also deferred a decisive victory in Italy for another six months and more, and it frustrated Mr. Churchill's design to make a lunge for the Danube valley.

An interesting feature of the assault on the Riviera coast was that the close air support was largely provided by a squadron of British and American escort carriers. This practice had been recommended because in the invasion of Sicily the support provided by shore-based aircraft had not been altogether satisfactory, and we had first tried it out in the Salerno landings.[1] There it had not been an unqualified success—largely because the Royal Navy possessed no really suitable ship-borne fighters. Off southern France the aircraft carriers did much better. Yet it was the Americans in the Pacific who proved beyond doubt that, just as a mercantile convoy needed to carry its own air defence along with it, so could the needs of an amphibious expedition best be met by incorporating in it the ship-borne aircraft needed to give protection overhead and provide close support to the assault troops.

We saw earlier how, in January and February, 1944, the American Central Pacific forces had assaulted and seized the key islands of the Marshall group. After that important success our Allies planned to leap 1,000 miles farther to the west, and strike at the Marianas, which barred the road towards the Philippines from the east. The assaults on Saipan and Guam were originally planned to take place on 15th June—nine days after the landings in Normandy: but

[1] See pp. 202-3 and 205.

when the Japanese Navy's full strength began to move out from the Philippines the Americans cancelled the Guam operation, and disposed their main fleet to protect the Saipan invasion force. The 'Battle of the Philippine Sea' that followed is an extremely interesting example of a fleet action during the period when the carrier-borne aircraft was the dominant weapon at sea. First the American reconnaissance submarines won their side a great advantage; for they not only signalled accurate and timely reports of the enemy's preliminary movements, but also sank two of his big carriers. Then there followed an interval during which each side was trying to locate and attack the other's main force. The Japanese actually got their blow in first: but the Americans were ready to meet their air striking force, and repulsed it with very heavy losses on 19th June. Next day the American aircrews struck back, and sank one carrier, after which the Japanese retreated to the north-west. But the American fleet was handicapped by the duty of protecting the Saipan expedition; and it was this, combined with slowness in sending out reconnaissance aircraft to re-locate the enemy, that enabled the surviving Japanese ships to escape. Though the battle cannot thus be classed as a decisive victory, the Japanese plan to catch the American fleet at a disadvantage, while it was hampered by the need to protect the amphibious forces, failed completely; and that sealed the fate of the Marianas. By the end of July, 1944, all the key islands were in American hands. They now held airfields from which their heavy bombers could open a direct offensive against targets on the Japanese mainland: and their strategy had progressed one stage nearer to the assault on the Philippines themselves. In mid-September, only six weeks after the end of Japanese resistance in the Marianas, MacArthur seized Morotai in the Halmahera group, while the Central Pacific forces assaulted the key islands in the western Carolines and the Palau group. Thus did the Central and South Pacific forces finally join hands in the Philippine Sea in the autumn of 1944—less than a year after the former had struck their initial blow at the Gilbert Islands some 2,500 miles to the east

The Americans, however, were determined to allow their adversaries no pause in which to recover their strength and reinforce their defences, and they therefore advanced the date of the invasion of the Philippines from 15th November to 20th October. Furthermore they decided to strike directly at Leyte, in the heart of the group, instead of seizing the southern island of Mindanao as they had first intended. While the assault forces, which had been placed under General MacArthur, were assembling at Manus and Hollandia, the Fast Carrier Task Force struck repeated blows at enemy airfields and shipping in the Philippines, in Formosa and in the islands stretching south from the Japanese mainland, thus cutting the route by which reinforcements might reach the Philippines. These far-ranging preliminary blows, and the careful attention given to softening the defences by air and sea bombardments, enabled the assault forces to establish themselves on shore in Leyte Gulf on 20th October at very small cost. But the Japanese realised that, if the Philippines were to be successfully defended, they must strike back with all the resources they possessed, and had therefore ordered almost all their surviving warships to move against the invasion forces. Their plan was designed to draw the American main fleet away to the north, so allowing two powerful squadrons to reach Leyte Gulf by way of the narrow San Bernardino and Surigao Straits to the north and south of Leyte island. Though the southern force was virtually annihilated in a series of fierce, close-range night actions, the northern force actually emerged into the Philippine Sea early on 25th October, to find only a few small and weakly-armed ships present to bar the way into Leyte Gulf. For Admiral Halsey had swallowed the bait of the decoy force sent south from Japan, and had set off to the north with the whole of his fleet in pursuit of it. Fortunately the Japanese Admiral failed to seize the chance and, after fighting a somewhat desultory battle with the American light forces, he retreated by the way he had come. Though Halsey's carrier aircrews almost wiped out the Japanese decoy force, his impetuous pursuit did produce a very critical situation off Leyte

Gulf, and one may feel that the Americans were lucky to escape so cheaply. None the less the series of battles fought on 24th and 25th October, 1944, together constituted so decisive a victory that never again was the Japanese Navy able to offer effective opposition to the development of Allied strategy. Thenceforth they relied mainly on the 'Kamikaze' suicide bombers to attack our amphibious expeditions: and although those novel instruments (which gave a foretaste of the era of the guided missile) caused us a good deal of trouble, and at times inflicted unpleasant losses, they were incapable of acting as substitutes for the sea power of which Japan had, by the end of 1944, been almost totally deprived.

In Admiral Mountbatten's South-East Asia theatre the last six months of 1944 saw the re-establishment of our control of the Indian Ocean and the Bay of Bengal. Supplies and reinforcements for the Fourteenth Army in Burma thus flowed in almost unhindered, and by September the last of the U-boats, which had inflicted quite substantial losses earlier in the year, had withdrawn. Though the lack of combined operation vessels still prevented the Supreme Commander mounting any considerable amphibious enterprise, our reasserted maritime supremacy did prevent Japanese reinforcements and supplies reaching Rangoon by sea; and the long and difficult overland route from the ports on the South China Sea across Siam was quite incapable of meeting the needs of the enemy's land forces. Furthermore in South-East Asia, as in the home theatre, the long-range minelaying aircraft proved very effective instruments of blockade; and by the end of 1944, they and our submarines, which constantly patrolled off the enemy's more distant ports and bases, were imposing severe delays and disruption on his seaborne traffic. Lastly the loss of nearly four million tons of shipping during the year —mostly at the hands of the American submarines in the Pacific— had left the Japanese with a tonnage which was quite inadequate for the maintenance of their large overseas forces. Although in Burma, as in the Pacific, they continued to contest every position almost to the last man, there comes a point at which even the utmost self-sacrifice on the part of the individual can avail nothing; and when the flow of the barest essentials of food, fuel and ammunition has been reduced by blockade to an uncertain trickle, as was the case with the Japanese in South-East Asia by the end of 1944, that point has surely been reached.

In our home waters the Arctic convoys ran very successfully for the first three months of 1944. But by March we believed that the *Tirpitz* had repaired the damage inflicted by the midget submarines in September, 1943, and it therefore became very desirable to put her out of action again. On 3rd April, a powerful carrier air-striking force accordingly attacked her in Altenfiord. Complete surprise was achieved, and she was hit by no less than 14 bombs: but they were not heavy enough to do lethal damage, and in fact she was repaired within three months. It was the lack of really suitable strike aircraft in the Royal Navy—a consequence of the pre-war policy towards the Fleet Air Arm—that deprived the aircrews of a decisive success on this occasion. It is difficult not to feel that, given good aircraft, they would have been as successful against the *Tirpitz* as the American naval aircrews were against the giant Japanese battleships *Musashi* and *Yamato*—both of which were sunk by carrier air attacks in the Pacific.

After the April convoy had reached Russia safely we had to devote all our resources to the Normandy invasion, and no more were sent until August, by which time the success of the undertaking was assured. Simultaneously with restarting the convoys the Home Fleet carriers made a whole series of new attacks on the *Tirpitz*. However bad weather, and the difficulty of achieving surprise, deprived them of any significant success. Then in September, R.A.F. heavy bombers were sent to a Russian airfield, and they obtained one hit on the battleship with a 12,000 pound bomb, which inflicted such damage that the Germans shifted her to Tromsö to serve as a coast defence battery. But in that base the Lancasters could reach her from British airfields, and on 12th November, they finally sank her at her moorings. Though the

Tirpitz never played a very active part in the war, and the only time she fired her big guns against an enemy target was in a brief bombardment of Spitzbergen in September, 1943, she had a profound influence on our disposition and strategy. As long as she lay in Altenfiord we had to give every Arctic convoy heavy ship cover; and that meant that reinforcements which were urgently needed by the Eastern Fleet had to be retained at home. Moreover the need to blockade her in harbour absorbed a very big effort by a wide variety of instruments, such as carrier-borne and shore-based aircraft and midget submarines. The long blockade of the *Tirpitz* in her Norwegian bases did, however, reinforce the lessons derived from the blockade of the battle-cruisers in Brest in 1941-42—namely that the ancient strategy of establishing a firm hold over the enemy's main units had lost none of its effectiveness, and had indeed been strengthened by the addition of the strike aircraft to the instruments available for such purposes.

In western Europe the break-through by the Allied armies in August, 1944, and their rapid advance across France and Belgium produced the need for the sea services to open up new ports of supply: since the artificial harbours off the original assault area, and Cherbourg (which was still the only major port we held in northern France), were now too far from the fighting front. Most of the Channel ports were captured early in September; but they were so blocked and damaged that many weeks were bound to elapse before appreciable quantities of stores could be disembarked in them. On 4th September, however, the British Army captured the great port of Antwerp virtually intact; but as the Germans held both banks of the River Scheldt, we were able to make no use of it whatsoever. We will return shortly to the causes of the long delay in opening the Scheldt to the supply traffic without which the Allied armies were almost immobilised.

Well before the break-out from Normandy in August, we had been tightening our hold over the German bases on the coast of the Bay of Biscay. This was another example of a blockade established by sea and air forces; for cruisers and destroyers patrolled close off-shore, Coastal Command aircraft swept and searched for enemy shipping, and Bomber Command attacked the bases themselves. No enemy surface ships broke through the blockade. But the Germans did succeed in transferring most of their U-boats from their Biscay bases to Norway—chiefly because the development of the 'Schnörkel' breathing tube enabled them to stay submerged for very long periods, and greatly reduced the effectiveness of the short-wave radars from which our escort vessels and aircraft had derived such great benefits in the earlier phases. Thus, in spite of the loss of the Biscay bases, the U-boats were able to open a new campaign in our inshore waters in September, 1944: and although the losses they inflicted were never serious, they caused us a good deal of trouble right up to the end of the war.

An important benefit derived from the enemy's expulsion from the Biscay coast of France was that our north-south Atlantic convoys no longer had to make a wide detour out into the ocean, but could approach and leave British ports passing to the south of Ireland. This enabled us to revert to a convoy organisation very similar to that which had been introduced at the beginning of the war, but which the fall of France had forced us to abandon in 1940; and the saving of tonnage was considerable. Thus do favourable developments on land often ease the burden of the maritime services.

With their surface fleet reduced to impotence and their U-boats constantly harried by our sea and air escorts and patrols, the Germans produced a large variety of small assault craft, such as explosive motor-boats and human torpedoes, with which they tried to contest our control of the narrow seas. We had actually encountered some of these craft earlier in the Mediterranean combined operations at Anzio and on the French Riviera coast; but in the Channel the enemy employed them in far larger numbers, and with great persistence. Though they caused us a certain amount of trouble they never seriously impeded the flow of our shipping, and they themselves suffered heavy losses. The lesson seems to be that, although special assault craft can sometimes achieve an important success by penetrating into an enemy anchorage to attack a particularly important target, as substitutes for the conventional instruments of sea power they are quite ineffective.

To return to Antwerp, the long delay over opening the Scheldt arose partly from the disagreement between Field-Marshal Montgomery and General Eisenhower over the strategy to be adopted for the advance into Germany, partly from the slowness with which the British Second Army reacted to the opportunities which arose immediately after the capture of Antwerp to seize the key points to the north of the river, and partly to the First Canadian Army being given tasks beyond its capacity—namely to capture the Channel ports and also clear the south bank of the river. With General Eisenhower's approval Field-Marshal Montgomery first concentrated his effort on seizing a bridgehead over the lower Rhine at Arnhem, and on opening up a corridor to the north-east from Antwerp in order to keep the bridgehead supplied: but by September 25th, the parachute operation at Arnhem had failed. Yet it was not until 16th October that Montgomery switched his full offensive power to clearing the river Scheldt, and by that time the enemy had so far recovered his balance that he was able to offer stubborn resistance. Walcheren, the key island at the river mouth, was assaulted from the sea and land early in November, and on the 4th of that month the Navy was at last able to start sweeping the 80 miles of estuary and river leading to Antwerp. On 28th November, nearly three months after it had been captured, the port was open to deep draught ships.

To-day two conclusions appear inescapable. The first is that the banks of the River Scheldt could have been cleared very much earlier: and the second is that the navies could not restore the armies' mobility until they had gained the use of Antwerp. Though it is a long-standing tradition that, once the Army is ashore, all naval considerations shall yield to meeting the soldiers' needs, it is difficult not to feel that in the autumn of 1944, that principle was carried too far. And in view of the great part that Antwerp has played in British history, from the time of the Spanish Armada down to Napoleon's attempt to develop it as ' a pistol pointed at England ', it is surprising that in none of the high level documents dealing with plans and policy can one find any mention of the importance of the port until some days after it had been captured. Thus it seems true to say that there was a failure in long-term Allied planning, as well as in inter-service co-ordination. And it may be that on the planning side it was the Naval Staff at the Admiralty who should have raised the issue at a high level, and that Admiral Ramsay's operational staff should have represented the naval needs earlier and more forcefully to the Supreme Commander and to Field-Marshal Montgomery. But the clash of purposes in the military hierarchy, and the slowness with which the Canadian and British Army commanders reacted to the opportunities which arose on their fronts probably contributed to the difficulties which arose.

While the Allied armies in north-east Europe were held up in the approaches to the Scheldt, in the Mediterranean the Germans were withdrawing from Crete, southern Greece, and the Aegean islands, where they could no longer maintain their garrisons in the face of our overwhelming maritime superiority. Thus the islands which we had tried to seize a year earlier, as well as the far more valuable bases in Crete and the Peloponnese, all fell to us at very small cost—once we had established a high degree of command over the adjacent waters. In October we occupied Athens, and it was our sea power that enabled us to transfer forces quickly from Italy and Egypt when the Communists attempted to usurp power in war-torn Greece. The prompt execution of the British Government's purposes on this occasion provides a classic example of a far-sighted statesman using the instruments which he had ready to hand to resolve a potentially dangerous threat to his country's interests. To-day, with Greece a staunch member of the Western Alliance, we may be thankful for the vigour and determination with which Mr. Churchill acted in the autumn of 1944—though with scant sympathy from his American colleagues.

By the end of 1944 our command over the Adriatic was almost as complete as it was in the Aegean. With the Germans confined to a toe-hold on the Istrian peninsula, the communications of all their forces in Yugoslavia, Albania and western Greece were gravely imperilled. It was basically the extension of our maritime control to the waters on both sides of the Balkan peninsula that forced the Germans to admit that they could no longer hold what they had gained in 1941: and the same influence brought Turkey, Egypt and other states of the Levant belatedly into the war on the Allied side in February, 1945. Looking back to-day it seems surprising that the Germans made such poor use of the commanding strategic positions which they gained in 1941. Just as in the central Mediterranean the capture of Malta should not have been beyond their capacity, so with southern Greece, Crete and Rhodes in their hands they should surely have striven to drive us right out of the eastern basin before turning on Russia. Had they accomplished those two purposes, North Africa would have been theirs, and the route to India and the Far East, where they could have linked up with the Japanese, would have stood wide open. But after June, 1941, the titanic campaigns in Russia absorbed more and more of their resources, detachments from the Luftwaffe and the U-boat fleet were only thrown into the Mediterranean campaign piecemeal, and the opportunity was allowed to pass. Though it is true that we suffered substantial losses at the hands of the German bombers and U-boats, their effort was never strong enough, nor applied sufficiently consistently, to tilt the scales. And by developing a joint sea-air defensive system we finally overcame them both. In the end the Mediterranean campaign cost the Germans thousands of valuable aircraft, and no less than 68 U-boats.

With the enemy confined to the north Ligurian Sea and the head of the Adriatic we were able to cancel most Mediterranean convoys, and the escort vessels thereby released joined the steady flow of warships now proceeding by way of Suez to the Indian Ocean. There the Eastern Fleet was conducting a rising offensive across the Bay of Bengal, and was also preparing to carry out the combined operations which, at the third attempt, were to regain us the long-disputed, jungle-clad Arakan coast, which commanded the approaches to the Irrawaddy delta from the west. In November, 1944, the British Pacific Fleet, which we had been endeavouring to assemble for more than a year, was officially formed in Ceylon; and in the following January its main units left for Sydney, attacking the oil refineries in eastern Sumatra on the way. To understand what the formation of a new main fleet on the other side of the world entailed, we must retrace our steps to the second Quebec Conference in September, 1944. Although the deployment of British naval forces in the Pacific after the defeat of Germany had been discussed long previously with the Americans, it was not until that meeting that our Ally finally agreed that our fleet should take part in the main operations against the last enemy, and should not be relegated to a subsidiary theatre in the South Pacific. The chief opposition to this proposal, which lay very close to Mr. Churchill's heart, came from Admiral E. J. King, the American Chief of Naval Operations. It is a fair deduction that his predominant motive was determination that the Royal Navy should have no share in the glory of the final victories over Japan—to accomplish which the U.S. Navy disposed of ample forces of its own. Happily President Roosevelt, whatever his misjudgments may have been in his dealings with British and Russian long-term purposes in the European theatre, and in spite of the chronic mistrust which he, in common with many of his countrymen, displayed towards British imperial interests, took a wider and more generous view on the issue of our participation in the final phase of the conquest of Japan; and at Quebec Mr. Churchill's proposals for the fleet were 'no sooner offered than accepted' by him.

However, the despatch of the fleet to the east was a far more complicated matter than merely assembling the warships in Ceylon.

For we had promised the Americans that our ships would be self-supporting in all important respects. Unfortunately Sydney was not well equipped to serve as a main base for so large a fleet, and we possessed no 'intermediate' or 'advanced' bases nearer to the waters where it would be required to work. The problem of finding a suitable 'intermediate' base was solved reasonably satisfactorily by the Americans agreeing that we should use Manus in the Admiralty Islands: but the needs of the fleet while in that base and during its periods of active operations could only be met by putting its supply or 'logistics' organisation afloat. Because of the vast distances in the Pacific, and the lack of developed bases, the Americans had devoted great attention to their mobile 'Fleet Train': and by 1944 it had reached a very high pitch of efficiency. Our fleets on the other hand, had always relied to a far greater extent on fixed bases: and although the Admiralty had realised long before the British Pacific Fleet was formed that its supply organisation had to be built on the American model, it was extraordinarily difficult to find ships, and especially fast tankers, which were capable of meeting the needs. The Fleet Train of some 60 ships finally assembled was a very heterogeneous collection of merchantmen and auxiliaries of many types and nationalities: and if they did in general manage to meet the requirements of the operational warships, the margin was so small that, had the Americans not interpreted very liberally the dogma of self-sufficiency agreed at Quebec, it might have disappeared altogether. Thus it was again proved that, as Sir Herbert Richmond remarked about our earlier wars, 'hygiene and supply are fundamental elements affecting both strategy and tactics'.

It had always been MacArthur's intention to invade the large island of Luzon, where lay the capital city of Manila, as soon as possible after securing Leyte. In mid-December, 1944, as a stepping stone to Luzon, he seized the island of Mindoro, and on the following 9th January he carried his plan for the reconquest of the Philippines one stage nearer to fulfilment by landing in strength in Lingayen Gulf, Luzon, only 100 miles from Manila. But it was not until early March that he recaptured the city from which he had been expelled in defeat in 1942. A few days after the landing on Luzon, the main American fleet broke into the South China Sea, and for ten days the carrier aircrews played havoc among the merchantmen which they encountered off the Asian mainland. This foray may be said to mark the final severance of the Japanese mainland from all the conquests in the South Pacific which they had won so cheaply three years earlier.

After the recapture of Manila MacArthur mounted a series of minor amphibious assaults in the southern Philippines and Borneo, which lasted almost to the end of the war. Though the Americans felt a moral obligation to liberate the whole of the Philippines with the least possible delay, and they also attached importance, which was actually exaggerated, to recovering the oil-fields of Borneo, from the military point of view these operations had little significance. For the Japanese garrisons were by this time so completely isolated that they were bound to lapse into total ineffectiveness.

As to the strategy to be adopted after the reconquest of the principal islands of the Philippine group, one school in America, of which Admiral King was the most powerful representative, wished to seize a base on the China coast near Amoy, partly with the object of supporting Chiang Kai-shek's armies in China, and also invade Formosa. However General MacArthur, as ever the chief protagonist of amphibious strategy, preferred to leap to the Bonin and Ryukyu islands, which lay directly on the sea road leading to the Japanese mainland; and in the end he had his way. In retrospect it is plain that the Americans attached excessive importance to the land campaign in China. For the truth was that, although the Chinese were certainly containing large Japanese forces, the fate of the latter depended—not on depriving Admiral Mountbatten's command of its essential transport aircraft in order to fly in supplies from Burma, nor on establishing a base on the China coast, but on command of the western Pacific. Once such command had been firmly established the whole of the Japanese forces on the Asian mainland would be, to use Mr. Churchill's vivid simile again, 'like cut flowers in a vase'. Apart from the fact that, because the South-East Asia command's purposes were inextricably intertwined with British imperial interests, the Americans preferred to support Chiang Kai-shek, their attraction towards the mainland of China is a curious, though not a unique example of their periodical hankerings after a continental strategy.

The first American leap to the north was to Iwo Jima in the Bonin Islands, only 650 miles from Tokyo, on 19th February, 1945. But before they had actually overcome all Japanese resistance on that tiny volcanic outcrop, much larger expeditions had sailed from the far away Solomon Islands and from Leyte Gulf to seize Okinawa in the Ryukyu group. The importance of both those islands lay not only in their proximity to Japan proper, but in the fact that the possessor of them would command the whole of the East China Sea and the approaches to Japan from North China, Manchuria and Korea—the last sources from which they could draw supplies. Furthermore the capture of Okinawa would isolate the strong garrison in Formosa, which would have been a very difficult objective to seize by assault from the sea.

It was in the assault on the Ryukyu group, which opened on 26th March, 1945, that the British Pacific Fleet first came into action. Although it would be quite wrong to suggest that, had our ships not been there, the outcome would have been any different, their presence did show the Americans that the British Government's determination to fight on until the last enemy had been defeated was fully shared by the men of the fleet: and in the end their courage and skill won the admiration of their Allies. Furthermore one may remark how it was the instruments of sea power that made British purposes and policies tangibly felt throughout the vast Pacific theatre during the closing months of the war.

While the struggle for Iwo Jima and Okinawa were at their height, events were moving to a climax in the Home and Mediterranean theatres. Throughout the winter of 1944-45, we continued to build up the strength of the armies in western Europe, chiefly through Antwerp and Marseilles: we kept a fairly effective grip on the U-boats which were lying concealed all around our coasts: we dealt with the large numbers of specially designed assault craft which the Germans sent out to attack our coastal traffic: the Arctic convoys sailed steadily to north Russia: while the blockade of Germany was all the time being tightened by surface warships and submarines, and by the strike and minelaying aircraft of the R.A.F. The long-range air minelayers were now able to reach out to the western Baltic, over which the enemy had enjoyed almost undisputed control ever since the beginning of the war; and there is no doubt at all that, taking the war as a whole, they proved the most successful and economical instrument of blockade. Second to the air minelayers in sinking enemy merchant ships came the shore-based and carrier-borne strike aircraft; but, in proportion to the successes achieved, they suffered far higher losses than the minelayers. Third in accomplishments stand our submarines: but they were handicapped by the severe restrictions imposed on them during the first two years of the war; while our surface warships, though they sank or captured comparatively few enemy merchantmen after the first six months, were undoubtedly chiefly responsible for sweeping them off the seas and oceans of the world.[1] By their joint efforts the various instruments of blockade had, by the end of April, 1945, brought German seaborne traffic to a virtually complete standstill. As to the U-boats, on 4th May, when Admiral Dönitz ordered them to cease operations, there were still 45 at sea, about a dozen of which were lying in ambush in our coastal waters: nor had we succeeded in sinking any of the new types with much higher underwater speeds. But in the final phase of the Atlantic Battle they caused us relatively few losses: and if they forced us to deploy very

---

[1] The relevant figures for the Home Theatre are:—

Enemy merchant ships sunk by	air-laid mines:	604 (660,000 tons).
„ „ „ „ „	direct air attacks:	289 (574,000 „).
„ „ „ „ „	submarines:	104 (318,000 „).
„ „ „ „ „	surface warships:	86 (303,000 „).

large numbers of escort vessels and maritime aircraft, we did find that, once they had revealed their presence by making an attack, we were generally able to bring them to book. It is worth quoting a few figures regarding the most intensive *guerre de course* that the British sea services have ever had to face. Of the 1,162 U-boats completed by the Germans, 785 were destroyed; and, of the 631 sunk *at sea*, British ships and aircraft shared almost equally in the destruction of no less than 500. The strategic bombing campaign had virtually no effect on the Atlantic Battle until the autumn of 1944, when it did delay the completion of the new types of U-boat. The final statistics show that only 63 U-boats were destroyed in bombing raids, and all but two of those successes were achieved during the last 17 months of the war, when German anti-aircraft and fighter defences were steadily weakening. The strategic bombers did, however, destroy or damage a good many of the German Navy's surviving surface warships during the final weeks, when most of them were immobilised in various Baltic harbours. By far the most effective anti-U-boat instruments were the sea and air convoy escorts, who thus reinforced the old lesson that the escort-of-convoy strategy provides the most effective means both of defending our merchant shipping and of destroying raiders of all types. But the cost to the Allies of the long struggle at sea amounted to no less than 5,150 merchantmen totalling $21\frac{1}{2}$ million tons—a slightly greater tonnage than the entire British Merchant Navy had possessed in 1939: and it was the U-boats, with 2,828 ships of over $14\frac{1}{2}$ million tons sunk, that accomplished by far the greatest share of that prodigious destruction. Observing how shortage of shipping cramped all our strategic purposes throughout the offensive phase, it is difficult not to conclude that a greater emphasis on the provision of sea and air escorts, and a more consistent application of the convoy strategy, would have yielded substantial benefits, and perhaps brought victory earlier. But rare are the statesmen who, when faced by conflicting priorities and subjected to the pressure of an ignorant public which always clamours for more vigorous action and more visible results, will remember that the loss of one single merchantman does not end as she slides beneath the waves. For her entire cargo—perhaps 10,000 tons of it worth several million pounds —has gone too: and another ship must bring in another cargo to replace it. Nor does the loss end with the sunk ship and her cargo: for every future voyage she might have made, and every ton of goods she might have delivered safely at their end has been forfeited. The merchant shipping of a nation is a priceless asset—in peace as well as in war: and the nation that squanders it, and fails to nourish and protect it does so at its peril.

In the Far East the struggle for Okinawa, which began on 26th March, 1945, lasted until nearly the end of June: and during it the attacks by the Japanese suicide bombers rose to a climax. But such unorthodox methods could not possibly act in substitution for the conventional instruments of sea power, which by this time Japan almost totally lacked; and the 'Kamikazes', if they caused us losses and anxiety, were foredoomed to failure. In March, 1945, almost simultaneously with the assault on the Ryukyus, the Americans took steps to tighten the blockade of Japan to a stranglehold by cutting her off from her last sources of supply on the Asian mainland. While submarines infested the Sea of Japan, the main British and American fleets swept up and down the enemy's coasts, striking at shipping and at shore targets almost at will; but it was again the air-laid mine that contributed most to the final phase of the blockade. No less than 12,000 mines were laid in the shallow approaches to Japanese ports and harbours between March and July, 1945, and by the end of the latter month enemy shipping movements had been brought to a standstill, her economy was in chaos, her industries were grinding to a halt, and her people were starving. But, exactly as happened in the 1914-18 conflict against Germany, we did not realise how deadly our blockade had been until the war was over and we were able to enter the former enemy country to assess the results for ourselves. Had the effectiveness of the blockade been realised earlier (and a scientific study of the consequences of the destruction of Japan's entire merchant marine on her economy would surely have produced strong evidence of her inability to continue the war), it seems likely that the decision to use the atomic bombs would have been viewed differently. In that event the stigma of having been the first to employ weapons of indiscriminate mass destruction might not have stained the ideals for which the Allied nations were fighting. In fact it was the destruction of the Japanese main fleets off Midway Island, in the Solomons campaign, in the battle of the Philippine Sea, and off Leyte Gulf that made the Allies' offensive strategy possible; and it was the virtually complete destruction of Japan's Merchant Navy that brought her to the brink of collapse. Allied submarines sank more than half of the 8½ million tons of shipping which she lost, the rest being accounted for chiefly by direct air attacks and by mines. In fact it now seems clear that the war against Japan provides an example of how a skilfully-waged *guerre de course*, allied to an offensive maritime strategy, can bring victory: and it is worth remembering that the instruments employed in that *guerre de course* were identical to those used by Germany in her endeavour to bring Britain to her knees. The difference between success in the one case and failure in the other arose from the fact that, although both we and the Americans at times showed a surprising hesitancy in adopting the historical strategy of convoy, we did in general understand the need to conserve and protect our mercantile tonnage. On the other hand the Japanese regarded such ' defensive ' measures as inimicable to their pride, and that led them into a fatal error.

Once Japanese sea power had been destroyed the fate of all her outlying territories was sealed. Early in September, 1945, the combined operation planned to reconquer Malaya took place without encountering opposition: the rich islands of the Eastern Archipelago were recovered soon afterwards, and all the Japanese garrisons which had been left isolated and cut off in the wake of the Allies' seaborne advance surrendered. The futility of a maritime nation trying to maintain large military forces overseas whilst lacking the sea power necessary to keep them supplied, cannot better be demonstrated than by the fact that, at the time of her surrender, Japan had some five million soldiers under arms. It was not, of course, sea power acting in isolation that won the final victories in 1945. But it was sea power, employed in skilful conjunction with the other arms, that made those victories possible; and the strategy which brought about first, the downfall of Italy, then the surrender of Germany, and finally that of Japan, was always predominantly maritime. Yet the consequences of the series of shattering defeats inflicted on us and our Allies in the Far East during the early months—incidentally again by a skilfully-applied maritime strategy—were very long lasting, and are indeed still felt in the changed attitude of the Asiatic nations towards the white races. And those defeats all stemmed from our failure to provide in adequate numbers and up-to-date form the instruments of sea power by which we had grown rich and strong, and which had enabled us, though not without much fumbling and frequent error, to defeat the attempts of earlier dictators to secure for themselves the sources of our wealth, and to establish for themselves a hegemony over the weaker nations of the world.

VIII

Some conclusions regarding
the War of 1939-45, and a
glance at subsequent
developments

At the beginning of this survey it was suggested that the enjoyment of a flourishing trade in peace and the successful application of a maritime strategy in war depended on the possession of trained seamen, fighting instruments, the means of transport, and overseas bases. Here we will first briefly review how far the nation had provided itself with those essential elements in 1939, the deficiencies which were exposed by the test of conflict, and the steps that had to be taken to remedy them: then we will consider how far the principles which had slowly developed during the course of the preceding three or four centuries were confirmed or refuted by the recent struggle; and finally we will briefly review the strategic problems which have arisen since 1945.

In 1939, the Royal Navy was almost entirely manned by long-service men, whose life had been or was to be devoted to their vocation; they were familiar with all the vagaries of the fickle element on which they lived and worked, and they were masters of their specialised crafts. Furthermore the reserves of trained men, whose experience and qualities were the same as those on active service, were adequate to the immediate needs; and as the war progressed the sea-faring section of the population was able to meet the unceasing demand for more reserves. Nothing provides such convincing proof of the importance of the human element as the rapid expansion of the R.N.V.R., and the accomplishments of the civilians who flocked into it throughout the war. Nor can there be any doubt that in 1939, Britain was more richly endowed in the human than in any of the other elements.

In the field of fighting instruments, the long period of financial stringency had left the fleet with a high proportion of elderly ships, many of which had not even been adequately modernised. Moreover it now seems clear that the balance between the various traditional classes—the battle fleet, the cruisers, and the flotilla—had not been happily struck; and that too much faith continued to be placed in the big gun as the principal arbiter of defeat or victory at sea, and too little imagination had been shown towards the potentialities of ship-borne aircraft. In part this derived from the divided control from which the Fleet Air Arm suffered between 1918, when the Admiralty surrendered its responsibility for the development of naval aviation, and 1937, when the department regained full control. But the lack of what one may call a scientific approach to study of the capacities and limitations of aircraft in between the wars, the prejudices of some of the older school of officers, and the conservatism which has (by no means always disadvantageously) been an unchanging feature of the sea services' outlook, probably also contributed to the unsatisfactory equipment of the Fleet Air Arm, and to a miscalculation regarding the priority of the duties which would fall to it in war. Very similar misjudgments were also made with regard to the role of shore-based aircraft. For neither their offensive function as instruments of blockade, nor their great potential contribution to the success of the escort-of-convoy strategy was foreseen. On the other hand it is certainly the case that the excessive claims of the extreme enthusiasts for airborne weapons, who held that all seaborne instruments had become obsolete and that the bomber alone had become the decisive weapon, did not assist towards the achievement of a fair balance. For they forced those responsible for maritime policy and plans to expend too much of their effort on rebutting such arguments: and, in consequence, too little thought was given to arriving at a scientific assessment of the contribution of shore-based aircraft to an integrated strategy.

Mention of the part that scientific analysis could have played in solving the problems of the pre-war era leads naturally to consideration of the development of 'Operational Research' during the war.

For that new art, which is in fact a combination of the scientific with the historical approach, unquestionably came to exert a very wide influence on all aspects of tactics and strategy. To give only one example, it was Operational Research that discovered the optimum size of convoys, and the theoretical number of escorts necessary to afford them the best protection. Indeed as the conflict progressed it became ever plainer that such methods must replace the previous empirical processes by which staff officers had for many years been accustomed to arrive at their recommendations; and they have since become an accepted branch of staff work in all its forms.

In the classes of warship generically described as cruisers and flotilla vessels our instruments were more modern and better suited to their tasks than in the battle fleet. But, as in every earlier war, we quickly found that the wide variety of demands which at once arose far exceeded the capacity of the ships of those classes which had been provided. The shortage of long-range escort vessels was particularly acute, and it was not until American construction overtook the deficiency towards the end of the war that we were able to meet the requirements for trade defence really adequately.

In the matter of well-placed bases we still enjoyed the great legacy inherited from earlier times. Yet it is no exaggeration to say that neither at home nor overseas were any of our bases properly defended: and that greatly handicapped the fleets and squadrons which had to work from them. Furthermore the war had not been long in progress before the soldiers' and airmen's view that a base which lay in close proximity to enemy airfields was indefensible, was shown to be completely erroneous. Though the experiences of Malta provided the best refutation of that argument, both we and the Americans learnt that, given an adequate and co-ordinated defence system, a base could fulfil its functions in face of the heaviest enemy effort to neutralise it by bombing. But the threat to fixed bases from the air did have the result of directing attention to the need to make the fleet's supply system mobile. Before the war the Admiralty had therefore begun to put a proportion of the Navy's stores and supplies afloat, and had also made some provision for a mobile naval base organisation. None the less it is probably true to say that in 1939, and indeed for the greater part of the war, the Royal Navy relied too much on fixed bases. Certainly it was the Americans who taught us that, given good equipment, an efficient temporary base could be constructed very quickly; and that a floating 'logistics' organisation could meet all the essential needs of the fighting ships, and also greatly extend their sea-keeping capacity by enabling them to be replenished without returning to a fixed base. It is interesting to recall that Hawke's long blockade of Brest in the Seven Years' War was sustained by a floating supply organisation which, in principle, closely resembled the American Fleet Train of the last war; and similar practices were adopted in the Napoleonic War blockades of French and Spanish bases. It seems possible that it was our possession of so many overseas bases that caused us to neglect the possibilities of seaborne replenishment between 1815 and 1939.

To turn to the manner in which our strategy developed during the war, it is something of a paradox that it was our total expulsion from the European continent in 1940 that forced us to change from a predominantly continental to a predominantly maritime strategy: and the reason for the change simply was that no other means of achieving victory then remained to us. Thus the reversion to a strategy which strongly resembled that of the elder Pitt in the Seven Years' War, and also that adopted during the greater part of the Napoleonic War, took place not through any voluntary act on our part, but under the compulsion of the Axis victories on land. It is, of course, impossible to assess the comparative importance of the western Allies' maritime strategy and of Russia's continental strategy to victory over the European Axis partners. But the fact that the Russian leaders exerted constant pressure to obtain delivery of vast quantities of stores and equipment from the west, especially by the Arctic route, and were moved to violent protests whenever our convoys were delayed or postponed, suggests that, even though the attrition of the Wehrmacht's strength was largely attributable to the land campaigns in the east, the sea power of the western Allies made a larger contribution to that accomplishment than is commonly realised. Two other conclusions regarding the benefits derived from the maritime strategy adopted in western Europe after 1940, and in the Pacific throughout virtually the whole of the struggle against Japan appear indisputable. The first is that it brought the western Allies victory over the European Axis partners at far less cost in human lives than the ' carnage incomparable and human squander ' of the long struggles in France and Flanders during the 1914-18 war; while the second is that, once command at sea had been won in the Indian Ocean and Pacific, victory over Japan was achieved with amazing speed and economy.

However, the reversion to a maritime strategy in 1940 at once produced a whole crop of difficult problems for the British services: for we had made almost no preparations to exploit the traditional benefits of amphibious power. This arose partly from the tacit acceptance of the predominantly continental strategy which the alliance with France had imposed on us in 1939, partly from the pre-war claim of the extreme protagonists of air power, to the effect that the new instruments of war had made a landing on a hostile coast impossibly hazardous, and partly from recollections of the costly failure of the expedition to the Dardanelles in 1915. Yet to-day reconsideration of the evidence has led to a striking change of opinion regarding the Gallipoli enterprise; and the view is now widely held that faulty planning and innefficient execution nullified the most imaginative strategic idea of the period. Furthermore it is certainly the case that air power, far from inhibiting amphibious undertakings, can positively and decisively aid the fulfilment of their purposes—once its contribution has been properly integrated with those of the sea and land services.

Mention of Gallipoli leads one to consider how it came to pass that the official histories of the 1914-18 war made so little attempt to assess the causes of our various failures. Unquestionably one influential factor was the censorship of the historians' work by the departments concerned. But we have recently also become aware of the manner in which some senior officers who themselves took part in controversial events reacted to any criticism of their actions. Whether it is justifiable or desirable that official histories of a recent conflict should be written while the chief participants are still living, may be arguable; but it is surely beyond argument that, once a historian has been appointed, he should be allowed to state his conclusions without regard to the subjective views of departments or individuals. Sir Herbert Richmond, when told of the difficulties encountered over compiling the account of the Battle of Jutland, remarked that ' the narrative should not be interfered with by anyone who was concerned in the action. They are witnesses—not judges . . .'[1] And it is a sobering thought that we owe more to the work of impartial students of such events as Gallipoli, the third battle of Ypres, the first campaign against the U-boats, and the Battle of Jutland than we owe to the official historians. Furthermore it is difficult not to feel that some of the mistakes made in the first German war might not have been repeated in the second—had the historians of the earlier struggle been allowed free rein to state their conclusions. A future generation may, however, be thankful for the fact that the harsh criticism which Churchill made of the final volume of the official naval history of the 1914-18 war will not, I believe, be repeated with regard to any of the official histories of the last war.[2]

To return after this digression to maritime strategy, though it is true that Mr. Churchill's vivid awareness of the merits of amphibious warfare caused him repeatedly to press for adventurous enterprises which were either premature, unnecessary or positively unsound, and that the powerful impact of his personality not seldom

[1] In his diary for 12th January, 1920. Quoted A. J. Marder, *Portrait of an Admiral*, p. 361 (Cape, 1952).
[2] ' The able historian has evidently had to submit his chapters to authorities and departments; and important personages in the story have clearly applied their pruning knives and ink erasers with no timid hand. The result is a sort of official amalgam which seems to be neither a plain, fearless narrative nor a fair and searching analytical examination of the great disputes'. *Thoughts and Adventures*, p. 123 (Thornton, Butterworth, 1932).

made it difficult, and even dangerous, to resist his proposals, it none the less remains true that much of the credit for the prompt adoption of the new strategy in 1940, and for the full exploitation of our sea power to land armies *in theatres of our own choice*, must surely remain his. And in President Roosevelt he found, or perhaps instructed, a powerful ally of similar outlook to himself. It is not surprising that, with a leader such as Churchill in power, there should have been failures as well as successes in amphibious enterprises. But those at Dakar in September, 1940, and at Dieppe and Tobruk in August, 1942, can confidently be attributed to neglect of one or more of the basic requirements for success in such undertakings mentioned earlier.[1] Furthermore we may be thankful that not a few other undertakings of a similar nature for which Mr. Churchill had vigorously pressed, such as the expedition to the Baltic planned at the beginning of the war, and the projected attempt to seize Pantelleria and the Dodecanese Islands in 1940, were overtaken by events.

In sum the experiences of the last war seem to suggest that, provided all the basic requirements for success in amphibious enterprises are met, they can bring as great benefits as were derived from them in earlier conflicts—both in the field of minor strategy (through small-scale raids) and in that of major strategy (by large overseas expeditions). However, the hazards of such undertakings remain as high as ever; and one must also face the fact that, while soldiers will never submit themselves enthusiastically to a form of warfare which subjects them to the discomforts as well as the risks of sea transport, the protagonists of air power are likely to place greater faith in the effects of long-range bombing than in the close air support which is needed by the naval and military participants in a combined operation. Yet the last war proved that the real contribution of air power to an amphibious enterprise lay firstly in defeating the enemy's reconnaissance, secondly in providing air escort and cover to the assault convoys and thirdly in helping, in

[1] See p. 28.

conjunction with heavy naval bombarding ships, to neutralise the enemy's coast defences before the troops were landed. Another lesson of the last war was that the opinion, long held in British military circles, that the possibility of achieving surprise would be improved by making the final approach and the actual assault in darkness, and also by sacrificing preliminary air and naval bombardments, was entirely mistaken. Not only did landings in daylight prove to possess great advantages in the avoidance of error and confusion, but the bombardments enabled the soldiers to establish their beach-heads, even on a heavily defended coast, at astonishingly small cost. Furthermore the bombarding ships showed their ability to act as heavy mobile artillery for the Army until its own guns were ashore, or its advance inland had taken it out of range from the coast. But in truth none of those experiences was new, and ample precedents for them can be found in history. Rather are they all extensions of ancient principles to which the new instruments of war had to be adapted.

No experience from the past received stronger reinforcement from the last war than the effectiveness of the escort-of-convoy strategy against every form of attack—air, underwater and surface— on merchant shipping. Indeed the decisive manner in which a properly integrated and well-trained escort proved capable of dealing with the new as well as the old forms of the *guerre de course* exceeded the expectations even of those who believed in the validity of historical principles. And every time that we or our American Allies deviated from that principle in search of a more ' offensive ' strategy we were quickly proved wrong. The most long-lasting deviation arose from the belief that bombing enemy bases and construction yards would have greater effect than providing the strongest possible air escorts to the convoys. But we now know that, whereas very few ships were lost from convoys when both sea and air escorts were present, the bombing campaign had, almost to the end of the war, very little effect on the enemy's effort. Just as in amphibious enterprises the sea and air services had to work in close co-ordination to meet the Army's needs, so did the combination of naval and air instruments in applying the escort-of-convoy strategy achieve success against every form of the *guerre de course*.

To turn to economic blockade, which we described earlier as the second method whereby a maritime strategy can produce the conditions in which victory can be won (the first being amphibious expeditions), its influence depended on the extent to which each of the three principal enemy countries was dependent on overseas trade. Thus against Italy, which had to import all her oil fuel and most of her raw materials, our blockade was extremely effective, her fleet was finally almost immobilised for lack of fuel, and her industries could only be kept in production by the diversion of raw materials from Germany. On the other hand, though our blockade of Germany produced many shortages, the country as a whole did not suffer to anything like the extent that it had during the later years of the previous struggle. This arose partly from the ruthless exploitation of the conquered continental countries; but the ingenuity the Germans themselves displayed in finding and manufacturing substitutes for the raw materials which they could not obtain from overseas undoubtedly helped to reduce the impact of our blockade. Yet their constant endeavour to bring home particularly valuable cargoes, for which purpose they even constructed a special class of submarines, proves that they suffered more than inconvenience. As to Japan, there is no doubt at all that the Allied blockade was the chief factor in bringing about her downfall: for it first of all severed all communications with her vast land conquests, and finally cut her off completely from the Asian mainland.

Naval blockade, whose traditional aim is to contain or neutralise the enemy's principal warships, was employed at various times against all our enemies; and it was here that the new instruments of war, and especially airborne weapons and mines, proved extremely effective. Thus the naval air attack on the Italian battleships in Taranto in November, 1940, the R.A.F.'s prolonged offensive against the German Brest and Norway squadrons, and the many American carrier-borne onslaughts on Japanese naval bases, can all be said to have been modern extensions of this ancient strategy. But the airborne weapons, if the most effective, were by no means the only instruments employed: for submarines, minelayers, and various special assault craft all took a hand in enforcing the blockades. We should also note how at the beginning of 1942, when unfavourable developments on land in the Middle East, and the heavy losses recently suffered by our fleet, forced us to relax our blockades of the Italian naval bases, they were at once able to run several important convoys to Africa; and their safe arrival further jeopardised our situation on land. There is a parallel between those developments and the effect of our failure to blockade the French Brest and Toulon fleets on the colonial campaign in the War of American Independence.[1] In most conflicts our naval and economic blockades have, however, overlapped; and they again did so in the recent struggle—notably in the continuous effort we made to stop the enemy's coastal traffic. Although in that campaign air minelaying and direct attacks by shore-based and carrier-borne aircraft achieved the biggest results, a wide variety of other instruments, including submarines and fast torpedo craft, were employed on the same duty. In sum it seems true to say that as long as the mercantile and military traffic of a belligerent nation is chiefly seaborne, the stoppage of that traffic will be a strategic requirement of great importance; and we should note that in the last war this was accomplished by attacks at *sea* to a considerably greater extent than by bombing raids on the enemy's ports. Nor should we forget that, at the beginning of the war, the Germans attempted to apply a similar strategy against our own coastal traffic. But once we had developed a co-ordinated naval and air defence system, we mastered every one of the instruments which they deployed for such purposes. Indeed the success with which our vital coastal traffic was kept moving in spite of all the enemy's endeavours to disrupt it, is not the least remarkable feature of the war. Yet the *guerre de course* on the oceans, and the attempt to

[1] See pp. 60 and 62.

blockade these islands, did together cause us great anxiety, and enormous losses of merchant shipping; and at two periods (at the beginning of 1941, and in the early spring of 1943), the enemy's efforts brought him within what now seems to have been measurable distance of success—as indeed they had done in 1917. With Britain's vulnerability to such methods of waging war thus twice proven, it is difficult to believe that the lesson has escaped the attention of another possible adversary.

Tactics being one of the methods by which strategy is applied, we may here review the influence of the new instruments of war on their development. We saw earlier how, from the mid-18th century, when the naval Fighting Instructions were made ' permanent ', down to very recent times, there has been a tendency for such a code to impose a high degree of rigidity on the handling of fleets and squadrons in battle;[1] and it was only when the leadership of men of genius, such as Anson, Hawke and Nelson, had been available to the Royal Navy, that a more flexible system was adopted. The 1939 naval Commander-in-Chiefs' Fighting Instructions, though prefaced by a statement that they were *not* mandatory, showed little less rigidity than the Grand Fleet Battle Orders of the 1914-18 war; and they were quickly proved to be quite unsuited to modern conditions. In many actions fought by our ships (notably in the River Plate battle, and in virtually all convoy battles) they were, however, completely disregarded; and senior officers allowed, and even encouraged, a wide measure of initiative by their subordinates. In a few instances, however, of which the first fight with the *Bismarck* is the outstanding example, the principles laid down in the Fighting Instructions were followed: and on that occasion the results were disastrous. Though it is difficult to say what factors caused senior officers to follow or disregard the instructions on various occasions, in a fleet where training has been based on a common doctrine, and a high degree of mutual confidence exists between officers, it is difficult not to feel that their

[1] See pp. 46-7 and 80-1

existence is more likely to be dangerous than beneficial—certainly if they go beyond stating very broad principles. As examples of undesirable rigidity, the 1939 Instructions stated that 'prior to deployment the Admiral will control the movements of the battle fleet as a whole. He will dispose the guides of divisions on a line of bearing at right angles to the bearing of the enemy fleet . . .'; and again that, if a convoy was attacked by a superior force, ' the ships in convoy should be ordered to scatter and the escorts to concentrate '—a decision that should obviously be left to the discretion of the senior officer. Perhaps the greatest influence in breaking the long thraldom of the Fighting Instructions was the impact of air power on naval tactics. For once attacks could develop suddenly and from many directions simultaneously, captains could not be expected to remain in close order awaiting a signal from the flagship. Be that as it may, nearly all the actions fought by the Royal Navy in the last war were conducted on lines which exponents of the ' Chase' and of the hard-fought battles of the Seven Years' and Napoleonic Wars would surely have approved. It may be for that reason that, at the conclusion of the struggle, there was none of the disappointment at the service's performance, nor any repetition of the controversies regarding the causes of failure, which had been so marked a feature of the early 1920s.

In the summer of 1945, the maritime Allies were in secure control of all the oceans of the world, and it seemed that the peaceful interchange of goods between the nations would proceed unhindered—to the vast benefit of mankind. Yet within a few years much had happened to shatter all such optimistic hopes: and to-day it seems that a new challenge on the seas is by no means impossible, since Russia has, for the first time in her history, emerged as a mercantile state with, apparently, a lively awareness of the importance of sea power. Furthermore all strategic principles have been thrown into the melting pot, and all the lessons of history have been called in question by the development of weapons of mass destruction. What, then, are the purposes to which Britain and her Allies should work at the present time?

The first inescapable factor in the problems which we have to face to-day is that, through the North Atlantic Treaty Organisation, we are entirely committed to the support of the western European nations on the continent; and that has reproduced the strategic situation created by our alliances with France in 1914, and again in 1939. Secondly, these islands are to-day more dependent on sea-borne supplies of food, fuel and raw materials than ever before, and so more vulnerable than ever before to an attack on our merchant shipping; and, thirdly, the military forces immediately available to the West are greatly outnumbered by those of the Communist countries. Thus the over-running of the whole of western Europe could happen very rapidly. It was to counter that threat that the ' deterrent ' strategy, which took advantage of our initial superiority in nuclear weapons was conceived; and although it is not susceptible to scientific or historical proof, it can reasonably be argued that it has been mainly our ability to retaliate with nuclear weapons that has preserved the precarious peace of the last fifteen years. Where the makers of our defence policy now seem to have erred is, first, in not foreseeing that the day was bound to come when Russia also became possessed of nuclear weapons; and, secondly, in accepting the argument that the deterrent strategy would be effective against minor as well as major aggression, so justifying drastic reductions in our conventional forces. As new developments in the field of weapons by one country have always been followed by similar developments in other advanced countries, the likelihood of East and West reaching a stage of nuclear parity should surely have been foreseen, and our defence policy adjusted in time to forestall the worst of its consequences—which is that the stalemate in the nuclear field acts as an incentive to minor aggression, which the deterrent strategy is powerless to prevent. The success of the Berlin air-lift in 1948-49, and the frustration of the Communist purpose in Korea in 1950-52, both of which were accomplished entirely by conventional instruments, undoubtedly proved that in limited conflicts the ancient needs for highly mobile forces of that type had in no wise declined; yet the lesson went unheeded.

It is worth investigating how the error of placing excessive reliance on the deterrent appears to have won acceptance. In the first place, although past and recent conflicts have proved beyond doubt that only by combining the contributions and capacities of all services can strategy be made really effective, the claims of what may be called the 'One Big Weapon School' were apparently accepted without adequate investigation of the probable consequences in other directions. It is also likely that the argument that weapons of mass destruction would act as guarantors of peace clouded popular judgment on the issue. For mankind has always been ready to snatch at the illusion that strife between nations can be eliminated. Secondly it is a fairly safe guess that reliance on one weapon, instead of on a variety of traditional instruments, must have held considerable attraction for the politicians—both on account of the apparent simplicity of the solution to a perennial problem that it offered, and because of the economies that it seemed to promise in other directions. Yet the argument that the increasing power of weapons would make war impossible is a very old illusion, which was certainly put forward during the latter part of the 19th century. Indeed history strongly indicates that the claims of the protagonists of any one instrument of war should always be treated with scepticism; and the error of the Royal Navy in allowing the big gun to dominate all its strategic and tactical thought for so many years, to the comparative exclusion of underwater, and later of airborne weapons, may be being repeated to-day by the Air Force's too dogmatic propagation of the deterrent strategy. As to the consequences produced by acceptance of that doctrine, it is surely now clear that the expected economies have proved elusive; and, secondly, that the interests of the western alliance have suffered very seriously. For in spite of having equipped ourselves with adequate nuclear

weapons to curb a major aggression, we have repeatedly found ourselves outflanked and forced back by the skilful and ruthless application of a strategy based on conventional military and economic
power. Nor is the reason for the succession of reverses which our
excessive reliance on the deterrent strategy has brought about far to
seek. For they can surely be attributed to the fact that the Russian
leaders know perfectly well that, unless they provoke us to an
altogether insupportable extent, it is inconceivable that we should
initiate the use of nuclear weapons. Thus, while we have armed
ourselves with a deterrent which (however valuable it may have
been before nuclear parity had come to pass) can never be used to
support our policy on any secondary issue, they are able to proceed
with their plans to extend their zones of political and economic
domination with little hindrance.

It seems indeed that, in the first flush of enthusiasm for the
nuclear strategy, we forgot that all *visible* instruments of power
have in them an inherent deterrent capacity of a far more flexible
nature, and have in the past constantly and successfully been used by
British statesmen to make known their views and purposes. This
was because the power of visible instruments *could be used*, initially
with moderation, and then, if necessary, with gradually increasing
pressure, culminating perhaps in the application of a carefully controlled degree of force; and the nation whose actions had attracted
their presence *knew that such instruments could be used*. Their arrival
gave early warning of the purposes of the statesmen who directed
them, while the pressure they exerted could be increased or relaxed
from day to day and even hour to hour. It is hard to understand how
such a concept has come to be discredited as ' gunboat diplomacy ',
what time a large section of the British people is apparently prepared to accept that, in certain not very clearly defined circumstances, weapons of mass destruction might be used to achieve
similar ends. The conclusion is inescapable that in the era of nuclear
parity, in a period of ' cold war ', or in a conflict for limited purposes,
a strategy based mainly on nuclear power cannot be effective.

On the other hand a strong case can be made out for the retention of the British deterrent until such time as an international agreement for the total abolition of strategic nuclear weapons can be achieved; since if history can point any lessons regarding the causes of the decline of nations, it surely indicates that a people who are not prepared to provide for their own defence are not truly free, and are doomed to a slow decay. Nor should we forget that, whereas coalitions of states have often shown unity and vigour during the offensive phase of a conflict, they have repeatedly shown a tendency to break up when attacked. Thus the much-canvassed suggestion that the deterrent should be left entirely in American hands might well contain the seeds of utter defeat for Britain and her European allies; since no one could possibly guarantee that the United States would act with the necessary promptitude to stop an act of major aggression against western Europe. It is probably true that we could with advantage integrate more closely with the United States the costly processes of research and, in some measure, the production of nuclear weapons and of the means of delivering them; but that should never be allowed to go so far as to leave us totally reliant on our Ally for the application of one aspect of our strategy. It may also be the case that the deterrent strategy could be applied with little loss of efficiency, with far less destruction, and with substantial economy by non-nuclear weapons, such as gases which produce only temporary disablement.[1] But if that is the case the possibility should surely be placed squarely before the British people; and the principle that a nation must provide its own means of defence is in no way altered.

What one may regret is, first, that our statesmen present these burning issues to the nation in so hesitant, even apologetic a form—as though they themselves are unconvinced whether or not our survival depends on the nation being properly armed. Secondly, that the delivery of the independent deterrent has come to be re-

[1] This possibility, and its advantages, are cogently argued in Captain B. H. Liddell Hart's *Deterrent or Defence* (Stevens, 1960), and the capabilities of a biological deterrent are discussed in *Naval Research Reviews* (U.S.A., 1961).

garded as the sole proprietary right of one service; and, thirdly, that the maritime needs of the nation have recently been placed at so low a priority in relation to other purposes.

We have now reached a stage at which the principles which should govern defence policy may be restated. If it be accepted that the independent deterrent must be retained, then the ancient requirement for mobility in the means of delivery must be met. The reason is that, to maintain the credibility of the deterrent, it is essential that it should be immune to destruction by pre-emptive attack. In other words it must be able to survive the first onslaught and then strike back. To-day mobility can be achieved either in the air, on the surface of the sea, or beneath the sea. Mobility in the air may one day be possible through the use of earth satellites: but that is still a long way off, and in the meantime it can only be achieved by keeping a proportion of the deterrent force continuously airborne—an extremely costly proceeding. Furthermore the shore bases from which manned bombers must work are scarcely less vulnerable to pre-emptive attack than the fixed missile sites on which, in flagrant disregard for the most valid of traditional principles, we had until recently decided to rely for delivery of the deterrent. Though the development of vertical take-off may somewhat reduce the vulnerability of shore bases it is difficult to see how it can ever be eliminated. Mobility on the surface of the sea suffers from similar disadvantages to mobility in the air: for warships, and especially large aircraft carriers operating in a strategic role, will be inviting targets for air and underwater attack. There remains mobility beneath the sea: and the full extent of the revolution brought about by the arrival of the nuclear or true submarine equipped with long-range missiles still seems to be scarcely appreciated in Britain. Suffice it to say that, for the first time in history, we have in it a weapon which is mobile in three dimensions. True the initial cost is high: but if it enabled us to dispense with new generations of large aircraft carriers and heavy bombers the probability is that, over a term of years, it would turn out to be the most economical step. One has only to consider the vast supporting organisation required to keep such warships and aircraft in service to realise the extent of the economies which would be effected by their disappearance; for the maintenance of very large graving-docks, of aircraft repair and maintenance yards, and of all the traditional apparatus of the naval or air base must account for a high proportion of their cost, in men as well as in money. The needs of the true submarine, though it would certainly require some supporting organisation, could surely be met far more economically. Furthermore from the British point of view the numbers required would not be great: since a force capable of keeping two such vessels permanently at sea in the Far East, and the same number in the Indian Ocean and in our home waters would suffice to constitute a very effective strategic deterrent.

The second cardinal need is for this country to provide itself with two up-to-date, highly mobile joint service task forces capable of landing and supporting a Brigade Group or its equivalent strength at very short notice wherever a sudden demand for the presence of conventional power may arise. It is obvious that, with the introduction of the Commando Carrier, we have taken a first step in that direction: but, in its present form, the task force is neither sufficiently strong nor sufficiently inter-service. Thus one may question the wisdom of leaving amphibious warfare solely in the hands of the Royal Marines—unless we are prepared to go the full distance, and adopt the virtually self-sufficient United States Marine Corps as our model. Moreover to allow the Army to become wholly wedded to a continental strategy, and divorced from amphibious warfare, would be merely to repeat the error of the pre-1914 period and the years between the wars. Two task forces of the type suggested would be necessary in present-day world conditions—one based in the Indian Ocean and the other at home: but within a reasonable time it should be possible to build up at any rate the nucleus for a third, formed largely of trained reservists. Between them they would ensure that the torch of amphibious warfare, which has so often been extinguished in times of peace, when each service always tends to go its own way, would be kept alight: and that would make it possible to create larger forces for major combined operations, should the need arise, with far less delay and difficulty than has been experienced in the past. Efficient sea and air transport would, of course, play a great part in the rapid supply and reinforcement of the amphibious task forces. But in an age when the right to fly through other nations' air space is being increasingly denied, and the arrangement of staging bases for refuelling aircraft has become extremely difficult, it is hard to see how the close air support which will be essential to the land forces can be guaranteed except by having it immediately available in carrier-borne form. Indeed as long as the use of nuclear weapons in a limited conflict is prohibited (and one can see no likelihood of the ban being lifted by this country) there can be no alternative to the manned fighter's present function of supporting the Army and destroying the enemy's air forces. Herein lies the justification for development of a new class of support carrier, which would be considerably smaller than the ships equipped to operate in the strategic role.

The third great need to-day is to improve and strengthen our sea-air trade defence forces; and to understand the urgency of that requirement it is necessary to review briefly how Britain stands to-day in the matter of the vital 'transport element' of maritime power. Though our mercantile marine has increased from approximately 17 million tons (excluding Commonwealth ships) in 1939 to some 21 million tons, the increase in tanker tonnage has concealed the drop in dry cargo ships, which has amounted to no less than a million tons; and it is our coastal fleet, which will be extremely important in the event of inland transport being disrupted, that has suffered the worst. Furthermore the proportion of large passenger liners (over 20,000 tons) in our mercantile fleet is now much greater than in 1939. And they may well prove of doubtful value, or even no value in war, when aircraft will surely prove the most efficient means of moving men quickly over long distances, and fast vessels capable of carrying heavy cargoes will be needed both to transport their equipment and to bring to this country the food and raw materials on which its survival utterly depends. Nor does the fact that our tanker tonnage has doubled since 1939 give grounds for complacency, since our oil imports have quadrupled in the same period, and our economy is now much more geared to the use of oil. We should also remember that the speed of merchant ships has always been critically important in the defence of shipping against every form of the *guerre de course*. But the increase of merchant ships' speed from an average of 11½ knots in 1939, to about 13 knots to-day has brought little or no strategical or tactical benefits, since it has not been in any way comparable to the increase of speed achieved by submarines and aircraft in recent years. Thus the vulnerability of the western nations, and especially Britain, to blockade has greatly increased—as our only possible adversaries must be well aware. British imports alone have risen from approximately 67 million tons in 1938, to nearly 112 million tons (including oil fuels) annually; and, to make matters worse, Russia herself is in all likelihood still relatively impervious to the pressure of blockade—as we learnt to our cost in the Crimean War, and rediscovered in the operations in support of the counter-revolutionary movement in the 1920s. Though it is likely that, with her fast-rising population and rapidly-increasing industrialisation, Russia's comparative invulnerability to blockade will decrease, it is certain that for many years to come she will be vastly less susceptible to such pressures than Britain and her European allies. Furthermore China is at present even less susceptible to blockade than Russia. There is, however, a plain need to undertake a continuous study of those nations' imports, in order that we may be possessed of accurate knowledge regarding the extent to which they are not self-supporting in food, raw materials and manufactured goods.

The maintenance of the flow of shipping in time of war has always depended greatly on the possession of adequate overseas bases, and it is on this necessity that the greatest anxiety may be felt to-day. For the upsurge of nationalism in formerly dependent territories has lost to us and our Allies the use of many of those which came to us from the 18th and 19th centuries, and our continued tenure of others is in doubt. Though it is perfectly true that the increased speed and endurance of ships should enable a maritime nation to do with fewer bases, and the last war proved that a mobile supply organisation could extend sea-keeping capacity to a greater extent than we had realised, it is surely inconceivable that command at sea can be exercised, and the flow of shipping maintained, with none at all. Yet that is the condition that the western alliance is to-day approaching. Nor can one draw any comfort from the fact that persistent American anti-colonial propaganda has helped to produce this state of affairs; for our principal Ally is to-day faced with exactly the same problem with regard to the overseas bases which she considers necessary to the exercise of her sea power. The recent withdrawal of South Africa from the Commonwealth on an issue of political principle, with scarcely a whisper from our side of the possible strategic consequences, shows how little the matter of overseas bases is understood by the British public—in spite of the fact that as recently as 1956, when the Suez Canal was closed, it was the ability and willingness of the South African bases to handle the greatly increased traffic that prevented the interruption of the whole of our eastern and Australasian trade. We may also remark how the Russian leaders never fail to seize an opportunity to acquire the use of an overseas base in fact if not in name (for ' base ' has become as discreditable a term as ' colony '), whenever western weakness or hesitancy has presented them with an opportunity. Indeed it seems quite probable that, for the first time since the end of the French wars of the 19th century, Britain and her allies may soon find themselves challenged by a rising maritime power who is well provided in the vital matter of overseas bases. Nor are the consequences of such developments difficult to foresee. In the Mediterranean, which admittedly may have lost some of its former importance as a trade route, our situation is precarious, and our ability to give adequate support to the nations belonging to the western alliance which border on its shores is at least doubtful; while in the northern Indian Ocean it will hardly be possible to safeguard our shipping with no developed base between East Africa and Singapore. If, moreover, the Persian Gulf is closed to our traffic we would become almost entirely dependent on the western hemisphere for oil supplies. It thus seems certain that, apart from a war by mutual annihilation, our survival will depend on control of the Atlantic. Yet without bases in Iceland or West Africa such control will be far harder to achieve than it was in the recent conflict. Indeed it can be confidently predicted that Iceland and the Spanish and Portuguese Atlantic Islands would, as so often in the past, again become critically important. The extent to which considerations of maritime strategy are ignored to-day cannot be better demonstrated than by our recent rather foolish quarrel with Iceland, and by our tendency to alienate Spain and Portugal because we dislike their form of government.

Whether we become wholly or only mainly dependent for our survival on control of the North Atlantic it is virtually certain that, in the event of a nuclear or non-nuclear conflict, we shall again have to employ the convoy strategy; and it is over the strength of the western alliance's sea-air escort forces that the gravest concern must be felt. Though some comfort may be drawn from the immunity of convoys to ballistic missiles discharged from fixed bases, they will be vulnerable to direct attack by missile-carrying aircraft and by submarines—which will surely necessitate a scale of defence at least as great as that needed to overcome the air and underwater threats of the last war. Yet to-day Britain and her allies (apart from the United States) are incapable of producing anything approaching adequate forces even to defend the vital North Atlantic shipping. It is moreover possible that our surface escorts may no longer be able to look for effective assistance from the shore-based aircraft which played so great a part in defeating the U-boats of 1939-45. For the arrival of the true submarine may well mean that airborne radar, which had already been deprived of much of its value by the 'Schnorkel' device of the last war, has become wholly obsolete. This would call in question the whole future of the fixed-wing aircraft in anti-submarine warfare: since, in the absence of some startling development in the field of sound location, the 'sono buoys', which are all that it can employ for detection, are greatly inferior to the supersonic Asdic device which a helicopter can lower into the sea and raise again at will. Plainly therefore the helicopter or hovering aircraft is the anti-submarine air instrument of the future, and the provision of escort vessels capable of operating them should stand first in the western alliance's trade defence needs. The second most important requirement is in all probability the provision of a long-range anti-aircraft guided missile. Unhappily the cost of ships capable of mounting and operating such instruments is to-day so high that it is difficult to see how adequate numbers could be provided to defend even the North Atlantic traffic—unless substantial economies can be achieved in other directions. We will return to that subject later; for the security of our shipping while on the open sea is not, unfortunately, the only problem to be faced in trade defence. The shallow waters of our long coastal routes and the approaches to our principal harbours have repeatedly been shown to be very vulnerable to minelaying; and bringing the ships through all the diverse perils encountered on the high seas will avail nothing if, at the end of their journeys, they are sunk by the underwater weapons which, in the present century, have proved such powerful instruments of blockade. In the last war we suffered heavy losses from mines, but managed ultimately to produce sweeps capable of dealing with all the many varieties of the influence-type except those actuated by the change of pressure produced by the passage of a ship; and to-day the only method of clearing such mines is still by counter-mining. It is therefore plain that a substantial force of coastal and inshore minesweepers remains a very important maritime need, and that improvement in the clearance of pressure-operated mines must stand high on the list of developments to which our scientists and technicians should bend their efforts. Incidentally it will certainly once again be necessary to sail all coastal traffic in convoy, in order to keep it within the narrow limits of the swept waters.

If then the priorities in defence here suggested are accepted the shape of our defence policy over the next decade becomes clearer. The deterrent would be retained in the form suggested, the need for mobility of conventional power would be met by the formation of the inter-service task forces, and a much stronger emphasis would be placed on the really urgent requirements of trade defence. Moreover such a policy would enable us to meet our commitments to the United Nations Organisation: for it is surely not inconceivable that another limited and local conflict, such as was waged in Korea in the 1950s, might arise. But the adoption of such a policy would demand statesmanship of a high order in the countries belonging to the North Atlantic Treaty Organisation, and in the councils of our own makers of defence policy. As to the former it cannot possibly be sound or economical for each member state to strive to create small balanced fleets on its own, when the real need is for the N.A.T.O. forces *as a whole* to be balanced and capable of jointly meeting the priorities here proposed. Thus the tendency for the smaller members of the alliance to provide themselves with large aircraft carriers, with which the U.S. Navy is already liberally equipped, must militate against meeting the deterrent aspects of western strategy in the most economical form, and also the requirements for mobility of conventional forces and trade defence. Furthermore the present N.A.T.O. command organisation, which appears to be based far more on satisfying national pride than on operational efficiency, must give grounds for concern: for it is difficult to believe that, in its present form, it would stand the test of war.

As to the British fighting services themselves, it is obvious that a much closer integration of their too often divergent policies is needed: for it is beyond doubt that to-day, as in the past, any strategy which is not truly inter-service is bound to suffer from fatal weaknesses. The attainment of such an ideal would, of course, demand a cessation of inter-service rivalry for funds, and a sacrifice by all three services of something of their perfectly natural but, from the national point of view, generally disadvantageous pride. Thus it seems essential for the Navy to face and accept that before the end of the next decade the large aircraft carrier capable of operating in a strategic role as part of the 'strike fleet concept' will become obsolete, such functions being taken over by the true submarine, which is unquestionably the 'capital ship' of the future. For the Air Force it will be necessary to swallow the very uncongenial pill that its claim to a proprietary right in the delivery of the deterrent can no longer be substantiated—if indeed it was ever truly valid. Furthermore the part of shore-based, fixed-wing aircraft in trade defence seems likely to decline, and that may well call in question the whole future of Coastal Command. On the other hand air transport undoubtedly has an immense part to play in a truly integrated strategy; and in the maritime field the need to blockade the enemy's ports and coastline will surely fall mainly on the Air Force. Air minelaying and direct attacks on enemy shipping at sea, which in the last struggle ultimately became the greatest contributions of Bomber and Coastal Command respectively to the enforcement of our blockade, appear to have lost nothing of their importance. But one may hope that the complicated compromises of 1939-45 for planning and executing such purposes will not be perpetuated. For the division of responsibility between two departments for operations concerned with the single function of blockade has little to commend it. Indeed so dominant will be the share of the Air Force in executing that important function that it could well be given full responsibility for all its aspects: but that would demand a much greater awareness of the maritime role of that service than seems at present to exist. As to the Army, although the need to continue the continental contribution to western defence cannot be disputed, it should not be allowed, as appears to be the case, to become so dominant as to exclude the need for mobility and for participation in amphibious warfare. Though it is natural for soldiers to view with some abhorrence the discomforts and uncertainties of working on an element with which they are unfamiliar, and at whose hands they have often received unkindly treatment, the merits of combined operations have been too often proven for it to be acceptable that they will not be needed again. In present conditions it appears that it is the strategic reserve, based in this country, that is most likely to be called on to meet such requirements; and it must be admitted that regimental traditions, however advantageous in other respects, militate against the formation of the compact, highly mobile and self-contained forces here proposed. To turn to the field where diplomacy and strategy overlap, we need to make a far more energetic attempt to convince the newly-born nations, nearly all of whom naturally wish to adopt a ' neutralist ' line, that their interests correspond fundamentally with our own; and that small and weak nations which endeavour to avoid involvement in a clash between giants nearly always succumb —at any rate temporarily—to the more ruthless of the contestants. Thus it is to their interests not to hinder, and if possible to aid the broad defensive purposes of the democracies. Because of the harbours they possess, and the strategic situation of their coasts, it is in the maritime field that they can best contribute to our cause.

The western alliance still possesses the great advantage of the predominant share in the world's mercantile tonnage, as well as by far the greater experience in and knowledge of the intricate skills of operating it economically. The ability to move goods and raw materials fast and efficiently all over the world could serve to help in fostering good relations with the ' uncommitted ' nations, all of whom are, very properly, anxious to increase their industrial capacity and raise their standards of living. By arranging favourable terms for the carriage of the imports they need and of the exports that they must sell, and by ensuring—so far as it is within our power— the expeditious handling of cargoes, we could bring home to them our common dependence on sea transport. That would surely help to awaken in them a clearer understanding of the influence of maritime power on the attainment of the aims they have set themselves in peace, and on their survival in war. Such a policy would in all probability require some degree of government direction and control of shipping; and although the British Merchant Navy cordially, and justly, dislike such measures, there would in fact be nothing exceptional in them in an era when most nations subsidise their shipping in one form or another. Furthermore since cargoes can be denied as well as facilitated, control of sea transport must surely still confer great political influence—as was shown by the belligerents' actions towards neutral nations in both wars of this century. Thus it seems possible that the ability to deny cargoes in a period of 'cold war' or 'conventional' conflict might prove powerful means of persuading neutral nations to grant us the use of the harbours which formerly served us so well as naval and mercantile bases. If that be accepted then the creation of a world-wide organisation for the control of all western mercantile tonnage and of seaborne cargoes must stand high on the list of the requirements which the nations of the western alliance can and should meet; and the measures necessary to ensure that the substantial tonnage at present sailing under 'Flags of Convenience' comes under western control also demand attention.

To sum up it seems clear that a new approach to the strategic needs of the western alliance in both the deterrent and the conventional fields is overdue. While retention of the independent deterrent is essential, in default of an enforceable international agreement for the abolition of strategic nuclear weapons, the vehicle for the delivery of the deterrent must be mobile; and the missile-firing submarine not only has plain advantages in that respect, but in the long view might well prove the most economic instrument. But our recent set-backs point very strongly to the need also to reshape our conventional forces, with far more emphasis on maritime needs. In the field of the N.A.T.O. navies the endeavour to acquire individual small 'balanced fleets' should be abandoned in favour of creating an integrated and balanced fleet within the alliance as a whole: and the N.A.T.O. command organisation should be put on a truly operational basis. In the particular field of the British maritime services the large aircraft carrier capable of operating in a strategic role will become obsolete within the next ten years: but carrier-borne air support, probably supplied from considerably smaller and simpler ships, will still be essential in combined operations. The money and men saved by the abandonment of the large carrier should be devoted to building up a fleet of true submarines capable of meeting the deterrent need, and in strengthening our escort forces. The latter must include a new class of vessel capable of operating hover-type aircraft, and equipped with long-range anti-aircraft missiles; and our present lack of overseas bases can only be mitigated by extending and improving the floating and mobile support for our escort forces. In the realm of amphibious warfare, the formation of two compact and highly-mobile inter-service task forces with self-contained air support, would fill an important need in 'limited' conflicts; and in the strategy of blockade the influence of strike and minelaying aircraft will be so great that it should become a responsibility of the Air Force. As to the shape of our Merchant Navy, the need for more fast dry cargo vessels is as plain as a revival of our coastal shipping and fisheries is overdue; and the present difficulty in manning the Merchant Navy, which has always proved a very important reserve of seamen, must give grounds for anxiety. But probably the greatest need of all is to reconstruct our strategy on a truly inter-service basis, eliminating the rivalries and jealousies which have so often bedevilled such purposes, and looking to each service for the breadth of outlook and statesmanship which the occasion and the opportunity demand. If it be said that in the proposals here put forward the emphasis is mainly on maritime needs and purposes, then it can be argued that the new defence policy is merely an extension and modernisation of the principles derived from recent and more distant experience, set out in the earlier chapters of this book. And it may well be that posterity will look back on the mid-20th century as one of those recurrent periods in Britain's history when her statesmen have neglected maritime needs—with dire consequences to her people.

THE END

Select Bibliography

The first section of this bibliography consists of books which cover the whole, or at least the major part of the subject. Later sections are divided into chronological periods, each of which produced developments in the understanding and application of maritime strategy. For each period one or two authoritative books of a general nature have been put first, followed by a selection of the more specialised works dealing with particular events, and biographies of the principal characters of the period. Only one biography of each person has been included, even though the choice in some cases (notably that of Nelson) is wide. An attempt has also been made to include at least one book in each period which deals with events from the point of view of England's adversaries. In many cases the books listed overlap into more than one period; but they have been placed under the heading to which they are chiefly relevant.

Nearly all the volumes published by the Navy Records Society (at present totalling 102) throw interesting and reliable light on the subject: but only the most important have been included. Nor can the serious student afford to neglect the great fund of historical information available in *The Mariners' Mirror* (the journal of the Society for Nautical Research), and the *Naval Review* (a private circulation journal): but references to those periodicals have been excluded, as they are only available to members. Mr. G. E. Manwaring's comprehensive *Bibliography of British Naval History* (Routledge, 1930), is quite invaluable to those who may wish to locate manuscript sources and articles in periodicals dealing with particular periods or subjects: but a good deal has been discovered and published during the thirty years since Mr. Manwaring's work appeared.

The choice of books and publications dealing with the wars of the 20th century is very wide indeed and it has been difficult to confine the list within reasonable bounds. An attempt has been made to select the most authoritative sources, and those which throw particular light on new developments, such as maritime air and submarine warfare. For these periods the student will find much valuable analysis and discussion in the monthly issues of the *Proceedings of the United States Naval Institute*. Finally a selection of the many books which deal with the strategic problems of the nuclear era has been included.

BIBLIOGRAPHY

1. GENERAL SOURCES ON MARITIME STRATEGY AND NAVAL HISTORY

H. W. RICHMOND, *Statesmen and Seapower* (Oxford U.P., 1946).
National Policy and Naval Strength (Longmans, Green, 1928).
(Ed. E. A. Hughes), *The Navy as an Instrument of Policy, 1557-1727* (Cambridge U.P., 1953).
A. T. MAHAN, *The Influence of Sea Power upon History, 1660-1783,* (Sampson, Low, Marston, 1890).
Naval Strategy (Sampson, Low, Marston, 1911).
J. A. WILLIAMSON, *The Ocean in English History* (Oxford U.P., 1941)
J. K. LAUGHTON, *Studies in Naval History* (Longmans, Green, 1887).
G. S. GRAHAM, *Empire of the North Atlantic* (Cumberlege, 1951).
W. LAIRD CLOWES and others, *The Royal Navy, a History* (7 vols., Sampson, Low, Marston, 1897-1903), though a valuable source of factual information, is too detailed for the lay reader: and as it contains errors caution is advised in making use of it.

More ' popular ' works are:—

C. C. LLOYD, *The Nation and the Navy* (Cresset Press, 1954).
G. CALLENDER, *The Naval Side of British History* (Christophers, 1924).
M. A. LEWIS, *The Navy of Britain* (Allen & Unwin, 1948).
The History of the British Navy (Allen & Unwin, 1959).
R. GRENFELL (as ' T.124 '), *Sea Power* (Cape, 1940).
B. TUNSTALL, *The Anatomy of Neptune* (Routledge, 1936).

2. FROM EARLY TIMES TO THE ACCESSION OF ELIZABETH I

J. A. WILLIAMSON, *Maritime Enterprise 1485-1558* (Oxford U.P., 1913).
The English Channel, (Collins, 1959).
The Voyages of the Cabots and the English Discovery of North America under Henry VII and VIII (Argonaut Press, 1929).
R. HARGREAVES, *The Narrow Seas* (Sidgwick & Jackson, 1959).
S. E. MORISON, *Admiral of the Ocean Sea* (Biography of Christopher Columbus) (2 vols., Oxford U.P., 1942).
F. BROWN, *English Naval Forces 1199-1272* (A. Brown & Sons, 1932).
M. OPPENHEIM, *The Administration of the Royal Navy, Vol. I, 1509-1660* (Lane, 1896).

BIBLIOGRAPHY

3. *ELIZABETH I AND THE WAR WITH SPAIN* (1558-1603)

J. E. NEALE, *Queen Elizabeth* (Cape, 1934).
A. L. ROWSE, *The Expansion of Elizabethan England* (Macmillan, 1955).
J. S. CORBETT, *Drake and the Tudor Navy* (2 vols., Longmans, Green, 1898).
        The Successors of Drake (Longmans, Green, 1900).
J. A. WILLIAMSON, *The Age of Drake* (A. and C. Black, 1938).
G. MATTINGLY, *The Defeat of the Spanish Armada* (Cape, 1959).
M. A. LEWIS, *The Spanish Armada* (Batsford, 1960).

Biographies

E. EDWARDS, *Life of Sir Walter Raleigh* (2 vols., Macmillan, 1868).
J. A. WILLIAMSON, *Sir John Hawkins* (Oxford, U.P., 1927).
        Sir Francis Drake (Collins, 1952).

4. *THE EARLY STUARTS* (1603-1641)

S. R. GARDINER, *History of England from the Accession of James I to the outbreak of the Civil War* 1603-1642 (10 vols., Longmans, Green, New Ed. 1894-5).
C. D. PENN, *The Navy under the early Stuarts* (John Hogg, 1920).
C. R. BOXER, *Journal of Maarten H. Tromp* (2 vols., Cambridge U.P., 1930).
C. DE LA RONCIÈRE, *Histoire de la Marine Française* (Vol. IV of six volumes, Paris, Librairie Plon, 1910).

5. *THE CIVIL WAR, THE COMMONWEALTH AND THE FIRST DUTCH WAR* (1642-1660)

S. R. GARDINER, *History of the Commonwealth and Protectorate* 1649-1654, (4 vols., Longmans, Green, New Ed. 1903).
C. V. WEDGWOOD, *The King's Peace* 1637-1641 (Collins, 1955).
        The King's War 1641-1647 (Collins, 1958).
C. WILSON, *Profit and Power. A Study of England and the Dutch Wars* (Longmans, Green, 1960).
S. R. GARDINER and C. T. ATKINSON (Eds.), *Papers relating to the First Dutch War* 1652-4 (6 vols., Navy Records Society, 1899-1930 and Corrigenda, 1932).
R. C. ANDERSON (Ed.), *The Journal of the First Earl of Sandwich* (Navy Records Society, 1928).
G. E. MANWARING and W. G. PERRIN (Eds.), *Life of Sir Henry Mainwaring* (2 vols., Navy Records Society, 1920-21).

BIBLIOGRAPHY

Biographies

J. S. CORBETT, *Monk* (Macmillan, 1899).

C. D. CURTIS, *Blake, General at Sea* (Barnicott and Pearce, 1934).

J. DE LIEFDE, *The Great Dutch Admirals* (Sonnenschein, Le Bas & Lowrey, 1886).

A. BRYANT, *Samuel Pepys*, Vol. I *The Man in the Making* (Cambridge U.P., 1933).

6. THE RESTORATION AND THE SECOND AND THIRD DUTCH WARS (1660-1688)

D. OGG, *England in the Reign of Charles II* (2 vols., Oxford U.P., 1934).

A. W. TEDDER, *The Navy of the Restoration. From the Death of Cromwell to the Treaty of Breda* (Cambridge U.P., 1916).

A. BRYANT, *Samuel Pepys*, Vols. II and III *The Years of Peril* and *The Saviour of the Navy* (Cambridge U.P., 1935 and 1938).

R. C. ANDERSON (Ed.), *Journals and Narratives of the Third Dutch War* (Navy Records Society, 1948).

F. R. HARRIS, *The Life of Edward Montague, First Earl of Sandwich 1625-1672* (2 vols., Murray, 1912).

7. WILLIAM III AND MARY: THE WAR OF THE ENGLISH SUCCESSION (1688-1697)

D. OGG, *England in the Reigns of James II and William III* (Oxford U.P., 1955).

J. EHRMAN, *The Navy in the War of William III 1689-1697* (Cambridge U.P., 1953).

E. B. POWLEY, *The English Navy in the Revolution of 1688* (Cambridge U.P., 1928).

R. D. MERRIMAN (Ed.), *The Sergison Papers* (Navy Records Society, 1949).

C. DE LA RONCIÈRE, *Histoire de la Marine Française* (Vol. VI of six volumes, Paris, Librairie Plon, 1932).

8. QUEEN ANNE'S WAR, OR WAR OF THE SPANISH SUCCESSION (1702-1713)

J. H. OWEN, *War at Sea under Queen Anne, 1702-1708* (Cambridge U.P., 1938).

G. A. R. CALLENDER, (Ed. S. Martin-Leake), *The Life of Admiral Sir John Leake* (2 vols., Navy Records Society, 1920).

G. S. GRAHAM (Ed.), *The Walker Expedition to Quebec*, 1711 (Navy Records Society, 1953).

B. TUNSTALL (Ed.), *The Byng Papers* (3 vols., Navy Records Society, 1930, 1931, 1932).

J. S. CORBETT, *England in the Mediterranean* (2 vols., Longmans, Green, 1904).

O. BROWNING (Ed.), *Journal of Sir George Rooke* 1700-1702 (Navy Records Society, 1897).

9. THE WAR OF JENKINS'S EAR AND WAR OF THE AUSTRIAN SUCCESSION (1739-1748)

H W. RICHMOND, *The Navy in the War of* 1739-1748 (3 vols., Cambridge U.P., 1920).

R. PARES, *War and Trade in the West Indies* 1739-1763 (Oxford U.P., 1936).
Colonial Blockade and Neutral Rights 1739-1763 (Oxford U.P., 1938).

B. McL. RANFT (Ed.), *The Vernon Papers* (Navy Records Society, 1958).

F. PARKMAN (Ed. S. E. Morison), *France and England in North America* (Faber, 1956). (NOTE: This abridgement by Morison of Parkman's 7 vols. covers the whole period of Anglo-French conflict in North America down to the fall of Quebec, 1759).

Biographies

W. V. ANSON, *Life of Lord Anson* (Murray, 1912).

C. H. HARTMANN, *The Angry Admiral. Edward Vernon, Admiral of the White* (Heinemann, 1953).

10. THE SEVEN YEARS' WAR (1756-1763)

J. S. CORBETT, *England in the Seven Years' War* (2 vols. Longmans, Green, 1907).

H. W. RICHMOND (Ed.), *Papers relating to the loss of Minorca* 1756 (Navy Records Society, 1913).

G. MARCUS, *Quiberon Bay* (Hollis & Carter, 1960).

C. C. LLOYD, *The Capture of Quebec* (Batsford, 1959).

J. S. CORBETT (Ed.), *Fighting Instructions* 1530-1816 (Navy Records Society, 1905).

BIBLIOGRAPHY

11. THE WAR OF AMERICAN INDEPENDENCE (1775-1783)

W. M. JAMES, *The British Navy in Adversity* (Longmans, Green, 1926).

H. W. RICHMOND, *The Navy in India, 1763-1783* (Benn, 1931).

A. J. PATTERSON, *The Other Armada* (Manchester U.P., 1960).

A. T. MAHAN, *Major Operations in the War of American Independence* (Sampson, Low, Marston, 1913).

Biographies

A. T. MAHAN, *Types of Naval Officers* (Sampson, Low, Marston, 1902).

M. BURROWS, *Life of Admiral Lord Hawke* (W. H. Allen, 1899).

J. BARROW, *Life of Richard, Earl Howe* (Murray, 1838).

D. HANNAY, *Rodney* (Macmillan, 1891).

D. HOOD, *The Admirals Hood* (Hutchinson, 1942).

S. E. MORISON, *John Paul Jones* (Faber, 1959).

12. THE WAR OF THE FRENCH REVOLUTION AND THE NAPOLEONIC WAR (1792-1815)

A. T. MAHAN, *The Influence of Sea Power on the French Revolution and Empire 1793-1812* (2 vols., Sampson, Low, Marston, 1892).

C. N. PARKINSON, *The War in the Eastern Seas 1793-1815* (Allen & Unwin, 1954).

M. A. LEWIS, *A Social History of the Navy 1793-1815* (Allen & Unwin, 1960).

G. E. MANWARING and B. DOBRÉE, *The Floating Republic* (Bles, 1935).

J. HOLLAND ROSE, *Lord Hood and the Defence of Toulon* (Cambridge U.P., 1922).

P. MACKESY, *The War in the Mediterranean, 1803-1810* (Longmans, 1957).

O. WARNER, *The Battle of the Nile* (Batsford, 1961).

D. POPE, *England Expects* (Weidenfeld & Nicolson, 1959).

J. S. CORBETT, *The Campaign of Trafalgar* (Longmans, Green, 1910).

E. FRASER, *The Enemy at Trafalgar* (Hodder & Stoughton, 1906).

T. ROOSEVELT, *The Naval War of 1812* (Putnam, 1901).

J. K. LAUGHTON (Ed.), *Letters and Papers of Charles, Lord Barham* (3 vols., Navy Records Society, 1907, 1910, 1911).

W. G. PERRIN and C. C. LLOYD (Eds.), *The Keith Papers* (3 vols., Navy Records Society, 1927, 1950, 1955).

W. JAMES, *The Naval History of Great Britain, 1793-1827* (6 vols., Bentley, 1847).

Biographies

C. OMAN, *Nelson* (Hodder & Stoughton, 1947).

W. CLARK RUSSELL, *The Life of Admiral Lord Collingwood* (Methuen, 1901).

E. P. BRENTON, *Life and Correspondence of John, Earl of St. Vincent* (2 vols., H. Colburn, 1838).

13. *THE NINETEENTH CENTURY*

D. B. SMITH and A. C. DEWAR (Eds.), *The Russian War*, 1854-55 (3 vols., Navy Records Society, 1943-45).

H. W. WILSON, *Ironclads in Action* (2 vols., Sampson, Low, Marston, 1896).

M. A. LEWIS (Ed.), *Sir William Dillon's Narrative of Professional Adventures* (2 vols., Navy Records Society, 1953, 1960).

R. CARSE, *Blockade: The Civil War at Sea* (Rinehart, U.S.A., 1958).

D. MACINTYRE, *The Thunder of the Guns. A Century of Battleships* (Muller, 1959).

14. *THE DAWN OF THE NEW ERA* (1900-1914)

A. J. MARDER, *From the Dreadnought to Scapa Flow* (Cape, 1961).

F. T. JANE, *The British Battle Fleet* (2 vols., Library Press, 1915).

H. W. WILSON, *Battleships in Action* (Vol. I of 2 vols., Sampson, Low, Marston, 1926).

LORD FISHER, *Records* (Hodder & Stoughton, 1919).

A. J. MARDER (Ed.), *Fear God and Dread Nought. The Letters of Lord Fisher of Kilverstone* (3 vols., Cape, 1952, 1956, 1959).

15. *THE FIRST GERMAN WAR* (1914-1918)

Official or 'Authorised' Histories

J. S. CORBETT and H. NEWBOLT, *Naval Operations* (5 vols., Longmans, Green, 1920-1931).

C. E. FAYLE, *Seaborne Trade* (3 vols., Murray, 1920, 1921, 1924).

A. HURD, *The Merchant Navy* (3 vols., Murray, 1921, 1924, 1929).

W. RALEIGH and H. A. JONES, *The War in the Air* (6 vols., Oxford U.P., 1922-1937).

The German Official History, *Der Krieg Zur See*, was published under seven subject headings and is extremely detailed. English translations of some parts are in the Admiralty Library, but no translation has been published.

Shorter Works

H. NEWBOLT, *A Naval History of the War*, 1914-1918 (Hodder & Stoughton, 1920).

W. S. SIMS with B. J. HENDRICK, *Victory at Sea* (Murray, 1920).

R. SCHEER, *Germany's High Seas Fleet in the World War* (Cassell, 1920).

LORD JELLICOE, *The Grand Fleet 1914-1918* (Cassell, 1919).
         The Crisis of the Naval War (Cassell, 1920).

A. MOOREHEAD, *Gallipoli* (Hamish Hamilton, 1956).

B. PITT, *Coronel and the Falklands* (Cassell, 1960).

Biographies

R. H. BACON, *Life of Earl Jellicoe* (Cassell, 1936).

W. S. CHALMERS, *The Life and Letters of David, Earl Beatty* (Hodder & Stoughton, 1951).

16. THE SECOND GERMAN WAR (1939-45)

A. Official or 'Authorised' Histories covering the whole War

S. W. ROSKILL, *The War at Sea* (4 vols., H.M.S.O., 1954-61).

S. E. MORISON, *The History of United States Naval Operations in World War II* (14 vols., Little, Brown, U.S.A. and Oxford U.P., 1948-60).

J. SCHULL, *War History of the Royal Canadian Navy, The Far Distant Ships* (Ministry of Defence, Ottawa, 1951).

G. HERMON GILL, *The Royal Australian Navy, 1939-42* (Australian War Memorial, 1958).

B. Shorter works covering whole War

S. W. ROSKILL, *The Navy at War, 1939-45* (Collins, 1960).

J. CRESSWELL, *Sea Warfare 1939-45* (Longmans, Green, 1950).

P. K. KEMP, *Victory at Sea* (Muller, 1958).

J. L. KERR and W. GRANVILLE, *The R.N.V.R.* (Harrap, 1957).

E. RAEDER, *Struggle for the Sea* (Kimber, 1959).

F. RUGE, *Sea Warfare 1939-45. A German view point.* (Cassell, 1957).

B. FERGUSSON, *The Watery Maze. The Story of Combined Operations* (Collins, 1961).

C. Battles and Campaigns

I. EVACUATION FROM EUROPE AND INVASION THREAT, 1940

L. F. ELLIS, *The War in France and Flanders, 1939-40* (Official History, H.M.S.O., 1953).

BIBLIOGRAPHY

D. DIVINE, *The Nine Days of Dunkirk* (Faber, 1959).
P. FLEMING, *Invasion 1940* (Hart-Davis, 1957).
D. GRINNELL-MILNE, *The Silent Victory* (Bodley Head, 1958).
R. WHEATLEY, *Operation Sea Lion* (Oxford U.P., 1957).
W. ANSEL, *Hitler Confronts England* (Duke U.P., U.S.A., 1960).

2. BATTLE OF THE ATLANTIC

D. MACINTYRE, *The Battle of the Atlantic* (Batsford, 1961).
U-boat Killer (Weidenfeld & Nicolson, 1956).
D. A. RAYNER (Ed. S. W. Roskill), *Escort* (Kimber, 1955).
S. W. ROSKILL, *The Secret Capture* (Collins, 1959).
R. SETH, *The Fiercest Battle. The Story of Convoy ONS.5* (Hutchinson, 1961).

3. THE PACIFIC WAR

S. W. KIRBY and others, *The War against Japan* (Official History, Vols. I and II, H.M.S.O., 1957, 1958).
K. ATTIWELL, *The Singapore Story* (Muller, 1959).
F. OWEN, *The Fall of Singapore* (Michael Joseph, 1960).
T. V. TULEJA, *Climax at Midway* (Dent, 1960).
M. FUCHIDA and M. OKUMIYA, *Midway* (Hutchinson, 1957).
M. OKUMIYA and J. HORIKOSHI, *Zero* (Cassell, 1957).
C. VANN WOODWARD, *The Battle for Leyte Gulf* (Macmillan, U.S.A., 1947).
R. INOGUCHI, T. NAKAJIMA and R. PINEAU, *The Divine Wind* (Hutchinson, 1959).

4. MEDITERRANEAN CAMPAIGNS

I. S. O. PLAYFAIR and others, *The Mediterranean and Middle East* (Official History, Vols. I, II and III, H.M.S.O., 1954, 1956, 1960).
I. CAMERON, *Red Duster, White Ensign. The Story of the Malta Convoys* (Muller, 1959).
S. W. C. PACK, *The Battle of Matapan* (Batsford, 1961).
W. VAUGHAN-THOMAS, *Anzio* (Longmans, 1961).
H. POND *Salerno* (Kimber, 1961).

5. HOME WATERS, ATLANTIC AND ARCTIC

R. GRENFELL, *The Bismarck Episode* (Faber, 1948).
D. POPE, *73 North* (Weidenfeld & Nicolson, 1958).
D. MACINTYRE, *Narvik* (Evans, 1959).
C. E. L. PHILLIPS, *The Greatest Raid of All* (Heinemann, 1958).

BIBLIOGRAPHY

G. WINN, *P.Q. 17* (Hutchinson, 1947).

I. CAMPBELL and D. MACINTYRE, *The Kola Run* (Muller, 1958).

D. POPE, *The Battle of the River Plate* (Kimber, 1956).

E. YOUNG, *One of Our Submarines* (Hart-Davis, 1952).

6. INVASION OF NORMANDY, 1944

D. HOWARTH, *Dawn of D-Day* (Collins, 1959).

C. RYAN, *The Longest Day* (Gollancz, 1960).

D. Biographies and Autobiographies

LORD CUNNINGHAM, *A Sailor's Odyssey* (Hutchinson, 1951).

W. S. CHALMERS, *Full Cycle. The Biography of Admiral Sir Bertram Ramsay* (Hodder & Stoughton, 1959).

Max Horton and the Western Approaches (Hodder & Stoughton, 1954).

D. MACINTYRE, *Fighting Admiral. The Biography of Admiral Sir James Somerville* (Evans, 1961).

P. VIAN, *Action this Day* (Muller, 1960).

E. J. KING and W. M. WHITEHILL, *Fleet Admiral King* (Eyre & Spottiswoode, 1953).

W. F. HALSEY and J. BRYAN, *Admiral Halsey's Story* (McGraw-Hill, U.S.A., 1960).

K. DÖNITZ, *Admiral Dönitz Memoirs* (Weidenfeld & Nicolson, 1959).

17. STRATEGY IN THE MID-20th CENTURY

B. H. LIDDELL HART, *Deterrent or Defence* (Stevens, 1960).

J. SLESSOR, *Strategy for the West* (Cassell, 1954).

The Central Blue (Cassell, 1956).

H. S. DINERSTEIN, *War and the Soviet Union* (Stevens, 1959).

R. L. GARTHOFF, *Soviet Strategy in the Nuclear Age* (Stevens, 1959).

E. J. KINGSTON-MCCLOUGHRY, *Defence* (Stevens, 1960).

MAXWELL D. TAYLOR, *The Uncertain Trumpet* (Stevens, 1960).

F. A. JOHNSON, *Defence by Committee* (Oxford U.P., 1960).

LORD TEDDER, *Air Power in War* (Hodder & Stoughton, 1948).

Index

Admiralty: Navy Board founded, 24; considers evacuation of Mediterranean in 1796, 71; decision to reinforce Mediterranean in 1798, 72; strategy of in Napoleonic war, 78, 80; remedies inefficiency after Crimean War, 92; "Blue Water School," 94, 104; arguments with War Office, 94-5; slow to develop submarines, 96; Fisher's reforms, 101-2; Naval War Staff established, 102-3; turns down patents for flying machines, 103; attitude towards C.I.D., 103; on blockade prior to 1914 war, 105; responsibility for escape of *Goeben* and *Breslau*, 113; signals during Battle of Jutland, 117-20; naval expedition to Gallipoli, 122; anti-submarine measures of, 129, 131; reluctance to adopt escort of convoy strategy, 130-1; adopts convoy strategy, 131; relinquishes control of R.N.A.S., 138; on capabilities of naval aircraft, 138; changes of First Sea Lord in 1914 war, 140; struggle for navy between the wars, 146-8; discussions with Air Ministry, 149; in sinking of *Bismarck*, 171; in movement of *Prince of Wales* and *Repulse* to Singapore, 174-5; operational control of aircraft in the Atlantic, 180-1; in disaster to PQ.17, 183; build up strength in Indian Ocean, 186, 209; clearance of Scheldt, 224; on providing bases and a Fleet Train in Pacific, 227; development of mobile naval base organisation, 239-40

Admiralty Islands: assault on, naval base established in, 208; use as intermediate base by B.P.F., 227

Aegean: reverses in 1943, 206-7; German withdrawal 1944, 224

Air Ministry: on functions of Coastal Command, 149; views on convoy, 152.

Air Power: influence on close blockade, 49, 105; Fisher's foresight on, 102; use of Zeppelins, 116; Admiralty's conservatism towards, 138, 238; functions of carrier-borne aircraft, 149; influence on

earlier strategic conceptions, 150, 238; prevents invasion in 1940, 167; application of for blockade, 169-70; German Air Force superiority in Greece and Crete, 172-3; efficiency of Japanese carrier air power, 175; superiority in Sicily does not prevent Axis evacuation, 204; lack of in Aegean in 1943, 206-7; Allied air superiority before invasion of Normandy, 212-13; of American carrier task-force, 208, 218, 228; as instrument of blockade, 230, 232; in amphibious enterprises, 243-4; contribution to the maritime war, 244-6; in the nuclear age, 253, 255, 261

Alexandria: capture of in 1801, 76; base for Mediterranean Fleet in 1939, 151; immobilisation of French Squadron in, 165; British battleships damaged at, 193

Algeria: capture of 1942, 191-4

America: New Amsterdam handed over to Britain, 35-6; fighting in, in Seven Years' War, 50-2; War of American Independence, 60-3; *see* United States for subsequent entries.

Amphibious warfare and operations: exploitation of under Elizabeth I, 27-8; lessons learnt from early operations, 28-9, 37; operations in the Seven Years' War, 52-4; Pitt's secret instruction to Wolfe, 53; operations in the War of the French Revolution, 74; failure of expedition to Constantinople in 1807, 83; operations in the war with America of 1812, 87; in the Crimean War, 90; neglect of in 19th century, 94-5; Fisher's views on, 103; war plans for, prior to 1914, 107-8, 122; operations in 1914, 114-15; the Dardanelles campaign, 122-5; reasons for failure of, 126; Zeebrugge and Ostend raids, 132-4; not mentioned in 1939 war plans, 149-50, 157, 241; Norway campaign in 1940, 162; failure at Dakar, 165-6; skill of Japanese in, 175, 188; development of, and operations in 1942, 184-7; essence of offensive strategy, 187-8; invasion of

Fisher as First Sea Lord, 125; succeeded by Jellicoe, 126

Japan: Anglo-Japanese Alliance of 1905, 146; rise of as a maritime power, 147; attacks on Malaya and South East Asia, 174-5; strategic errors in Pacific, 209; heavy losses of merchant shipping, 209, 219; cut off from conquests of 1941, 228; downfall of, 232-4; effect of blockade on, 232-3, 245-6

Japanese Navy: efficiency of carrier air power, 175, 188; raids on Ceylon, 186; defeats in battles of Coral Sea and Midway, 187-8; failure to adopt convoy strategy, 209; defeat in Battle of the Philippine Sea, 216-17; defeat at Battle of Leyte Gulf, 218-19; use of the Kamikaze suicide bomber, 219, 232; final destruction of, 233

Jellicoe, Admiral John, Earl: C-in-C Grand Fleet, 108, 114, 121-2; in Jutland, 117-20; becomes First Sea Lord, 126; reluctance to adopt convoy, 130; succeeded as First Sea Lord, 131; pessimistic views of, 132; proposes northern mine barrage, 134

Jervis, John, Earl St. Vincent: 69, 71-2

"Kamikaze": Japanese suicide bomber, 219, 232

Keith, Admiral Lord: 77

Kempenfelt, Richard: 64

Keyes, Admiral of the Fleet, Sir Roger: in Dardanelles campaign, 124-5; raid on Zeebrugge, 133

King, Admiral E. J., U.S. Navy: Chief of Naval Operations, opposition to a British Fleet in Pacific, 226; strategy to establish base on China Coast, 228

Kitchener, Earl: 122-5

Klosterzeven: convention of, 51

Landing Ships and Craft: designs for developed, 185; chronic shortage of in S.E. Asia, 209-10, shortage of for Anzio landings, 210

Laughton, Sir John: 61, 81

League of Nations: 145, 147

Leros: occupation and loss of, 206-7

Lewis, Professor M. A.: 46

Leyte: Americans land on, 218

Lion, H.M.S.: 115-16

Lisbon: expedition against in 1589, 28, 30-2; British base in War of Spanish Succession, 43-4; British base in War of French Revolution, 75

Lloyd George: forces Admiralty to adopt convoy, 131, 140; strategy of, 140-1; rejects doctrine of "Freedom of the Seas," 145

Logistics: problem of in blockading enemy ports, 38, 48; problem in the Pacific, 189; the American Fleet Train, 227, 240; difficulties in providing a British Fleet Train, 227

Londonderry: 40, 157

Louis XIV, King of France: 35-6, 40, 42

Louisbourg: capture and return of, 47-8; recapture of by Wolfe, 52

Lützow, German pocket battleship: 181

MacArthur, U.S. General: campaign in New Guinea, 190, 208-9; seizes Morotai, 217; invasion of Leyte, 218; reconquest of Philippine Islands, 227-8; protagonist of amphibious strategy, 228

Macaulay, Lord: 54-5

Madagascar: 186-7

Madeira: occupations of, 75, 83, 167

Madison, U.S. President: 86-7

Mahan, A. T.: on *guerre de course*, 42, 116; on the outcome of the Seven Years' War, 54; on convoy in Seven Years' War, 55; on Hotham's actions in War of French Revolution, 68, 70; works on Sea Power, 81, 95; on sea power in Napoleonic War, 82; on Britain's spirit of aggression, 84; on dealing with commerce raiders, 160; on maritime concentration, 165

Malaya: Japanese invasion of, 174, 186

Malta: blockade of in 1799, 73; capture of in 1800, 75; return to the Knights, 76-7; defence of in Second German War, 151-2; key to control of Mediterranean, 167, 173; reinforcements sent to in 1941-2, 173-4, 183; siege ends, 194

Manila: 54, 228

Mann, Admiral: 70

Mariana Islands: assault on, 216-17

Maritime Needs and Policy in 1960s: need for mobile joint service task forces, 254-5; need to improve sea and air trade defence, 255-8; need to retain bases, 257-8; defence policy for N.A.T.O., 260, 263-4; need for more integration of British fighting services, 260-2; interests of neutrals, 262-3

Maritime Power: function of, 15; history of growth of, 16-17; combined operations as means of exploitation of, 29; importance of realised by Commonwealth leaders, 33; use of 1700-40, 45; use of in Seven Years' War, 51; decline of British

INDEX

appointed, 209; shortage of landing craft in, 210, 219; blockade of Japanese ports in, 219-20

Spain: War with England (1585-1603), 27-32; in First Dutch War, 34; in War of Spanish Succession, 42-4; in war of Jenkins's Ear, 45; in Seven Years' War, 54; in war of French Revolution, 67-8, 75; in Napoleonic War, 77-8

Stalin, Russian Marshal: 183

Stopford, General: 125

Strategy: *see* Maritime Strategy, Deterrent Strategy, Maritime Needs and Policy in 1960s

Submarines and Submarine Warfare: slowness of R.N. to develop, 96-7; Fisher's foresight on, 102, 104; Wilson's views on, 103; German use of in war of 1914-18, 112, 121; Germans resort to unrestricted warfare, 129, 131-2; British attempt to block Zeebrugge and Ostend, 132-4; U-boat warfare in 1939, 158; U-boat warfare in 1940-41, 168; U-boat campaign off American coast and in Caribbean, 179; crisis in Atlantic in March, 1943, 195; U-boats withdraw from Atlantic, 195; operation of "milch cows," 196-7; U-boat operations in remote areas, 196; Bay of Biscay air offensive on U-boats, 196-7; midget submarines attack on *Tirpitz*, 198; American successes in Pacific, 209, 219; Germans develop "Schnörkel," 222; U-boats shift to Norway, 222; U-boat losses in Mediterranean campaign, 225; as instruments of blockade, 230; U-boats in final phase of the war, 230; figures of U-boat losses and results achieved, 231; Japanese tonnage sunk by Allied submarines, 233; submarines to replace aircraft for delivery of the nuclear missile, 253-4, 261

Suez Canal: 93, 257

Suffren, French Admiral: 61-3

Tactics, Naval: influence of Fighting Instructions on, 46, 81; study of in 18th century, 64-5; line of battle, 63, 71, 80, 108; discussion of Nelson's Trafalgar Memorandum, 80; slowness of Navy to change with technical progress, 96; at outbreak of 1914 war, 108-10; in Dogger Bank action, 115-16; in Battle of Jutland, 117-20; rigidity causes disappointing results in 1914 war, 141-2; problems studied and exercised between the wars, 149; influence of "Operational Research" on, 238-9; impact of air power on, 247-8

Tanga: expedition to, 115

Tangier: 35, 39

Texel: expedition against, 74

Tiger, H.M.S.: 116

Tirpitz, German battleship: threat to Arctic convoys, 182-3; attack on by midget submarines, 198; attacks on and sinking of by R.A.F., 220; influence of on British strategy, 221

Tobruk: raid on, 185

Torpedoes: influence on close blockade, 49; on tactics, 119-20

Torrington, Earl of: 40

Toulon: attempt to capture in War of Spanish Succession, 42-3; action off in 1744, 46-7; action at in 1793, 67, 69; blockades in war of French Revolution, 70, 72-3; blockade in Napoleonic War, 48, 77-8, 82, 85, 93

Tourville, French Admiral: 40

Trade: leads to development of maritime power, 15-19; expansion under Elizabeth I, 26-7; principal cause of Dutch Wars, 33-5; *guerre de course* against, discussion of, 40-2; expansion in spite of *guerre de course*, 54; Armed Neutrality against interference with, 61, 74; Napoleon's Continental System and Milan decree, 82-3; Britain's "Orders in Council," 82-3, 86, 111; neutral nations benefit during war, 111

Treaties, Naval: Five Power Naval, 145; Four-Power, 146; Naval Limitation of 1922, 146; of London, 1930, 147; Anglo-Egyptian of 1936, 151

Treaties of Peace: of Breda, 35; of Ryswick, 42; Methuen, 43; of Utrecht, 44-5; of Aix la Chapelle, 48, 50; of Versailles in 1783, 63; of Amiens, 76; of Tilsit, 82; of Ghent, 87

Tunisia: campaign in, 194

Turkey: expedition to Constantinople of 1807, 83, 123; *Goeben* and *Breslau* escape to, 112-13; in Dardanelles campaign, 122-6; neutrality of in Second German War, 182; Aegean campaign in 1943, 206; enters war in 1945, 225

Tyrwhitt, Admiral Sir R.: 133

U-boats: *see* Submarines and Submarine Warfare

United Nations Organisation: 260

United States of America: (*see* under America for entries previous to 1783) Louisiana Purchase, 77; War with

EPILOGUE

MARITIME DEVELOPMENTS SINCE 1962

There have been many political, economic, legal and technological changes in the world scene since 1962 when *The Strategy of Sea Power* first appeared. The world, and the role played in it by navies has altered markedly over the past twenty years or so. The effects of political and economic change have been nowhere more apparent than for the British. Within a few years of the publication of Roskill's book, the British Government declared its intention to withdraw from defence commitments East of Suez and opened a determined campaign to join the European community. These objectives have been largely achieved and Britain is more substantially wedded to Western Europe for its prosperity and security than it has been for many centuries. Nevertheless the recent Falklands war and current discussions about a Western, or indeed a West European role, in the Indian Ocean/Gulf region shows this to be more a switch in emphasis than a complete acceptance of a wholly Eurocentric defence policy. More ominously the relative decline in Britain's economic fortunes which was already apparent in 1962 has become markedly so since then. This decline is nowhere more evident than in the merchant shipping and shipbuilding industries. In consequence the capability gap between Britain and its main ally has widened considerably since 1962, when it was already great.

But the United States, and its Navy, faces a more complex and in many ways a more difficult world too. There has been a diffusion of military power and political initiative such that the long-established confrontation between East and West is far from being the only source of conflict involving navies. Since 1962 there have, in fact, been many naval wars, or wars with a substantial naval component; the Arab-Israeli Wars of 1967 and 1973; the Vietnam War; the Indo-Pakistan War of 1971; the Turkish invasion of Cyprus 1974; the Falklands War of 1982; the current war between Iran and Iraq, to name but a few. In these wars, many of the classical functions of sea power were once more displayed, but so far at least there have been no direct hostilities between the superpowers.

One of the occasions when they perhaps got nearest to this was in October 1962 a few months after the publication of *The Strategy of Sea Power* – the Cuba Missile Crisis. Its experience here persuaded the Soviet Government to make a determined push for parity in strategic nuclear weapons, a state most certainly achieved by the late 1970s. This achievement has considerably bolstered Soviet confidence and reinforced the perception that the consequences of a full-scale nuclear war would be unbearable for all concerned. This knowledge has naturally inhibited the behaviour of both: in the first place the superpowers have sought to avoid situations of confrontation. In the second, where these nevertheless occur, both have consented to follow a largely unstated set of rules which lessens the chance of inadvertent conflict or escalation. Nowhere was this more readily apparent than in the careful orchestration of naval activity before, during and after the Arab-Israeli War of 1973. But other sources of conflict remain, and indeed, in today's turbulent and volatile world, have multiplied. These will inevitably concern the superpowers whether they wish it or not and vastly complicate the task of naval planners who must prepare for a bewilderingly wide range of possible contingencies.

The Cuban Missile Crisis also reinforced another process in the Soviet Union that was already well underway in 1962 – a desire for a substantial global navy, because that crisis revealed the vulnerability of the strongest nation if it could not get its way at sea. Certainly the rise of the Soviet Navy over the past twenty years or so has been one of the most remarkable developments of the post-war era. Of course Soviet naval planners continue to operate under severe constraints: they have to cope with a grossly inefficient administrative and governmental system, a disappointing economy, an adverse maritime geography and the continued dominance of the Soviet military establishment by the Army. Nevertheless they have produced a Navy which has transformed the Soviet Union into a global superpower with an infinitely longer political and military reach than it had before.

This has resulted in a hugely increased maritime threat (perhaps involuntary, perhaps not) to Western security and prosperity. In times of peace the efforts of a busy and active Soviet navy are supplemented by those of a thriving merchant marine in challenging Western political and economic interests around the world. In times of war and tension the military threat to Western maritime security had vastly increased. It used to be the case that the United States and its allies could afford to assume that the West would command the sea and ponder merely on what to do with it. Now this is no longer true. The West would need to fight for command before being able to exercise it. Everything that might have to be done at sea in any future conflict would be far more difficult to achieve than it might have been before: since the facts of geography alone make NATO a predominantly maritime alliance which must command the sea in order to survive, this change in the strategic balance at sea is highly significant.

In addition to these political-economic-strategic changes there have been others too, not least in the legal sphere. The first United Nations conference on the Law of the Sea began in 1958 and there has since slowly developed a general acceptance of a territorial sea that has been extended from three to twelve miles. This has affected the legal status of over one hundred international straits. Furthermore some believe that the current almost universal practice of exercising rights over an Exclusive Economic Zone of

200 miles will in course of time and by a process of creeping jurisdiction lead to futher enclosure of the open oceans. There has been a good deal of controversy about the extent to which maritime operations are hedged around by an increasing corpus of international law and treaty obligation, and about the effects that this might have.

Some experts maintain that these legal, or quasi legal restrictions will reduce the value of navies by undermining their traditional mobility and flexibility. For instance, anything which significantly reduces rights of passage is bound to interfere with the ability of naval forces to get rapidly from one place to another and must therefore reduce their strategic value both in war and peace. On the other hand sceptics have pointed to recent mysterious submarine happenings off the coast of Sweden in support of a contention that no law of the sea which significantly reduced the value of navies would in fact be allowed to appear by those great powers whose interests would suffer if it did. In the meantime, with constant quarrels over disputed areas of the world ocean, such as the South China, Barents and Aegean Seas, to name but a few, evolving law is more likely to increase gainful employment for sailors than to decrease it. Moreover if and when lines of jurisdiction are eventually agreed, the resultant areas will need to be policed – and this will require naval forces too, if of a mainly constabulary kind.

But the most dramatic source of change has clearly been technological. The revolution in weaponry stands out most obviously, particularly with the development of nuclear weapons and their possible application to war at sea. Some radicals have argued that their advent would reduce the value of navies because future conflicts between the great powers would either *be* short because nuclear weapons were used or be *kept* short for fear that nuclear weapons might be used otherwise. Either way, it seemed, the war would be over before navies had time to exercise a decisive influence on its outcome, because, as all the traditional theories agreed, the exercise of maritime power is essentially a slow-acting business. Others, on the other hand, have argued that the catastrophic consequences of going nuclear would greatly inhibit the use of such weapons, and in fact might make unavoided wars long, or limited, or both. Conventional military operations at sea would therefore be perfectly possible. There has been even more uncertainty, and far less public discussion of another aspect of the nuclear issue, namely the ways in which naval warfare itself would be affected by the use of nuclear weapons – a cloudy issue of which the world has, happily, no experience.

There have been other dramatic sources of change in weapons technology as well. The sinking of the Israeli destroyer *Eilat* by the Egyptian Navy in 1967 confirmed the age of the naval missile as did the Indo-Pakistan war of 1971, the Falklands war of 1982 and the current war in the Gulf. These new weapons are more lethal, more accurate, of longer range, apparently capable of infinite development and launchable from the smallest of naval platforms. On the one hand they give the surface ship more power than it has ever had before (as in the case of the Soviet nuclear battle cruiser *Kirov* and when their Tomahawk cruise missiles are fitted, the U.S. Navy's reconstructed battleships of the *New Jersey* class) but on the other seem to make it more vulnerable to attack by submarine, aircraft and minor combatants of all kinds. Various means of defence of course exist, in the shape of technological deception, of active defence by means of the pre-emptive destruction of the enemy weapons platform or by destroying the incoming missiles *after* they have been launched. This possibility is quite a novel one. Nelson could not swat down cannon balls after the French had fired them at him but his successors do have some such prospect.

The lethality of modern weapons has increased the advantages of hiding if such is possible and many would argue that its particular combination of effective firepower, relative conceal-ment, high speed and long endurance through nuclear propulsion have elevated the importance of the submarine relative to the surface ship. Roskill himself believed that this would be so:

> The fleet of the future, as I see it, will probably not be a balanced fleet, but will be almost entirely a submarine and anti-submarine fleet, and I fancy that more and more warships will go underwater before many years are past.[1]

But in fact this has not proved to be the case so far, though there are persistent claims that it may yet be. In the first place, the capacity to use the sea positively (rather than simply to deny such uses to someone else) for the transport of men and materials across the oceans or to launch amphibious operations still requires the presence of surface ships, often of the largest kind. Moreover the surface ship still enjoys huge advantages in that other main dimension of technological change in naval warfare, the revolution in communications, sensors and command and control. The volume of potential reconnaissance and battle information has enormously increased over the past several decades thanks to the advent of surveillance and communications satellites, sensor technology and computer data processing. Of course such developments bring their own problems too, but they tend to be more manageable on surface ships, particularly large ones. As the French Admiral, Hubert de Moineville, has recently concluded: 'Thus missiles, data processing and helicopters have restored standard surface ships to their rightful place in combat at sea – something that would have seemed unlikely some years ago'.[2] For such reasons, Roskill's rejection of the balanced fleet still appears premature. Most current analysts believe navies need the kind of all-round capability that makes it difficult for their adversary to outflank them either by tactical or technical means. This is represented as a balanced fleet comprising a judicious mix of surface ships, submarines and aircraft. Admiral Gorshkov of

---

[1] In correspondence with R. E. Walters, 21 April, 1965 in Rosk 7/8, Churchill College, Cambridge.
[2] Hubert de Moineville, *Naval Warfare Today and Tomorrow*. (Oxford: Basil Blackwell, 1983), p. 73.

the Soviet Navy is quite clear on the matter. In his view, the Soviet Union needs the

> harmonious balanced development of the force of the ocean-going navy matching the demands of the time, capable of opposing any stratagems of foes and of confronting a potential aggressor with the need to solve himself the very problems which he is creating for our country[3]

All these technological challenges, when acting in conjunction with the related political, economic, strategic and legal changes discussed earlier, have created a climate of uncertainty about naval purposes and naval methods analogous in many ways to that of the late 19th Century, another era when naval men were faced with a bewildering plethora of competing developments. Such challenges have occasionally caused something of a crisis in confidence even in the biggest navies. As Admiral Gorshkov remarked,

> It turned out unfortunately that we had some very influential 'authorities' who considered that with the appearance of atomic weapons, the Navy had completely lost its value as a branch of the armed forces. According to their views, all of the basic missions in a future war allegedly could be fully resolved without the participation of the Navy.[4]

But despite these doubts the strategic importance of the sea has remained and we will conclude this brief review of the maritime scene since 1962 with a survey of some of the major functions of the world's navies together with some account of how they are performed today. We will start by addressing some of the peacetime ones.

The supervision of the sea immediately off the shore line has always been an important function and is now the main task of most of the world's navies. Militarily it is as important now to

---

[3] S. G. Gorshkov, *The Sea Power of the State* (London: Pergamon, 1979) pp. 154–5.
[4] Quoted in R. W. Herrick, *Soviet Naval Strategy* (Annapolis: U.S. Naval Institute Press, 1968) p. 68.

offer a last ditch defence against raids, minor attacks or incoming invaders as ever it has been. Nowadays this function calls for the employment of a host of minor combatants, patrolling aircraft, inshore submarines, coastal artillery, minefields and sensors. Its continued importance is exemplified by the fact that something like one ton in six of the Soviet surface fleet is devoted to the performance of such tasks. For recent examples, one can look at the efforts of the Swedish navy to prosecute submarines operating amongst its islands or to the radar picket/air defence Type 42 destroyers standing between the Falklands and Argentine airfields during and after the South Atlantic conflict of 1982.

This military function in coastal waters has been bolstered by the increasing need to manage the offshore estate because of the growth in relative importance of marine resources, competition for declining stocks of fish, the size and activity of the world's merchant shipping and the general increase of the leisure interest in the sea. This implies an increased possibility of jurisdictional disputes such as those over demarcation in the South China or Barents Sea as well as a need for positive policing of shipping against drugs smuggling, violation of fishing regulations, piracy, illegal immigrants, subversives, maritime terrorism and so on. No-one doubts that this must be done, although there are differences of opinion about the methods to be used. Some urge the U.S. Coast Guard model: a large civilian paramilitary navy for small tasks; most, though, include at least some of these functions within the range of 'normal' naval tasks. But their performance calls for large numbers of small ships whose design and operation requires flexibility and restraint; their requirements are often so specialised that these ships are not suitable for deep-water operations and so naval planners have to make difficult choices between competing priorities.

Admiral Gorshkov has also given considerable emphasis to the political role of naval forces in peacetime. This is no longer regarded as something of a bonus, but instead as a principal justification for having a navy in the first place. He has persuaded his political masters that the navy is an effective vehicle for spreading ideas, for winning allies and helping them, and for increasing the prestige and influence of the state. A whole range of naval activities serve these ends, ranging from friendly port visits, joint exercises, training and the conduct of sea-based trade. Gorshkov also emphasised the 'deterrent' functions of naval power as a means of dissuading potential adversaries from taking hostile action, by showing them that the costs of the action could well outweigh the benefits. This is done by the constant rehearsal and visible display of all military capacities at sea, with their moderation, incidentally, being one means of signalling a desire for better relations.

Finally sea power can be a means of coercion even in peacetime. Navies, Gorshkov tells us, can:

> demonstrate graphically the real fighting power of one's state . . . Demonstrative actions by the navy in many cases have made it possible to achieve political ends without resorting to armed struggle, merely by putting on pressure with one's own potential might and threatening to start military operations. Thus . . . the navy has always been an instrument of the policy of states, an important aid to diplomacy in peacetime.[5]

Naval diplomacy of this sort requires forces capable of performing a wide variety of tasks, possibly far from home and for extended periods of time. It is the natural function of the larger navies but has been regularly conducted by many small and medium navies, in a reduced way, throughout the postwar period.

Two points should perhaps be made about these peacetime functions of sea power. In the first place they have been much performed by the world's navies over the past generation or so: the stress on naval diplomacy may be in partial recognition of the

---

[5] Gorshkov, op. cit. p. 248.

greatly increased costs of actually using force in the modern age. Secondly they are functions for which the classical formulations of maritime strategy, Roskill's included, offer little guidance. Of necessity therefore there has arisen, especially over the past twenty years, a veritable library of modern literature full of suggestions as to how these tasks should be performed.

When considering the war-time activities of modern navies we enter a more familiar world. Command of the sea, or as it is now generally called, sea control, continues to be the immediate operational aim of navies in wartime situations. Modern weaponry may make it a more transient and geographically limited phenomenon than it often used to be, but its purpose remains as Roskill described it – the means by which one can use the sea for one's own purposes and prevent an enemy from using it for his. Current conceptions of maritime strategy also identify the concept of sea denial by which one aims simply at preventing the enemy from using the sea in certain areas. This is widely held to have been the rather modest aim of the Soviet Navy of the 1950s whose object was to prevent the U.S. Navy Carrier Battle Groups from using northern waters in order to attack Soviet territory.

Since 1962 control of the sea has been contested in the traditional way by naval battle, in terms dictated by modern technology. The preliminary encounters of the Argentine and British navies in the early days of the Falklands conflict, which resulted in the sinking of the *General Belgrano* were a modern example of an old style of battle, both the ship and the torpedo which sank it being of World War II vintage. A more typical modern example of naval battle would be the engagements between Arab and Israeli missile-equipped fast attack craft during the Arab-Israeli war of 1973. There the style may have been different, but the principle and the purpose were the same. Equally, the air/sea engagements of the Falklands and Gulf wars of course have parallels as well as dissimilarities to World War II experience.

Admittedly second-best navies have continued to opt instead for a fleet-in-being strategy of some sort. In 1973 for example the Egyptian navy kept two *Kotlin* class destroyers just about operational in Alexandria, thus occupying the attention of Israeli forces which would otherwise have been attacking the Arab interest elsewhere, in a manner distinctly reminiscent of the wartime career of the German battleship *Tirpitz*. The response of the stronger side to a weaker adversary deliberately seeking to avoid battle has always been to seek to neutralise his forces by some form of military blockade, and so it is now. In the Falklands campaign British submarines effectively sealed the Argentine fleet into its bases in just such a way. In any sustained East/West conflict Western forces would certainly seek to exploit the geographic vulnerabilities of the Soviet Union to try to cut its naval forces off from the world's ocean by blockading the various narrows through which they would have to pass.

The weaponry employed in modern struggles for sea control may be novel in some respects – the use of nuclear-propelled submarines, or naval missiles of long range and considerable lethality: the forces in contention may be smaller individually, or in the aggregate, or more spread about, relying heavily on satellite communications and computer technology. They seem nevertheless to be working to principles and purposes which the classical theories of maritime power would have found eminently recognisable.

This is much less true of one of the ways in which the great powers employ their capacity to use the sea – namely as an area from which to deploy the forces of strategic nuclear strike directed against the territory of the principal adversary and his allies. Although the Soviet Navy had deployed submarines with primitive long-range land attack missiles from the late 1950s, this new naval task really came to fruition with the commissioning of the first of the US Navy's *Polaris* submarines at the time Roskill was completing his manuscript for *The Strategy of Sea Power*. The advantage of putting the nuclear deterrent at sea in this way was that the missile-carrying submarine's invisibility made it difficult for the adversary to locate and destroy it. Accordingly, such submarines have provided the state with a secure means of devastating retaliation even if its long-range bomber bases and missiles fired from land were crippled by a surprise, preemptive strike. The certainty that an aggressor would be subjected to such destruction, however carefully or ruthlessly he planned his attack, has been at the heart of both sides' nuclear deterrent ever since. The modern nuclear-propelled ballistic missile firing submarine (the SSBN) has proved so suitable for this role that it has signally affected naval strategy and has attracted a very large slice of the naval effort of the major maritime powers. Since the early 1960s, the development has been in the direction of larger, quieter submarines and of longer range missiles with more penetrating power and destructive impact. Nowadays Soviet submarines of the *Typhoon* or *Delta III* type, for example, carry missiles capable of reaching the territory of the United States even when fired from Soviet waters – an extraordinary four-fold improvement in range over the past 20 years. Moreover, the *Typhoon* has 20 missiles with 12 warheads each, affording the theoretical capacity to destroy 240 targets in one broadside.

The potentialities of these modern descendants of the early *Polaris* submarines are such that efforts have been made on both sides to improve their capacity to locate and destroy them before they have launched their missiles. Amongst the many possibilities that must be included here are the attack of the SSBNs' command and control infrastructure (including anti-satellite operations), the destruction of their bases, their active trailing by hunter-killer submarines as they leave their bases and their location in the open oceans by means of complex sonar systems like the US Navy's bottom-mounted SOSUS system. In the 1960s, for instance, the US Navy deployed carrier task groups whose purpose was primarily to conduct anti-submarine warfare (ASW) operations of this sort, especially against those early Soviet submarines whose launch positions were relatively close to the United States.

These emerging vulnerabilities led to renewed efforts to improve the SSBN's survivability and were an important stimulus to the development of the very long range systems noted earlier and to various sets of naval dispositions. Oversimplifying, one of these might be called the *Trident* solution – the US Navy's practice of exploiting to the maximum the SSBN's extraordinary technological capacity for stealth, by sending its submarines out alone in the deepest parts of the most distant ocean where they hide until needed. In contrast, the Soviet Navy's *Delta* solution is to support the SSBN with the rest of the fleet; the SSBN stays in relatively well-known patrol areas, but is protected from hostile ASW efforts by friendly hunter-killer submarines, surface ships and aircraft. The Soviet Navy is, though, widely supposed to be developing a capacity to send its SSBNs under the Arctic ice, so this dichotomy in practice between the two navies should not be pushed too far. Whichever route is taken, however, the SSBN is generally thought to have kept ahead of measures to find and destroy it, and so continues to be the heart of the superpowers' nuclear deterrent posture. Were there to be a radical breakthrough in the means of detection, of course, this could all change.

But what is certainly clear even from this brief review of one of the newest naval tasks is the extent to which its performance is affected by other more traditional ones. Especially in Soviet practice, but for other navies as well, there remains the familiar need to protect relevant bases, depots and headquarters ashore from sea-based attack, to clear hostile units away from port exits, to protect SSBNs as they move to their patrol areas and so forth.

To complicate the matter a little, mention should be made of the advent of long-range nuclear-capable cruise missiles fired from surface ships such as the US Navy's *Tomahawk* deployed in the battleship *New Jersey*, or the Soviet Navy's SS-NX-21 missile, currently expected to be fitted to some of its newer hunter-killer submarines. Although such missiles are both nuclear and long range they are not generally considered to be part of the Superpowers' strategic nuclear arsenals but are instead regarded as theatre weapons deployed in direct support of the land/sea battle. But both from the point of view of the potential victims ashore and from that of the navies whose requirement is to deploy and protect their own such systems and to attack those of their adversary such distinctions might seem more than a little academic. In any case both strategic and theatre nuclear weaponry provide modern navies with a range of tasks where the old and the new intermingle in the most complex way. These new uses of the sea, in short depend on the capacity to control it to the necessary extent. In that at least they are like any other naval functions, ancient and modern.

With amphibious operations we are once again back on more familiar ground. Like most of their predecessors, wars fought since 1962 have been fought essentially about the control of land and so operations against the shore are one of the world's navies' most important tasks since this is where they directly influence the outcome of the land campaign. These operations have covered the whole spectrum, from isolated raids of the sort carried out by Israel and her Arab neighbours to full scale amphibious and ground attack operations of the sort carried out by the Americans in Vietnam and the British in the Falklands. It has always been arguably the most difficult and demanding maritime task of them all since it requires the coordination of completely different types of forces and their operation in large numbers and in positions of unavoidable risk, at places where an adversary may yet be strong – off his own shore line. Recent technological developments such as long range missiles seem to have made this function if anything even more difficult to perform – at least against sophisticated opposition, but it has nevertheless been a regular feature of naval operations over the past twenty years or so.

The same is true of that other classic use of the sea, as a means of transporting people and materials from one land mass to another. The importance of the task of protecting shipping is nowhere more important than it is for NATO. As Admiral Thomas Hayward, an American Chief of Naval Operations observed recently:

> Our strategic interests span continents and the interconnecting oceans. Virtually all our allies are separated from us by water. Our economic life depends increasingly on access to overseas markets and resources and our dependence upon the seas is growing not lessening.

The importance of shipping makes it a likely area for attack, and despite the scepticism about whether serious wars would last long enough for this to be a vital operation of war, both the attack and defence of maritime communications have been a regular feature of recent wars. Sometimes this has taken the form of an assault on the health of the adversary's economy – as in the case of the Iran-Iraq war, or to impede the flow of military supplies and personnel from one point to another as, in the 1973 Arab-Israeli War and the 1982 Falklands campaign. Methods used have included everything from the declaration of war and blockade zones, to the laying of mines (most successfully by the Americans off Haiphong harbour in Vietnam) to the direct attack of shipping by submarines, surface warships of all sorts and aircraft either at sea or in harbour. The continuities of naval operation between past and present are in fact especially obvious in this area.

This brief survey of naval activities over the twenty years or so since *The Strategy of Sea Power* first appeared shows an interesting mixture of the new and the old in terms of both the functions of naval power and the methods by which they are carried out. Things are neither completely different from what they used to be nor precisely the same. Deciding where to strike the balance in policy formulation between these two extremes is one of the most demanding of the many difficult tasks facing the modern naval planner and those interested in the results of their deliberations. This directly raises the question of the value of the guidance offered by historical experience especially when it is processed as it is in *The Strategy of Sea Power*.

Some of Roskill's readers believed quite firmly that the value of his book lay in the fact that it elucidated 'lessons from history which should never be forgotten and principles which, being absolutely sound, should be able to guide us in the future just as well as in the past'. Roskill had no quarrel with the verdict of his reviewer in the *Times Literary Supplement* that 'the principles of conducting maritime war are changed much less than has been supposed by technical innovations'. Nevertheless his view was that there was as much danger in blindly accepting the lessons of history as there was in neglecting them. As he wrote to one of his readers '. . . ancient principles must always be continuously called in question rather than be regarded as immutable'.[6]

The point was that the constructive juxtaposition of modern and historical experience isolates the things that need thinking about. Naval history is an indispensible aid to effective naval thought but mainly in that it provides insights and questions, rather than answers. The issue was put clearly by Sir Julian Corbett: 'The value of history in the art of war is not only to elucidate the resemblance of past and present, but also their essential differences'. Roskill always hoped that *The Strategy of Sea Power* would be read in this spirit.

[6] Letters from Admiral the Hon. Sir Reginald Plunkett-Ernle-Erle-Drax of 21 May 1962 and to Captain W. P. Carne of 28 Feb. 1969 in Rosk 7/9 and 7/8 respectively, Churchill College, Cambridge.